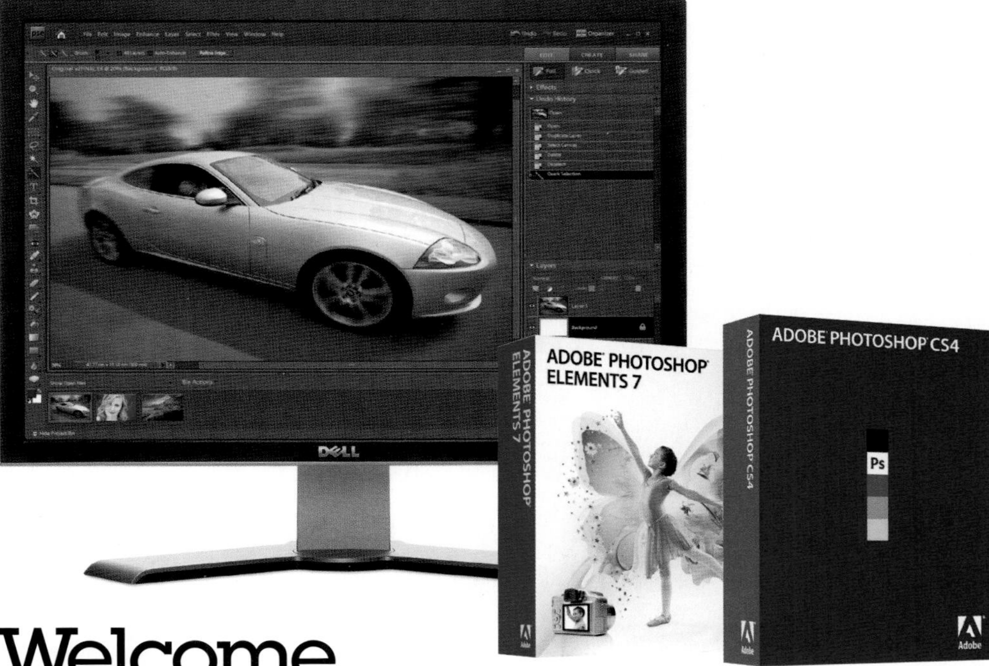

Welcome...

"Whether you take pictures on DSLRs, digital compacts or the latest range of hybrid cameras, you already know how easy and fast it is to produce great quality photos. You'll no doubt also be aware that once you've captured some great photos, if you want to get the most from your digital files, then the very best way to do this is to treat your images to a touch of Photoshop magic. Whether it's simply to tweak the shot, such as make some minor adjustments to exposure, contrast or sharpness, or to apply more wholesale changes, there is no other software that comes remotely close to Adobe's superb package. Available in different forms to suit all budget sizes, it's the most versatile and powerful application available for digital photographers. Of course, such a sophisticated tool requires time and effort to master, which is where *The Photographer's Guide to Photoshop* will help. Produced by photographers for photographers, this guide is the perfect introduction to Photoshop, guiding you through the key features and tools that you need to use, as well as providing you with a variety of techniques geared towards helping you make the most of your digital images. By following the jargon-free advice given by our team of experts, you can look forward to mastering many of the key Photoshop techniques that every photographer should know, and help lift your best images to new heights, while having fun as you learn new skills along the way. All the best!"

DANIEL LEZANO, EDITOR

Meet our team of Photoshop experts

All our experts are team members or regular contributors to *Digital SLR Photography* magazine. For more expert advice and inspiration, pick up the latest issue available on the second Tuesday of every month. For further information visit the magazine's website at www.digitalslrphoto.com

LUKE MARSH
A keen DSLR photographer, Luke's also the creative genius behind the look of *Digital SLR Photography* magazine and this MagBook as well as a Photoshop expert.

MATT HENRY
As a regular writer on photography and Photoshop, Matt provides expert advice on how best to use your camera, but also on the top post-production techniques.

IAN FARRELL
Ian has written for photography magazines for a number of years and specialises in Photoshop techniques. He's also the author of a best-selling book on digital post-production.

DANIEL LEZANO
Editor Lezano's passionate about photography and is the author of several books. His Photoshop expertise centres around the core techniques used by DSLR photographers.

The Photographer's Guide to Photoshop

Produced by Digital SLR Photography at:
6 Swan Court, Cygnet Park,
Peterborough, Cambs PE7 8GX

Phone: 01733 567401. Fax 01733 352650
Email: enquiries@digitalslrphoto.com
Online: www.digitalslrphoto.com

Editorial

To contact editorial phone: 01733 567401

Editor **Daniel Lezano**
daniel_lezano@dennis.co.uk

Art Editor **Luke Marsh**
luke_marsh@dennis.co.uk

Editorial Co-ordinator **Jo Lezano**
jo_lezano@dennis.co.uk

Editorial contributors:
Mark Bauer, Ian Farrell, Lee Frost, Matty Graham, Matt Henry, Ross Hoddinott, Lara Jade, Debbie Nolan, Paul Stefan, Bjorn Thomassen & Caroline Wilkinson

Advertising & Production

To contact advertising phone: 01733 293913
Display & Classifield Sales: 0207 907 6651

Advertising Director **Natasha Blatcher**
natasha_blatcher@dennis.co.uk

Advertising Sales **Guy Scott-Wilson**
guy_scott-wilson@dennis.co.uk

Production Controller **Dan Stark**
dan_stark@dennis.co.uk

Publishing & Marketing

NICKY BAKER DIGITAL PRODUCTION MANAGER
DHARMESH MISTRY BOOKAZINE MANAGER
ROBIN RYAN PRODUCTION DIRECTOR
JULIAN LLOYD-EVANS MD OF ADVERTISING
MARTIN BELSON NEWSTRADE DIRECTOR
BRETT REYNOLDS CHIEF OPERATING OFFICER
IAN LEGGETT GROUP FINANCE DIRECTOR
JAMES TYE CHIEF EXECUTIVE
FELIX DENNIS CHAIRMAN

The Photographer's Guide To Photoshop ISBN 1-907232-05-2

Printed by Benham Goodhead Print (BGP)

Contents

34

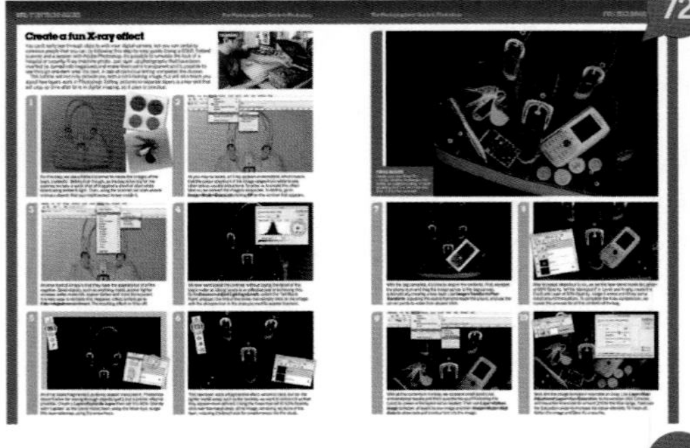
72

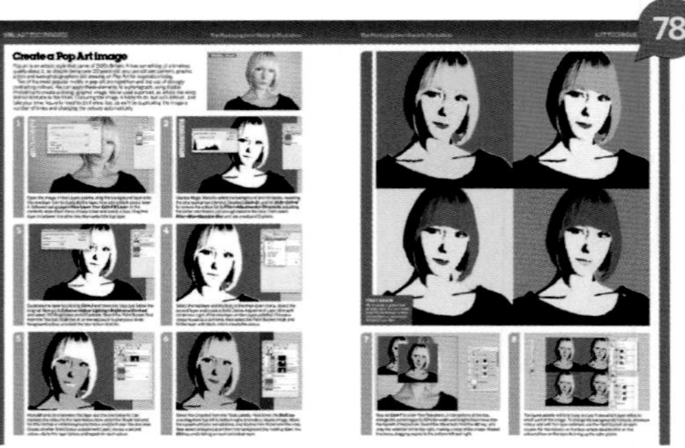
78

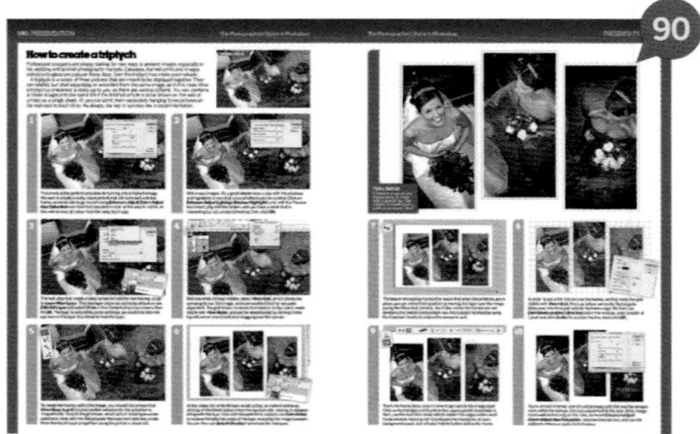
90

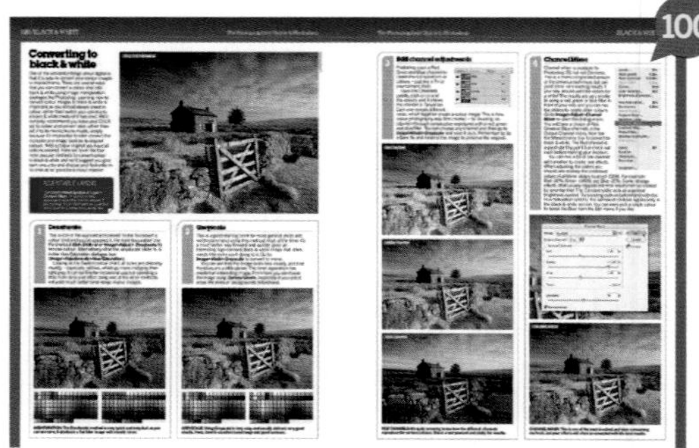
100

114

BJORN THOMASSEN

File Edit Image Enhance Layer Select Filter View Window Help
Undo Redo Organizer
final image for panel.tif @ 40% (RGB/8)
EDIT CREATE SHARE
Full Quick Guided
Effects
Histogram
Channel: RGB
Source: Entire Image
Mean: 132.52
Std Dev: 69.39
Median: 144
Pixels: 232263
Level:
Count:
Percentile:
Cache Level: 3
Undo History
Open
Layers
Normal
Background
40%
20 cm x 13.31 cm (300 ppi)
Show Open Files
Bin Actions
Hide Project Bin
Nikon
D90
ADOBE® PHOTOSHOP® ELEMENTS 7
Adobe

Photoshop. The digital photographer's choice!

IMPROVE YOUR SHOTS TODAY!

PHOTOGRAPHY IS ABOUT CREATIVITY, always has been. Since its very inception, photographers haven't been content to document their surroundings but sought to enhance, embellish, beautify and distort their imagery, be it via the darkroom or with in-camera techniques. Photoshop is just another tool in the creative arsenal, though it happens to be a damn good one, the best possible. Everything that was done in the darkroom can be recreated in Photoshop, and far more besides. Images that are now appearing in the digital age are really pushing the boundaries of the imagination. So if you haven't already jumped on the Photoshop bandwagon, it's really time to take that leap. You're missing out on the chance to really explore your creative self. Even if your ambitions are a little more modest, you'll find that there isn't an image in the world that can't be improved by Photoshop in some manner, even if it's a matter of a simple contrast tweak or basic blemish removal. And the best way learn is just to get stuck in. After, of course, you've familiarised yourself with the basics in our feature-packed guide to the best imaging software on the planet! Here are our favourite reasons for using Photoshop...

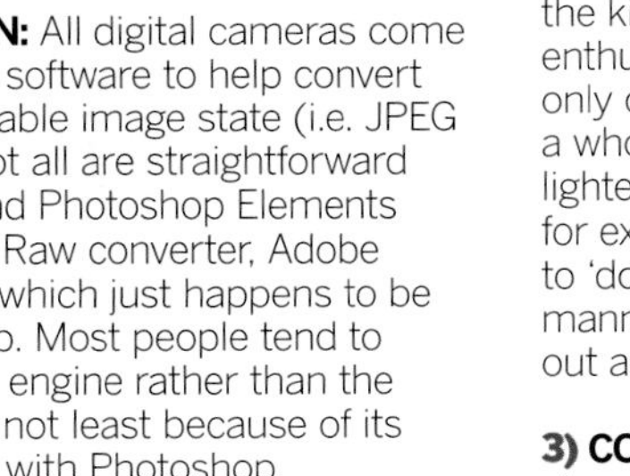

1) RAW CONVERSION: All digital cameras come with their own brand software to help convert Raw files into an editable image state (i.e. JPEG or TIFF). However, not all are straightforward to use. Photoshop and Photoshop Elements come with their own Raw converter, Adobe Camera Raw (ACR), which just happens to be rather good at the job. Most people tend to plump for the Adobe engine rather than the manufacturer's own, not least because of its seamless integration with Photoshop.

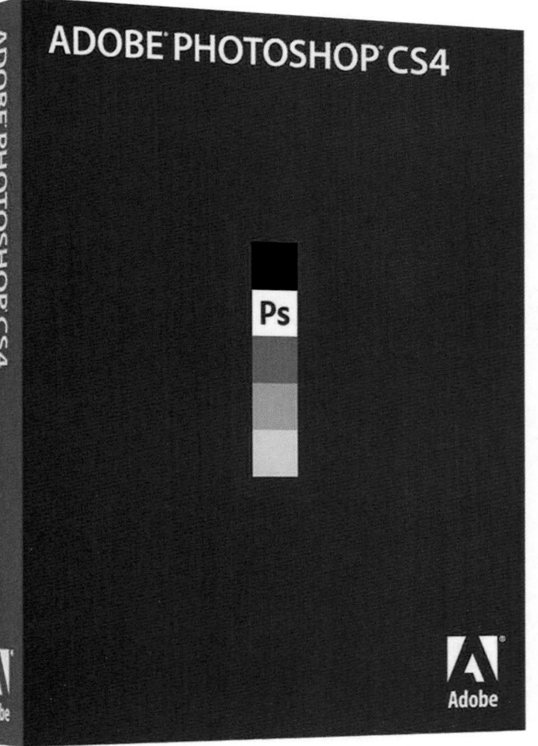

2) EXPOSURE CONTROL: Photoshop gives you the kind of control over exposure that darkroom enthusiasts could have only dreamt of. Not only can you lighten or darken the image as a whole, but you can work on specific tones, lightening the highlights or darkening shadows, for example. You can also work on specific areas to 'dodge' and 'burn' in the traditional darkroom manner – darkening a sky perhaps, or bringing out a bit more detail in a landscape foreground.

3) COLOUR CONTROL: We're not just talking about warming things up or cooling them down. You can tweak colours in any way imaginable and locally as well as globally, changing the colour of someone's eyes, hair, or perhaps the colour of a particularly bad tie. And you can control colour saturation as well as hue, so you can make those sunsets really burn.

4) BETTER BLACK & WHITE: Yes you can shoot black & white in camera but no it won't do. First you'll be shooting JPEG and secondly all you're doing is performing a basic desaturation, which means you'll be discarding vital information. Anyone who's ever printed in the traditional darkroom knows there's a bit more to mastering monochrome. Photoshop lets you control specific colour channels in the way that black & white filters did for film cameras.

5) BLEMISH REMOVAL: On a basic level this means polishing portraits up a little by removing spots, moles, and wrinkles but this process can be extended to pretty much anything with the clever combination of Clone Stamp and Healing Brush tools. You can remove a telegraph pole from an otherwise picture perfect landscape, an unwanted reflection from a window and so on.

6) MONTAGE: Layers allow you to montage different images together, in the same way that you might have once cut and pasted family photos. But Photoshop allows you to go that extra mile. You can change a cloudy sky for a clear one, add trees where there were none, or even place a person in a completely different scene. This type of montage is also known as compositing and has grown in popularity with amateur users and professionals alike.

7) SUBJECT ENHANCEMENT: Aside from taking things out that you don't really like and sticking stuff in that weren't really there, you've also got the option to enhance the things that you've already got. Aside from the colour and exposure controls for whitening teeth or pulling out a few grey hairs, you've also got the ability to change the shape and size of aspects of your image with the various Transform tools. And yes that can mean slimmer hips and bigger biceps but it could also mean ironing out the converging verticals of a tall building or scaling down a hand that's got too close to a wide-angle lens.

8) WEB PREPARATION: If you want to post your photos in a forum, an online gallery, your own website, or you simply want to email them, Photoshop certainly is going to come in handy. You can resize them, sharpen them, convert them to sRGB mode and save them with the appropriate JPEG quality setting.

9) SPECIAL EFFECTS: Photoshop has a massive array of filters to enable you to achieve all kinds of special effects. Turn photos into watercolour paintings, add frames and borders, add rain to a cloud scene, the list goes on.

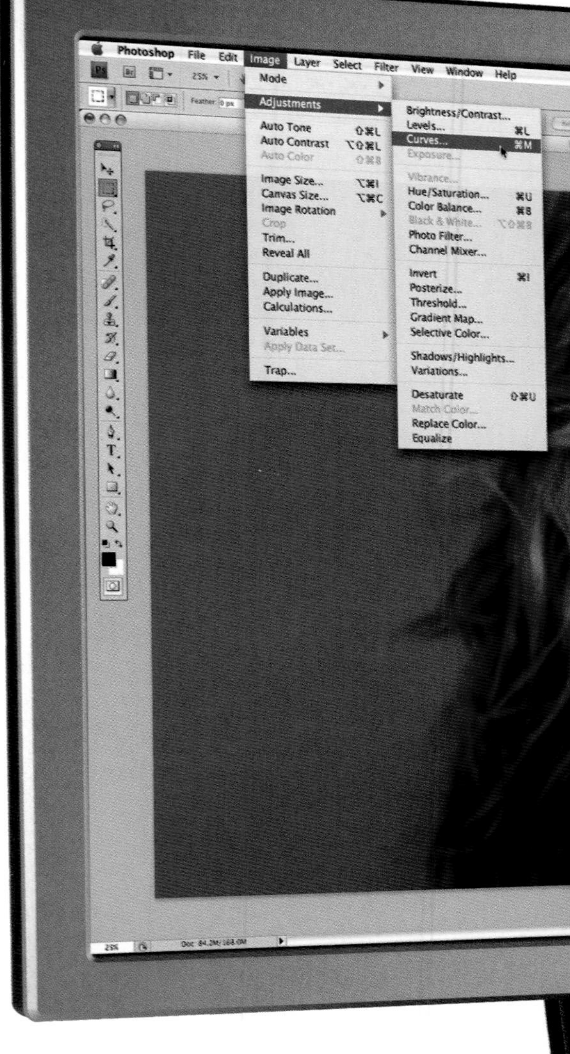

While the Elements interface is a little different to that found on Creative Suite there are enough similarities so that photographers migrating from one to the other won't find it too alien

Which Photoshop: Elements or CS?

PHOTOSHOP COMES IN two distinct flavours. Firstly you've got the full-blown 'Creative Suite' professional version, which has run from its first ever instalment back in 1990 all the way to Photoshop 7, then CS, CS2, CS3 and now CS4 (effectively Photoshop 11). Then there's the cut-down, beginner-friendly, consumer version called Photoshop Elements, now at version 7. To give you an idea firstly of the price difference, you can pick up a copy of Photoshop CS4 for anything between £200 and £500 online, whereas you can get hold of the latest version of Elements for as little as £30.

Truth be told, unless you're planning complex montages that involve cutting out intricate shapes, you'll be fine with Elements. If you're at the stage where you're good enough to be doing detailed cut-outs, you'll already know what the Pen Tool and the Channels palette are and how to use them and will probably already own or have access to a copy of Photoshop. You can perform all the edits you'll need as a beginner and intermediate user in Elements and for very beginners the learning curve will be much quicker. The only occasion you might as a first-time buyer want to plump for the full version is if you plan to use retouching as part of a semi- or fully-professional photographic workflow or have other ambitions for advanced retouching. In this case it's perhaps better to familiarise yourself with Photoshop from the start to save making the transition later on.

Which Photoshop: New or old?

IF YOU'RE A FIRST-TIME buyer, there's little incentive in buying earlier versions of either Photoshop or Photoshop Elements as there appears to be little differences in price and you have the added compatibility problems with newer digital cameras (for which updates are often only released for the latest versions). Owners of older versions may be forced to upgrade their copies for this very reason. If you're not planning on investing in the latest and greatest digital camera and already own a copy of CS, CS2 or CS3, you'll have to weigh the upgrade price against new features.

It's worth noting that there's certainly nothing spectacular that you couldn't be without in earlier versions – there are plenty of pro retouchers and photographers who refuse to upgrade. Many of the new features are quite gimmicky, though the Photomerge advancements were a big improvement for panoramic enthusiasts in CS3, and CS4's Clone Stamp Tool overlay is almost worth the upgrade alone if you do a lot of clean up work. The relatively low price of Elements makes holding out on newer versions slightly less worthwhile.

File formats

Check out the File Format drop-down list in the Photoshop Save As dialogue and get a shock at the multitude of options available. Panic not though; there are only really four formats worth discussing.

- ✓ Photoshop
- Photoshop EPS
- JPEG
- Large Document Format
- Photoshop PDF
- Photoshop 2.0
- Photoshop Raw
- Scitex CT
- TIFF
- Photoshop DCS 1.0
- Photoshop DCS 2.0

RAW
This is the catch-all terms given to the different proprietary file formats that come directly out of a digital camera when shooting in Raw (a Canon EOS 5D MkII Raw file, for example, has the extension .CR2). These files need converting into editable information via a Raw converter, such as Adobe Camera Raw (ACR), which comes packaged with both Photoshop and Elements. Shooting Raw allows access to the full range of information recorded by the camera sensor, giving more room to correct for exposure mistakes and to make edits to our image without chancing visible degradation. Raw files give you access to 16-bits of information, as opposed to a JPEG's 8-bit.

PSD
The PSD file is a Photoshop format that allows all Photoshop information, such as layers and saved selections, to be easily stored and re-accessed at a later date. It's an uncompressed format and maintains the full 16-bits of information. While TIFF files do give you the option of including Photoshop layers, the file size increases disproportionately, making the PSD the file format of choice for editing your images. When the image is finally flattened, it can be saved out as a TIFF or JPEG, though it's always a good idea to keep the PSD file with all the layers work you've done in case you need to make any additional changes at a later date.

JPEG
The JPEG is a compressed file format, designed to keep file size as low as possible with as little quality loss as possible. It uses what's termed a 'lossy' version of compression, meaning image information is thrown away for good. The amount discarded depends on the compression setting. A JPEG file retains only 8-bits rather than 16-bits of information, making it less useful as a format for image editing; the decrease in available information can produce signs of degradation if adjustments are pushed particularly hard. The reduced file size makes JPEG great for web reproduction, email and even magazine reproduction with a quality setting of 9 or more.

TIFF
The TIFF is generally an uncompressed file format (though there is a 'lossless' compression option), and an alternative to the JPEG for distributing images once you've made all your edits in Photoshop and flattened the layers. File sizes are considerably bigger than JPEGs, so it's used as a maximum quality option if you're prepared to distribute images on a CD or upload them via FTP – forget email! Those without a copy of Photoshop are normally able to open a TIFF file without any problems. It can hold 16-bit of information, but as it's not generally used for editing it's better to convert your images to 8-bit before saving as a TIFF to keep file size down.

The Toolbar (Elements)

Photoshop's Tools are generally quick and easy to understand as their descriptions usually outline their function well. A small black arrow to the bottom right of a tool icon indicates a sub-menu with further tools accessed by clicking and holding.

MOVE Can be used to move pixel information on a layer, text or an active selection. Just click and drag.

ZOOM Zoom in, zoom out. You may also choose to use ***Ctrl/Cmd*** and + or – with any other tool than select this one manually.

HAND Used for moving around your image when zoomed in or access quickly by holding down the spacebar instead.

EYEDROPPER Select a colour from your image or use any of the three tools housed underneath including Ruler.

MARQUEE Use these tools to make a selection based on a shape such as a rectangle or ellipse. Simply drag to size.

LASSO Draw your own custom selections with this tool, either freehand or using magnetic polygon points.

QUICK SELECTION Houses both the Quick Selection and Magic Wand tools for a semi-automated selection process.

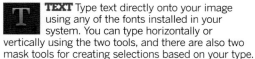

TEXT Type text directly onto your image using any of the fonts installed in your system. You can type horizontally or vertically using the two tools, and there are also two mask tools for creating selections based on your type.

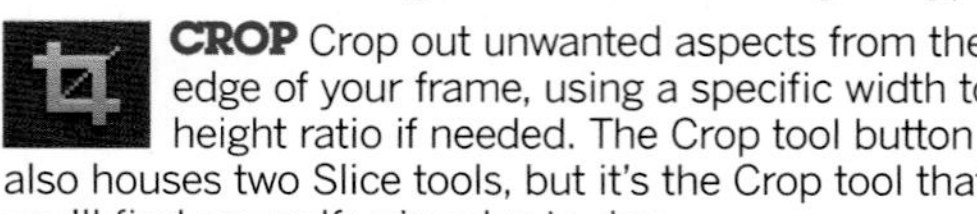
CROP Crop out unwanted aspects from the edge of your frame, using a specific width to height ratio if needed. The Crop tool button also houses two Slice tools, but it's the Crop tool that you'll find yourself using day to day.

HEALING Replace blemishes with nearby clean information and have it blended in with tools like Spot Healing.

CLONE STAMP Allows you to clone information from one area to another without the blending of the Healing tools.

ERASER Remove pixel information manually or in a semi-automated manner with Background or Magic Eraser.

BRUSH One of the most often used tools, particularly for painting information in and out on layer masks. You control its opacity and edge hardness via the Tool Options Bar. The Pencil Tool and Color Replacement sit underneath.

GRADIENT Draw gradients directly onto layers or their masks. Also houses the Paint Bucket tool for single colour fill.

BLUR Blur selected areas of your image or sharpen and smudge them with the two useful tools housed underneath Blur.

SHAPE Draw shapes using any one of the default shapes, or choose another with the Custom Shape tool.

DODGE & BURN The Dodge tool lightens and the Burn tool darkens. You can choose whether to focus on Shadows, Midtones or Highlights and there's also a Sponge tool for increasing or decreasing colour saturation.

HISTORY BRUSH (CS4) Go back in time by painting previous states into your image in conjunction with the History palette.

PEN (CS4) Allows the user to create curved as well as straight-edge selections to accurately outline solid-edge subjects.

DIRECT SELECTION (CS4) This tool and the one it hides are for selecting and moving paths created with the Pen or Shape tools.

Menus, tools and palettes

THE PHOTOSHOP WORKSPACE can be a daunting place at first, with its vast array of features, it can be enough to scare off the bravest of digital photographers. However, once you grasp a basic understanding of just a few key areas, you'll be up and running in no time. Here we'll be looking at the workspace of Photoshop Elements and although there are differences between this interface and that of CS4, Adobe does a great job with crossover between packages to encourage a progression for users as they become more experienced. The three key areas to understand are the Tools bar, which runs vertically down the left side and incorporates the Tools Options bar running horizontally above it; the Menu bar, which runs horizontally along the top of the workspace and finally, the palettes which run down the right side. All these items can be hidden or made visible in the Window tab of the Menu bar allowing users to customise the workspace to their individual needs.

QUICK MASK MODE (CS4) View selections as a translucent red mask rather than marching ants. When active, you can paint onto your image with a black or white brush to add or subtract from the selection. Press ***Q*** to turn it on and off.

The Menu bar (Elements)

EDIT As well as hosting options for general preferences and keyboard shortcuts, the Edit menu is home to Cut, Copy and Paste, though all these are accessed easier via their keyboard shortcuts. The Transform commands are located here too allowing you to perform things such as Scale, Rotate and Skew.

IMAGE All the popular image adjustments such as Levels and Curves can be found here, though usually you'll want to add these as adjustment layers via the button in the Layers palette, rather than applying them directly to pixel information. The Image menu also lets you alter size via the Image Size command.

LAYER The Layer menu is home to popular layer-based commands like Convert to Smart Object, Merge Layers and Flatten Image and you can also add adjustment layers from here. In truth virtually everything here is better accessed by keyboard shortcuts or buttons on the Layers palette itself.

SELECT Everything to do with selections is here, such as Select All, Deselect and Select Inverse. You can also modify selections via this menu with commands like Expand, Contract, and most commonly Feather. This menu also gives access to the very useful Transform Selection and Color Range commands.

FILTER Along with being home to a variety of special effects filters, the Filters menu also includes two of the most often used filters in Photoshop – Unsharp Mask and Gaussian Blur. These two filters are integral to much of the work done in Photoshop and can be employed for a variety of purposes.

Palettes (Elements)

There are several interchangeable palettes accessed in the Window tab of the menu including Colour Swatch, Histogram, Info, Navigator and Styles and Effects. Here's two you won't be able to live without...

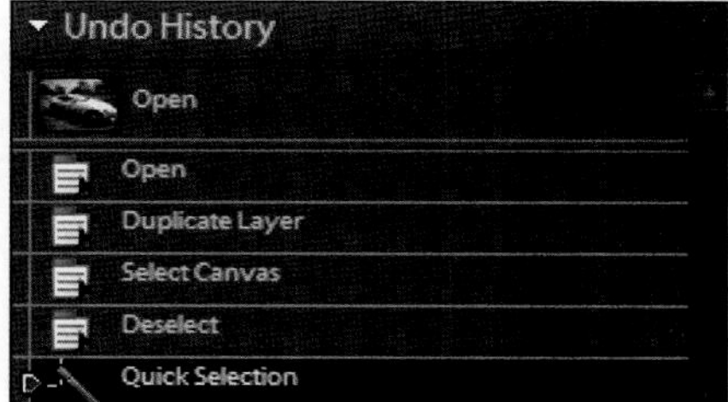

UNDO HISTORY Everything you do in Photoshop, whether it be applying a brush stroke, filter or deleting a layer, is recorded in the History palette. The number of steps kept in memory is specified in the Preferences palette (the default is 20, but 40 is safer). Click to go back or use ***Ctrl/Cmd+Alt/Option+Z*** to go back one step at a time (Multiple Undo).

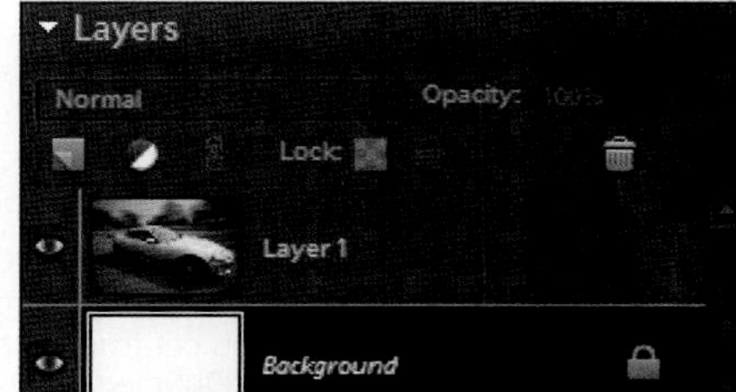

LAYERS This palette contains all your pixel, vector and adjustment layers, as well as their masks. You can re-order and delete these layers at any time, organise layers into Groups, turn them on and off with the visibility icon and, of course, add Layer Styles from the palette itself. There's also a context menu for more layer commands such as Flatten Image.

Photo Bin (Elements)

The Photo Bin in Photoshop Elements is an organisation tool that shows thumbnails of all the files you have open in the workspace. Underneath the thumbnail you'll see the file name and when you click on a thumbnail that file becomes the active document. A right click on a thumbnail gets you to a shortcut menu where you can minimise, close or rotate the image, create a duplicate file or access the image's original camera data.

PRO TIPS

CUSTOMISE YOUR SPACE

The Photoshop interface is fully customisable. If there are palettes you don't use simply hide them in the Window menu. Also, you can drag and drop them into positions that suit you!

The Clone Stamp tool

The Clone Stamp tool samples one area of an image and replicates it exactly over another area, or from one image to another if you wish. You simply click ***Alt/Option*** to define the source area that you want to use (in the same or a different image) and then click to 'clone' that new information somewhere else. You can select the size of the Clone Stamp tool's brush as you would a normal brush (use the ***[*** and ***]*** keys for speedy size changes) as well as changing the Hardness of the edges, though 0% Hardness is the usually the best choice to ensure the cloning isn't too obvious. It has a standard mode and an Aligned mode which you can select in the Tool Options bar at the top of the screen. Aligned mode returns the source point to the original area once you release the mouse button, no matter where you are in your image. In the standard mode, cloning always takes place in relation to the distance from the source point to the area you first moused down on to clone. If this sounds confusing, have a play and you'll see. The Clone Stamp tool was somewhat superseded for blemish removal by the Healing tools (see below), at least in areas of even tone. However, where the Clone Stamp tool still excels is for removing blemishes that are close to areas that change suddenly in tone. The Healing tools attempt to blend the new information in with the old, so they are prone to dragging in unwanted information. An example might be that you have a pimple right next to the hairline. In the middle of the forehead, the Healing tools do a great job, removing the pimple and blending the new information seamlessly. However, if you click the pimple near the hairline, you'll find that you'll end up with a smudged patch or a piece of hair replacing the pimple, as tools such as the Spot Healing brush will try to blend with the hair itself. The Clone Stamp is king for these situations; there's no attempt at blending, so as long as you source from an area that looks very similar in tone, the pimple can be removed effectively.

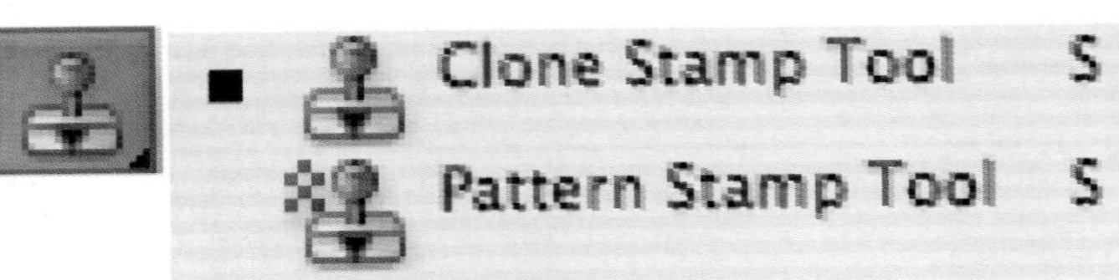

ADAM BURTON

ATTACK OF THE CLONE! To use the Clone Stamp tool you must first select a source point from the image by holding the *Alt* key. The tool will repeat the area you've sourced exactly so there's a bit of trial and error involved!

The Healing tools

The Healing tools comprise of the Spot Healing Brush tool, the Healing Brush tool, Patch tool (not in Elements), and the Red Eye tool. The Healing Brush tool was the original and works in the same way as the Clone Stamp tool, requiring a source point to start, only it uses complex algorithms to blend the sourced information with the new area. Spot Healing Brush was the follow-up and bypasses the need for a source point, although this means a sacrifice in control. The Patch tool is best for large areas of blemishes like wrinkles and works by allowing you to make a selection of the blemish area, which is then dragged to the clean source area (or vice versa via the options bar). The Red Eye tool is a simple one-click tool for red-eye removal.

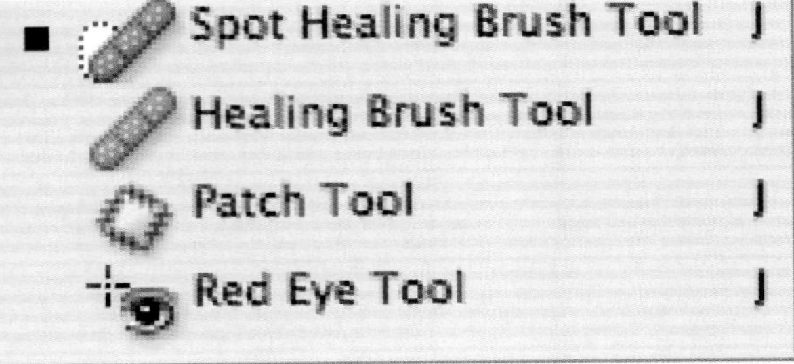

BJORN THOMASSEN

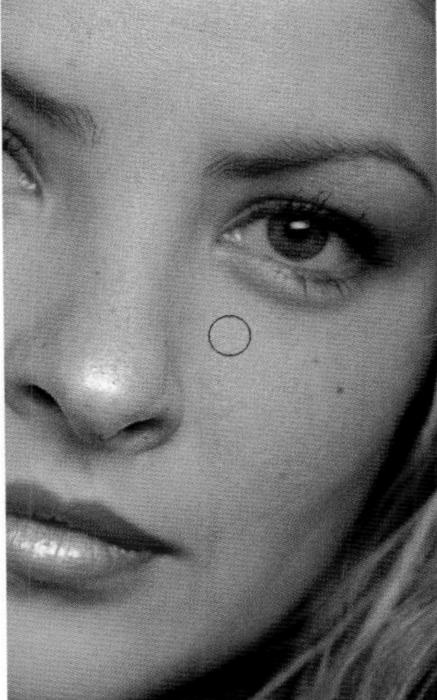

HEALING HANDS! Unlike when using the Clone Tool, you don't need to set a source point for the Spot Healing Brush. With the brush size set appropriately for the job we can just click over areas to be healed, ideal for skin touch-ups!

Curves

Curves is probably the single most important adjustment tool in Photoshop and one that you'll find yourself using time and time again. It allows you to tweak the tonal range in your image in a whole number of ways. For example, you can lighten or darken the image as a whole by adding and moving a single point on the curve. Or you can focus on specific areas of the image by adding further points. Add one point in the shadows and one point in the highlights, for example, and you can manipulate the two separately. One common use for this two point set-up is to push highlights upwards to lighten them, and shadows downwards to darken them. This 'S' curve produces an effective increase in contrast. Or you may wish to manipulate the mid-tones only, so you add a single point in the shadows and another in the highlights to fix them still, before adding a further point in the middle of the curve that is pushed either upwards or downwards to lighten or darken the mid-tones only.

You can add as many points as you like to focus on a very specific range if required. The whole idea behind using a curve is that tones are altered gradually, so that you don't notice a sudden jump which can lead to problems such as posterisation. By moving the end points at the top and bottom, you also gain control of the darkest and lightest points of your image, which effectively does the same as the white and black Input and Output sliders in Levels. You can clip tones at the end of each scale to pure black or white, or conversely weaken your darkest and lightest tones. Pretty much everything you can do in Levels, you can do in Curves (although the reverse isn't true) so it's down to personal preference as to which you use for specific tasks. The final thing Curves is also capable of is adding colour casts by moving the individual colour channels from the drop-down menu. You could add a blue cast to shadows (or remove one for that matter) and a red cast to highlights, for example.

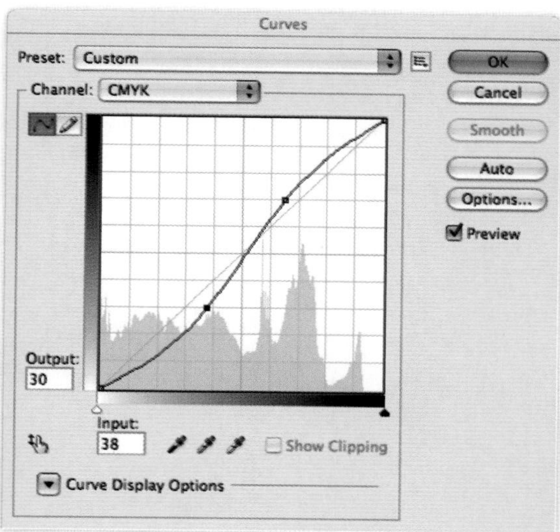

CHECK OUT THOSE CURVES! Using Curves is quite an advanced manner in which to improve the appearance of your image, although it does deliver excellent results for those prepared to sit and play for a while. The 'S' Curve, created by adding two points to the diagonal line of the grid, is a tried and trusted method for producing great results.

Levels

Levels displays an easier to use histogram than Curves, showing the range of tones that your image contains, from 0 at pure black to 255 at pure white. Its middle slider works similar to moving a curve upwards or downwards with a single point to lighten or darken, although it would also involve a slight shift in the end points on that curve to weaken blacks or whites. The black and white sliders on the same ramp define your darkest black and your lightest light. By moving those inwards to meet the histogram information, you are ensuring that you have 0 and 255 tones (pure black and pure white). By moving them past that information, you effectively clip more tones to pure white and black. The black and white Output sliders below do the reverse, weakening your blacks and whites.

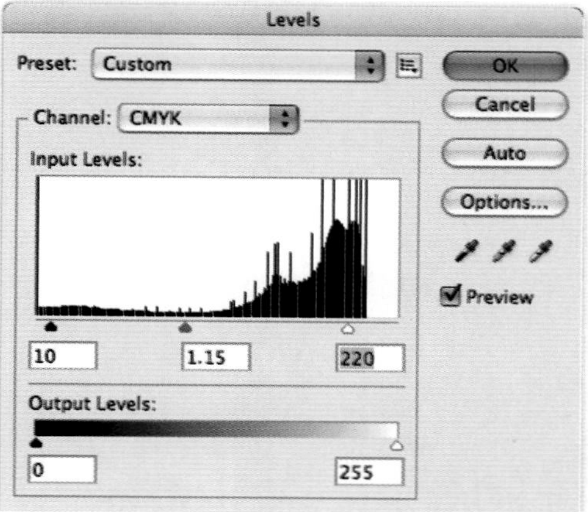

LEVEL WITH ME! Levels are an excellent way in which to adjust and control brightness, contrast and tonal range in one window by viewing the images histogram. Experiment by moving the Black Point, Mid-tone and White Point sliders to get the best results. Alternatively, you can use the Auto function or try the droppers icons to sample from the image itself. When you find a system that works for you why not save it and use it on more of your images in the future!

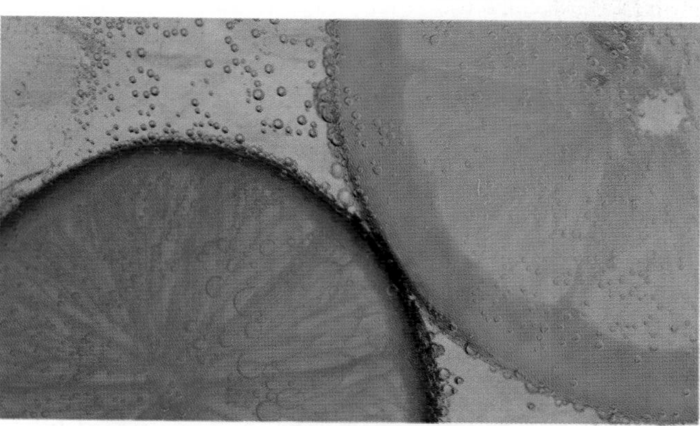

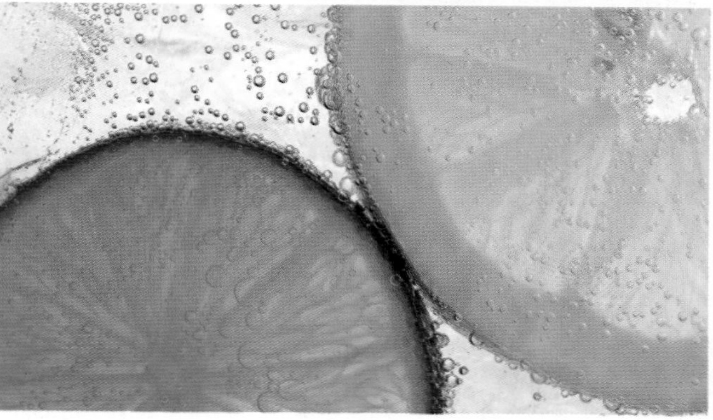

The Selection tools

THE ABILITY TO MAKE isolated selections within your image is a key aspect of using Photoshop. There are several different ways to make selections from those that are done manually, such as the Polygonal Lasso, to those that are semi-automated like the Magic Wand or Quick selection tools. Once made, the selection area is defined by a series of moving black and white pixels widely referred to as 'marching ants'. Each of the selection tools comes with a number of options that you'll find located in the Tool Options Bar that's located by default under the menus at the top of the screen. Among the most important are the New Selection, Add Selection (or press ***Shift*** while making selection), Subtract Selection (or press ***Alt*** while making selection), and Intersect Selection buttons (the Quick Selection Tool doesn't have the latter). These determine how multiple selections interact together. Here's a quick look at the selection tools and the way in which they function.

NATURAL SELECTION: This image is perfect for the Magic Wand tool as there is high contrast between colours. Due to the large areas of solid colour we can set the Tolerance to 100 pixels in the Options bar, then select the blue of the background by clicking it. Next, while holding the Shift key, we select the remaining blue areas to add them and then alter the background as we see fit.

RECTANGULAR MARQUEE

Allows you to create a selection based on a rectangular shape of any size or proportion. Simply click and drag to size. If you hold down the ***Shift*** key you can also constrain the proportions, allowing you to create an exact square selection. This tool is great for selecting easy, solid-edges.

ELLIPTICAL MARQUEE

The Elliptical Marquee tool allows you to create a selection based on an ellipse, again of any size or proportion. Click in your image and drag to get the size and shape to suit. Hold down ***Shift*** to draw a perfect circle. This tool has less practical selecting applications than Rectangular.

SINGLE COLUMN MARQUEE

Works in the same way as the Single Row Marquee tool, only it creates a vertical selection rather than a horizontal one. The selection is just one pixel wide and is useful for cleaning up straight-edged subjects masked or pasted via selection that are showing unwanted pixels.

SINGLE ROW MARQUEE

The Single Row Marquee tool creates a row type selection that is just 1 pixel in height. It can prove useful for cleaning up the edges of a previous selection that are showing stray colours of pixels that shouldn't be there – the top edge of an added doorway for example.

LASSO

The Lasso tool enables you to draw a selection free hand. As it's virtually impossible to trace around a subject freehand with 100% accuracy, it tends to be more useful for drawing rough selections that you plan to modify further down the line or for selecting areas that require erasing.

MAGNETIC LASSO

Works in the same manner as the Polygonal Lasso tool in the sense that anchor points are used to draw straight-edge shapes, only this time the anchor points are placed automatically by Photoshop as you move around an image edge. You can also plot points manually.

POLYGONAL LASSO

This tool allows you to draw your own selection manually, and has a distinct advantage for accuracy over the straight Lasso tool as it works by plotting anchor points to create polygonal based shapes. It can only draw straight lines; use the Pen tool for curved edge selections.

MAGIC WAND

The Magic Wand was the originally semi-automated tool, allowing you to simply click into an area and let Photoshop guess the area to be selected. As with the other two tools, you can control factors like Tolerance via the Tool Options Bar, but it's also best left for simple tasks.

QUICK SELECTION

Introduced in CS3, this tool allows you to quickly 'paint' a selection. As you click and drag, the selection expands and automatically finds and follows defined edges in the image. It's another semi-automated tool like Magnetic Lasso and Magic Wand that offers varying degrees of success.

The Crop tool

THE CROP TOOL is possibly the most widely used tool amongst digital photographers as composition is the key to a great image. As its name suggest, the Crop tool allows you to select a specific area of an image and discard all information outside this area. Although cropping reduces the dimensions of an image, it is not the same as resizing as the process does not reduce the pixel quality. There's no easier tool to use in Photoshop! Firstly you need to drag the cursor to create a crop preview area, then, resize if needed by moving any of the corner points, and finally apply the crop by pressing the ***Return*** key or double-clicking inside the active crop area. Simple! The crop preview can be rotated as well as resized by moving outside the active crop area until the cursor changes to indicate rotate is enabled. If you wish to crop and resize your image in one go, you can type in a specific size into the Crop tool options bar before making a preview selection.

MOVING, SCALING & ROTATING: You can make as many alterations as you wish before applying the crop. Move the crop area by clicking and dragging, resize by moving any corner point or scale by holding *Shift*. You can also rotate by moving the cursor outside the crop frame until the cursor changes indicating that rotate is enabled.

USING THE CROP TOOL INFO BAR: Before you make your initial crop selection you are able to type in width and height to create the precise size of your image once the crop is applied. Once the crop previews is active, the info bar changes with options to control the preview shield. You can turn it off, change its colour or adjust its opacity.

APPLYING THE CROP: Once you're happy with the crop preview it's time to apply the crop. To do this you can either go to *Image>Crop* in the menu bar or you can simply double click inside the crop area, better still press the Return key. If you decide to exit the crop preview use right click and select *Cancel*. If you're not happy press *Ctrl+Z* to undo.

Sharpening

OWING TO THE WAY that DSLRs work, digital images all need to be sharpened at some point, be this in-camera or afterwards in Photoshop or Elements. Put simply, you can break down 'sharpness' into two components. The first is resolution – the amount of detail a lens and sensor are able to resolve between them. There is nothing you can do to enhance this aspect in post-processing. The second is acutance – the amount of edge contrast in a picture. This is the part of sharpness we can enhance digitally.

There are many tools to do this in Photoshop's ***Filters>Sharpen*** menu, but the only two worth bothering with are ***Unsharp Mask*** and ***Smart Sharpen*** (found in the Enhance menu in Photoshop Elements) Unsharp mask lets you adjust the edge contrast so an image appears sharper (in reality you don't have any more resolution than you did before). There are some simple rules of thumb: set the Amount to 100 per cent and the Threshold to 0. Work out the correct Radius setting by dividing the intended output resolution by 200. In other words if you are printing at 300ppi sharpen with a Radius of 1.5; if you are outputting to the web, where people will look at your work on screens with a resolution of about 100ppi, the correct Radius here is 0.5. Be warned though, go too far with the Radius control and you'll see nasty looking halos around the edges in your picture.

Smart Sharpen (***Filters>Sharpen>Smart Sharpen*** in Photoshop or ***Enhance>Adjust Sharpness*** in Elements) does the same job but in a slightly more refined manner. Select Lens Blur from the Remove menu to have the filter only sharpen edges and not areas of continuous tone (like skies) that don't need it.

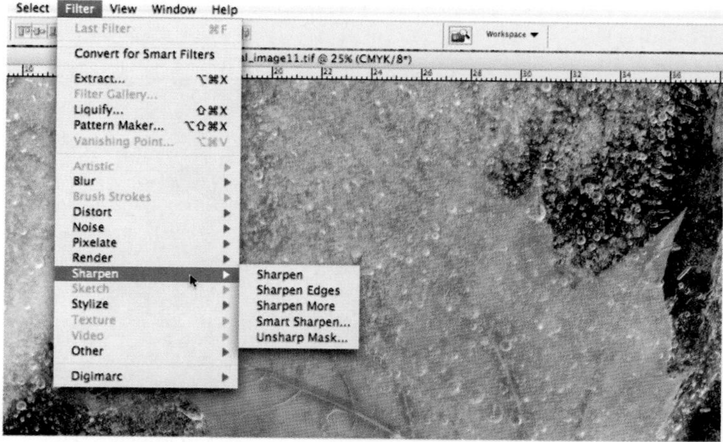

Many photographers do not realise the benefits (and dangers) of using the Sharpen tool. Try making an A4 print with and without sharpening applied and note the detail. Take care not to oversharpen as this can have an adverse effect on image quality. If you're submitting images to magazines or stock libraries, check if they prefer unsharpened or sharpened images as most prefer you not to have appied any sharpening.

The importance of using Layers

IT'S FAIR TO SAY that Photoshop would be nothing without Layers – just a standard paint program of the sort you might find free online. Sure there are plenty of complex features and commands available, but it's the functionality of Layers that lets you put them to use. Think of your background layer like a paint canvas, and then layers as pieces of clear acetate that you lay on top one by one. You can paint on the acetate or the acetate can be coloured or have lightening or darkening properties that affect everything else below. You can swap the acetate layers around, reposition them and you can remove and add information on each as you wish. Without these layers, you'd be forced to work directly on the canvas, limiting the flexibility of your work as if you mess up – which you will frequently do while learning – you will be forced to start again from scratch.

So Layers offer you the chance for a 'non-destructive' workflow, ensuring the background layer is kept in its original state, as well as the chance to make alterations down the line. Imagine you paste a player onto an empty football pitch, for example. When he's on a separate layer, you can move him around at any time or use Transform to flip him or scale him up or down in size, for instance. If the player is merged onto the background layer, you can't perform any such commands without also affecting the pitch itself. And if you decide later down the line that you prefer the pitch to be empty, you face going back through the history, and removing any other good work that you may have done, rather than simply deleting the additional layer.

There are three types of layers: those that contain pixel-based information (including text), those that contain vector information (such as shape layers), and then adjustment layers that contain embedded adjustment commands. It's the first and third that you'll mainly come up against for photo-based work. You can create a new pixel-based layer using the relevant button on the Layers palette or with the shortcut Ctrl/Cmd + Shift + N. You can paint on it as you like as long as it's selected. It's worth noting that you can duplicate a layer at any time with Ctrl/Cmd + J, and if you make a selection prior to using this shortcut, only the selected area is duplicated to the new layer – very useful. If you paste information from another document, it's automatically pasted onto a newly created layer. See the panels for information on adjustment layers and the indispensable layer mask.

The only disadvantage of layers is that they increase file size and can be memory-intensive. Images with huge stacks of layers can end up slowing down all but a very high-specified machine, and can take up precious hard drive space when saving. So, if you're running an older machine, and don't have oodles of hard disk space to spare, it's a good idea not to go crazy with the numbers you add. You can merge layers down that need no more work using Ctrl/Cmd + E (though avoid merging into the background layer).

When you're finished and want to save a reduced file size TIFF or JPEG version for distribution you can flatten all the layers with ***Layer>Flatten Image*** (just remember to save the non-flattened version as a PSD file).

USING MULTIPLE LAYERS
Layers allow you to apply different effects with the benefit of being able to make changes to individual layers without affecting the other layers, which allows you to fine-tune the overall result to your liking.

Navigating the Layers palette

The Layers palette is where you select the various Layer commands and tools. Here we explain what each does

1) BLENDING MODE This determines how the layer interacts with the information below it. It can be changed on a layer-by-layer basis from the default setting.

2) OPACITY Controls how opaque or transparent the active layer is. As you reduce opacity, the layer starts to fade and the beneath layer starts to show through.

3) LOCK TRANSPARENT PIXELS Check this button to prevent any blank areas on a layer being affected by further brush work. Handy if you've floated a selection to a new layer and want to work on these pixels alone.

4) LOCK IMAGE PIXELS Use this if you want to prevent altering anything on that layer with the painting tools. Useful to stop accidental changes to a layer that needs no further work.

5) LOCK POSITION This button prevents the contents on the layer being moved using the Move Tool. It's useful if you've floated a new piece of information, positioned it, and don't want it to be accidentally nudged.

6) LOCK ALL Combines both Lock Image Pixels and Lock Position, preventing anything on the layer being either painted on or moved. It also stops the layer from being deleted.

7) LAYER CONTEXT MENU Access further layer functions by clicking this context menu. You can get to commands like Merge Visible and Flatten Image as well as Convert to Smart Object from here.

8) VISIBILITY The eyeball icon allows you to turn visibility on and off for that particular layer. When visibility is off, the layer has no effect on information below.

9) ADD LAYER MASK Allows you to add a mask to a pixel-based layer so that you can reveal and conceal pixel information on that layer using a black or a white brush.

10) ADJUSTMENT LAYER You can add all of the fill and adjustment layers via this button, which is quicker than using the main Layer menu. Click once for the menu to appear then click your layer of choice.

11) FILL Works in a similar manner to Opacity but while Opacity works on the layer as a whole, Fill only works on pixel information, ignoring layer effects added via Blending Options.

12) LINK LAYERS Click this button with the relevant layers highlighted to link them together so that any subsequent Move or Transform commands affect all layers together.

13) ADD A LAYER STYLE This gives you the option of applying one of the layer styles available in the Blending Options dialogue.

14) NEW GROUP Creates a new group that you can drag and drop layers into. Use for organising the palette or focusing adjustments on certain layers only.

15) NEW LAYER Creates a blank layer above the selected layer. Hold down Ctrl/Cmd when clicking to create the layer underneath instead or use Alt/Option to bring up layer options.

16) DELETE LAYER Click this to delete the active layer, or drag the layer to the button itself. The Delete key also works (except with certain tools selected).

While you don't need to use Layers to improve your pictures, it's only when you start working with Layers that you're able to do more than just scratch the surface of Photoshop's potential.

Adjustment Layers

WHENEVER YOU MAKE any sort of adjustment to your image with the ***Image>Adjustment*** commands, you discard some of your original image information. The greater the adjustment, the more info you discard. This information can never be retrieved without going backwards in the History palette. If you keep applying Curves adjustments one after the other, for example, the image will eventually degrade beyond recognition, and at a much faster rate with 8-bit than with 16-bit images as you're starting with much less information.

We can't avoid throwing away information, but we need to try and keep it to a minimum. If we apply our adjustments directly to pixel-based layers, we can run into problems if we change our minds later and have to apply counter adjustments to correct the ones we've already made. Eventually we'll run into trouble and have to go back in the History and start from scratch, which is the reason why Adobe added the adjustment layer. The adjustment layer sits above our original information, showing its effect in real-time without affecting underlying information (until we flatten the image). If we want to change the adjustment at anytime, we simply double-click it. To add an adjustment layer, click the half-black, half-white circle at the bottom of the Layers palette or select ***Layer>New Adjustment Layer***.

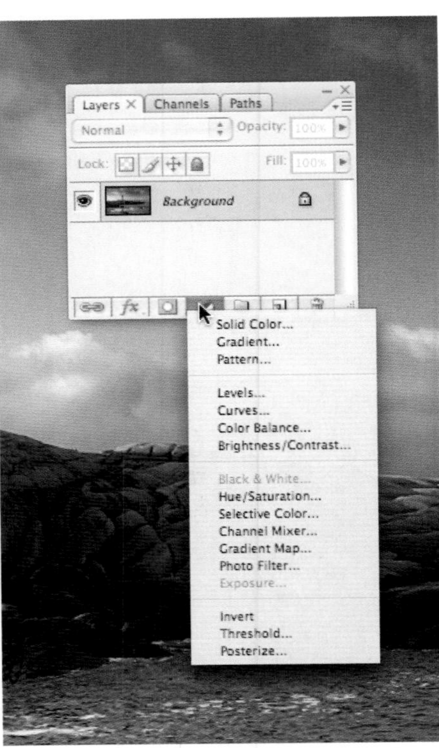

FINDING ADJUSTMENT LAYERS: Creating a new Adjustment Layer can be done in one of two ways. Firstly, you can use the top menu bar by going to ***Layer>New Adjustment Layer*** and selecting the desired function from the drop-down list (above left). Secondly, you can click and hold the Adjustment Layer Icon in the Layers palette (above right), where you'll find the same drop-down list of functions.

PUTTING ADJUSTMENT LAYERS INTO PRACTICE: To create this adjustment layer we used the icon at the bottom of the Layers palette as shown in the example above. For the purpose of this example we select Hue/Saturation from the drop-down list and a new adjustment layer is created containing a copy of the original image, which sits hidden beneath on the Background Layer. The Hue/Saturation function window opens automatically and for this example we reduce the saturation of the image and click OK. That's it! The best thing about Adjustment Layers is that all the original information remains stored in the layer, to alter we simply click the Adjustment layer icon (A) on the layer in the Layers palette and the Hue/Saturation window opens again.

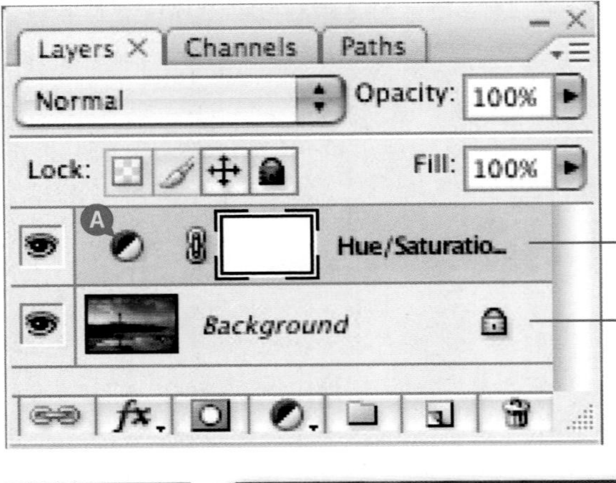

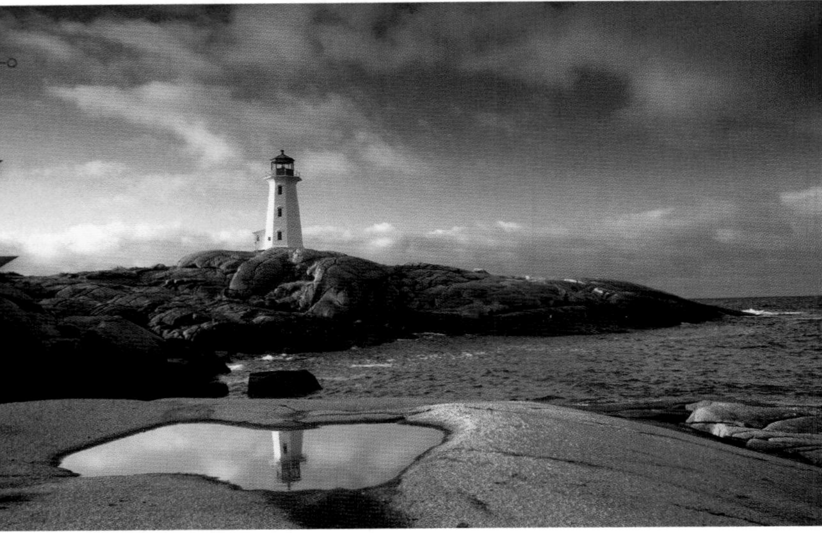

LAYER STRUCTURE: By default the original image is on the Background Layer. The adjustment layer created, in this case the Hue/Saturation adjustments, sit on the Adjustment Layer above the background. Any alterations to this layer will not effect the state of the original image beneath it.

Layer Mask

THE LAYER MASK is the blank rectangle that sits next to the adjustment layer icon (there's a chain link between them). All adjustment layers come with a layer mask as standard. Pixel layers don't, so you have to add one manually with the Add Layer Mask icon at the bottom of the Layers palette (though you can't add one to the Background Layer). The mask effectively tells Photoshop to hide certain parts of your layer. It's white by default, which means it's totally transparent and reveals everything on the layer. If you paint anywhere on the image with black and the layer mask selected, you'll find the information you've painted over on the active layer will become hidden, and you'll see the corresponding black area appear on the mask. Painting back over the white area will reveal that information again.

It's worth noting that you can also use any tones between black and white, so you can work with black and white at reduced brush opacity to partially conceal or reveal. The function of the layer mask is pretty simple then; to hide parts of a layer or adjustment layer. You can apply a contrast Curves change to the eyes of a portrait for example, or alter the hue of the sky only. And it saves you permanently erasing unwanted pixels on pixel based layers only to find you need them later down the line. Mask them out instead, and you can bring them back in anytime you like.

Layer Mask: Reveal All, Hide All, Reveal Selection, Hide Selection, Delete, Apply, Enable, Unlink

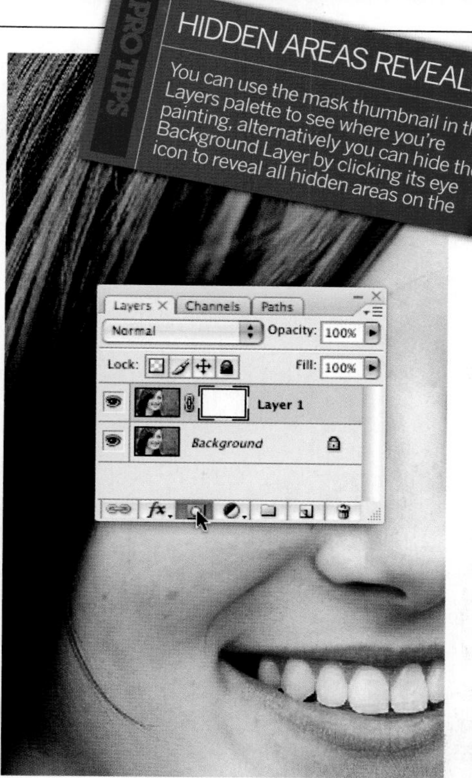

PRO TIPS

HIDDEN AREAS REVEALED!

You can use the mask thumbnail in the Layers palette to see where you're painting, alternatively you can hide the Background Layer by clicking its eye icon to reveal all hidden areas on the

FINDING LAYER MASK: Creating a new Layer Mask can be done in one of two ways but before you start you need to go ***Layer>Duplicate Layer*** to create a copy of the image, as a Layer Mask can't be created on the Background Layer. Next, you can use the top menu bar by going ***Layer>Layer Mask>Reveal All*** (above left), or you can click and hold the Add Layer Mask Icon in the Layers palette (above right).

USING LAYER MASK: For this example, we'll show you how to alter the background of this without affecting the girl's face. With a duplicate layer created and the Layer Mask activated as shown above we ensure the image part of the layer is active (A) by clicking it, then we use Levels to improve the overall vibrancy of the image with the intention of boosting the background. With this done we now click on the mask part of the layer (B) and select the Brush Tool, choose a suitable size and with it set to Black, we paint over the face area. In the areas of this layer where black is painted the information is hidden revealing the original information from the background layer beneath. To make hidden data visible again, simply paint over again with the brush set to white.

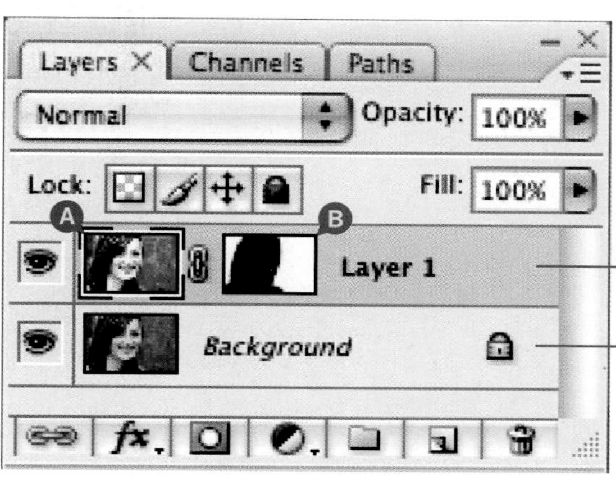

LAYER MASK

BACKGROUND LAYER

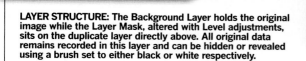

LAYER STRUCTURE: The Background Layer holds the original image while the Layer Mask, altered with Level adjustments, sits on the duplicate layer directly above. All original data remains recorded in this layer and can be hidden or revealed using a brush set to either black or white respectively.

Why shoot in Raw?

AS ALL EXPERIENCED photographers are aware, the very best images are a combination of great in-camera technique followed by top Photoshop skills. One of the most important steps forward that you can take is to shoot in Raw rather than JPEG to capture the maximum amount of information. There's no such thing as a .RAW file in the same way that there's .JPEG and .TIFF. Instead, 'Raw' is a catch-all term used to describe the data captured directly from a camera sensor, that comes in a variety of different flavours, depending on the brand of camera. Examples include .CR2 for Canon and .NEF for Nikon. Data in this form is greyscale, and not a lot of use to the camera user on its own. There are two methods of converting Raw files into usable image data. The first happens automatically in-camera whenever you select the JPEG setting. The second method is to shoot in Raw mode and convert your Raw files post-capture using a PC or Mac and a Raw converter such as Adobe Camera Raw. The latter is the best option for maximum quality, as it gives users access to the full 16-bit range of information, giving you more latitude to make adjustments and correct for problems like under and overexposure. To use a film analogy, the Raw file is much more like a negative that you can interpret in the darkroom in the manner that you wish. If you let the camera do the conversion to produce a JPEG image, you've effectively produced a print already and thrown the negative away! Raw files also allow non-destructive editing. You produce an editable image in Photoshop from your Raw file – the Raw file itself is never altered. The principle disadvantage of shooting Raw is the extra time involved. JPEGs are ready to roll straight out of camera. Raw files on the other hand require the extra step of opening in Camera Raw, making necessary changes and then processing.

What cameras shoot Raw files?

All digital SLRs allow you to set your camera to shoot in Raw, but you'll also find most hybrid cameras as well as high-end zoom compacts and DSLR-type cameras allow you to switch from JPEG to Raw shooting for improved image quality. If you're unsure, check the instructions (or the Quality setting on the camera) to see if it offers this useful function.

RAW POWER! DSLRs, such as the Nikon D90, aren't the only type of camera that allows for Raw shooting. Top-end bridge cameras, such as the Fuji FinePix S9500, as well as premium compacts like the Canon PowerShot G11, are designed with more advanced photographers in mind and so offer Raw capability.

PRO TIPS

RAW FILES NAMED!

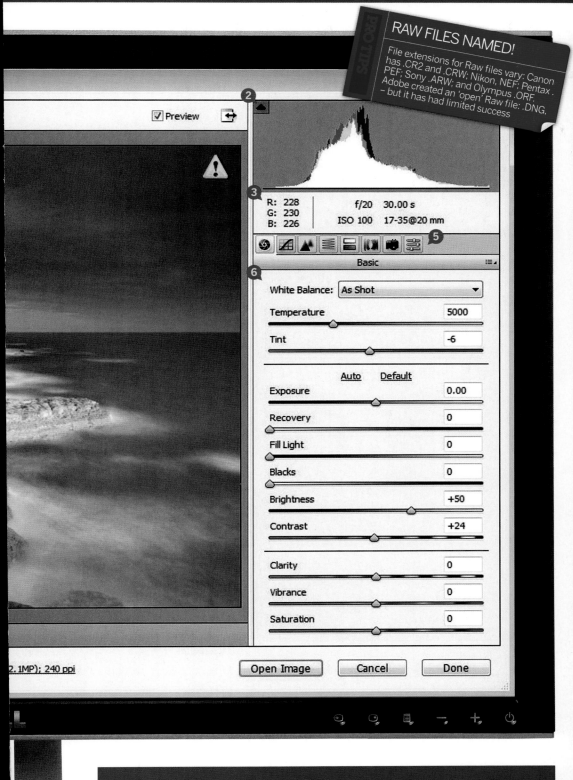

File extensions for Raw files vary: Canon has .CR2 and .CRW; Nikon, NEF; Pentax, PEF; Sony .ARW; and Olympus .ORF. Adobe created an 'open' Raw file: .DNG, – but it has had limited success

Raw interface

Open a Raw file in Photoshop and you're presented with the following interface. Here we explain the main commands that are displayed.

1) TOOLBAR Contains all selectable tools such as Zoom Tool, Hand Tool and Crop Tool. Users of the latest version of Photoshop also have access to the Adjustment Brush and Graduated Filter. Like the main Photoshop program, all Tools have single letter keyboard shortcuts that are worth getting to know.

2) HISTOGRAM The histogram tells you exactly what is happening to your Raw information in real time as you alter the dialogue controls. It takes the form of a graph, representing colour in numbers from 0 to 255, going from left to right, darkest to lightest. The white shade represents the combined red, green and blue channels and gives you the foremost indication of exposure.

3) INFO PALETTE Shows the pixel readings for red, green and blue channels from 0 to 255 when the cursor is placed in the main window, and also contains image metadata information such as aperture in f/stops, shutter speed in seconds, ISO rating and focal length.

4) IMAGE WINDOW The main preview window for the open image. You can zoom in using the Zoom Tool or the plus and minus buttons or drop-down menu underneath and can move around the image using the Hand tool or by holding down the Spacebar and dragging. Check the Preview box to see your image with and without current edits.

5) CONTROL TABS You can negotiate between the different control tabs by clicking on each. The first tab is labelled Basic and contains the controls that you will use most often, such as the Exposure and Blacks sliders. Other tabs are Tone Curve, Detail, HSL/Greyscale, Split Toning, Lens Corrections, Camera Calibration and Presets. Elements users have only Basic, Camera Calibration and Presets.

6) CONTROL WINDOW This is the main dialogue window that contains the controls for each of the specific control tabs. They're all slider based, other than the Point Curve section of the Tone Curve tab (which allows you to plot points on a curve) and the Preset tab, which involves simply selecting listed Presets.

7) OUTPUT BUTTONS Along the bottom you'll find all the buttons for doing what you choose once you have finished your edits. You can Save, Save As, Open, Open a Copy or use Done to store your edits without actually processing the Raw file. Holding down Alt/Option gives you access to the extra options.

Which quality level is best, 8-bit OR 16-bit?

Most digital cameras capture 12 or 14 bits of data per channel, which equates to a total of 4,096 or 16,384 levels in each colour channel. Think of levels as tonal information – the more levels you have the more tonal information is available. When you shoot in JPEG mode, you discard large amounts of this information to produce an 8-bit image, which retains just 256 levels per channel. Raw files can be edited in 16-bit mode, giving you access to the full 12- or 14-bits of information. The extra information won't be immediately obvious on screen or in print but really comes into play when you're making your edits. Adjustments such as Curves, Levels and Colour Balance all discard information each time they are put to use. So, while you may not be able to tell the difference on-screen and in print between 4,096 levels and 256 levels, you will be able to see a marked difference between the 2,000 versus 40 you may have left after heavy editing. In short, 8-bit files give you very little editing headroom before images start to visibly degrade.

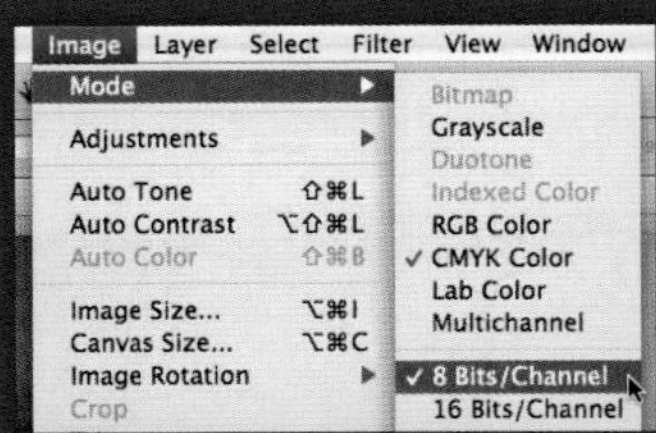

How to process a Raw file

The best thing about shooting Raw is how you can process the file to give a far better result than if you had captured the scene as a JPEG. While the preview of a Raw file on your camera's LCD monitor may look identical to a JPEG, the truth is that all the additional information is hidden with the file and impossible to display on your camera's screen. It's only when you open the Raw file on your computer that you'll be really able to see the wonders retained in this purest of image file formats.

Our step-by-step guide shows how processing Raw files in Photoshop allows you to extract an amazing amount of information from a Raw file that leads to a far superior result than if the image had originally been captured in JPEG.

1

The first thing we do when we open our Raw file is to see how the histogram looks with the default Camera Raw settings. We can see here that contrast is fairly low with the bulk of the information sitting in the middle. The preview window confirms this – the image looks quite muted and would benefit from extra contrast to add colour and detail.

2

There's a little bit of highlight information approaching the end of the histogram so next we see if there's any highlight detail that might be clipped. Click the triangle on the top right of the histogram to turn on the highlight clipping display. The whites of the distant lighthouse are clipped, which means we might potentially lose some highlight detail.

3

We could recover this information using the Recovery slider, but this would be at the expense of the highlights elsewhere, which would effectively reduce contrast. The small amount of clipped information isn't that important, so we decide to leave things be. Exposure looks spot on so we don't need to adjust this slider either.

4

At the other end of the histogram the darkest tones are a long way from the left edge, which represents pure black. There are areas in the rocks that should in reality be pure black, so we need to alter the black point. Hold down Alt/Option and move the Black slider until the rock cracks show black on the white background.

5

Now these areas are black, we have effectively clipped detail. We're normally looking to avoid clipping, but here it's necessary to strengthen the dark tones and improve contrast. We wouldn't expect to see detail in the rock face cracks. We set Contrast to +60 to boost contrast further without clipping too much more shadow detail.

6

We can now use a +25 on the Vibrance slider (or +15 on Saturation in earlier Photoshop versions without Vibrance) to pump the colour up a little. Press I to access the White Balance tool and check that we have got the correct White Balance by clicking on a neutral white or grey – the lighthouse in the foreground is good here.

FINAL IMAGE
It's clear to see the benefits of shooting your images in Raw, as it's possible to extract far more detail than if you had taken the shot as a JPEG.

7

This actually makes things look a little too cool, so we can use the Temperature slider to warm things up a little. We can strengthen contrast a little further if we wish by negotiating from the Basic tab to the Tone Curve tab. Select Point rather than Parametric and change the drop-down menu from Medium to Strong Contrast.

8

We can also bring out the sky and sea a little more with a selective Saturation and Luminance increase. Choose the HSL/Greyscale tab and select the Saturation sub-tab. Set Blues to +40. Now choose the Luminance sub-tab and set Blues to +40 here too. As you can see, these tweaks all result in the image delivering far more impact.

9

We negotiate to the Detail tab next and use the Zoom buttons to zoom in to 100%. We now work the Sharpness slider to get the image looking crisp on screen. We settle on Amount 100, Radius 1.0 and Detail 30. We don't need to worry about the image suffering from high levels of noise as the image was captured at ISO 100.

10

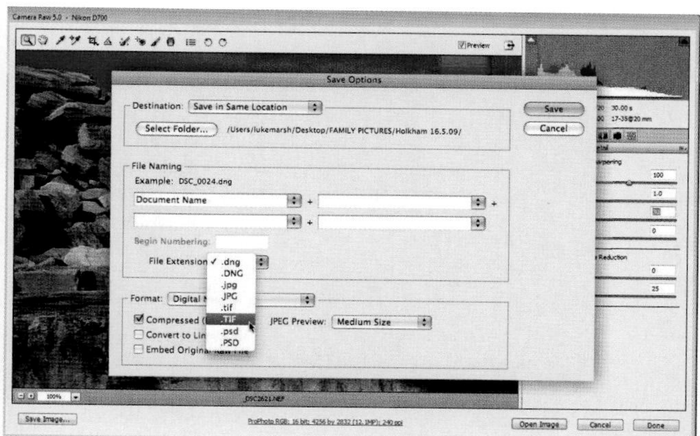

Once you're finished, you can either open the image to continue manipulation in Photoshop or save it for later. By saving the image as a .TIFF or .PSD format you will leave yourself with a 16-bit file as opposed to compressing the image to an 8-bit JPEG, which reduces the amount of information and thus flexibility when editing in the future.

Combining Raw files

Setting your DSLR to shoot in Raw means you're able to recover hidden detail from areas of the scene that are overexposed, such as bright sky. The Raw converter in Photoshop Elements can be used to create two different images at different exposures from the same Raw file and then recombine them for the perfect result.

Techniques used in this easy-to-follow step-by-step tutorial include exposure adjustment, layer creation and editing, level adjustment, sharpness control using the High Pass filter, opacity effects and colour adjustment. This method is also especially efficient as you are only working with image data captured in the original single exposure. This means you can revisit any of your old Raw files to try it.

1

If you've never used the Elements Raw converter before, the first thing you'll notice on opening files is the image opens in the Raw control window (above). For the first step, simply click ***Open***, leaving the settings as they are, then go ***File>Save As*** and create a Photoshop file (.psd) as we are going to be working with layers.

2

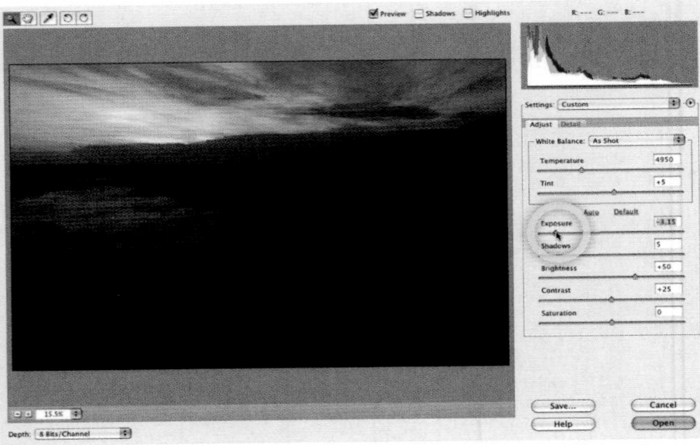

Next, reopen the original Raw file, and again the Raw control window appears with the image. This time, use the Exposure control (circled) and move the slider left, to underexpose the image, pulling back the detail from the sky area hidden on the original image. When you're happy with the results, click ***Open*** to take the image into Elements.

3

You now have two files open. One contains the original exposure and the other is the new underexposed image. With the underexposed file active, click ***Select>All*** then ***Edit>Copy*** placing the image into the pasteboard memory. Now you can close this file and use ***Edit>Paste*** to place this image into a new layer on the original file.

4

With the two exposures in place, we now want to combine the correctly-exposed foreground with the newly-exposed sky. With the sky layer active and using the Rectangular Marquee, select a large area of foreground, just short of the horizon. Next, use ***Edit>Delete*** to remove the area noting the effect in the Layer palette preview (inset).

5

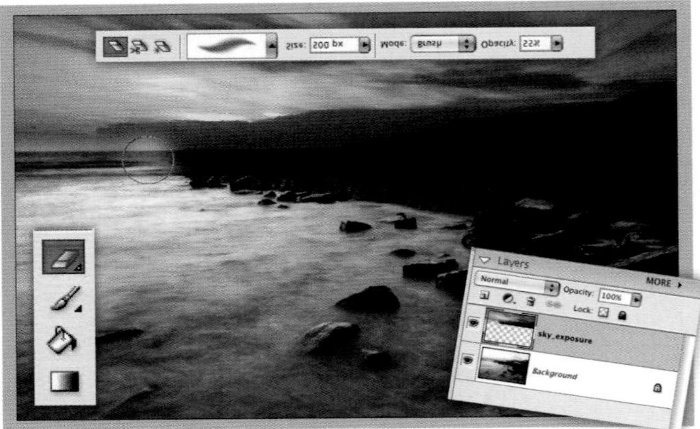

Now it's time to tidy up the horizon, so with the Eraser tool set to a medium-sized, soft-edged brush at an Opacity of 55%, gradually erase areas of the newly-exposed layer, revealing the original horizon exposure. The slight feathering effect between the two layers creates a misty effect that further enhances the image's mood.

6

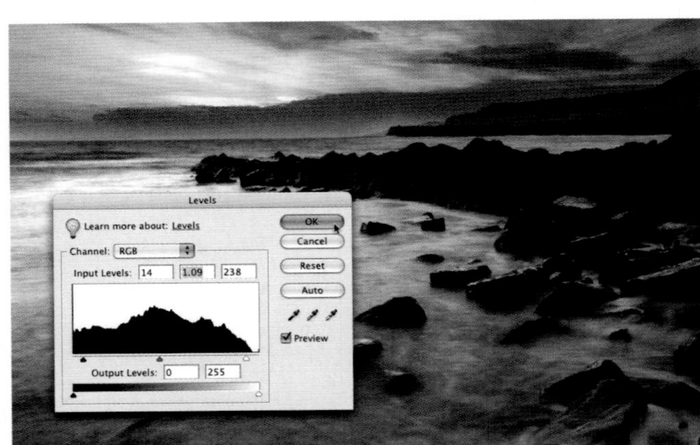

The initial layer work is complete, so to save your work so far, go ***Layer>Flatten Image*** then ***File>Save As*** to create a new file. With both layers merged, it's time for some overall enhancement, so click on ***Enhance>Adjust Lighting>Levels*** to lighten up the image and improve the definition. Click ***OK*** to apply the changes.

FINAL IMAGE
Stormy skies ahead! It's clear to see the benefits of shooting your images in Raw, as it's possible to rescue more detail than if you'd captured the scene as a JPEG.

7

The High Pass filter is a far more forgiving way to enhance detail than sharpening. To use it, first go to ***Layer>Duplicate Layer*** to preserve the original image. Then go to ***Filter>Other>High Pass,*** adjusting the Radius to around 20 pixels before clicking ***OK***. Now you need to change the Blend Mode in the Layer palette to Soft Light.

8

Use ***Layer>Flatten Image*** again, saving a copy if required. Now, using the Burn tool (inset right) with a large soft-edged brush and the Opacity at approximately 25%, darken the exposure of specific areas, which helps to improve the depth of the image. Focus on the edges of the frame and gradually build the effect up.

9

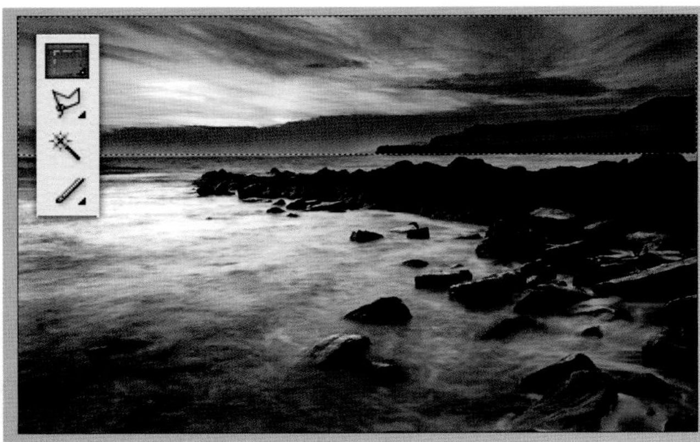

The image is predominately blue in hue and we'd quite like to inject a different tone to the sky area. Using the Rectangular Marquee tool, select the area above the horizon and ***Select>Feather,*** entering an amount of 50 pixels to soften the selection, before clicking ***Edit>Copy*** then ***Edit>Paste,*** placing the selection into a new layer.

10

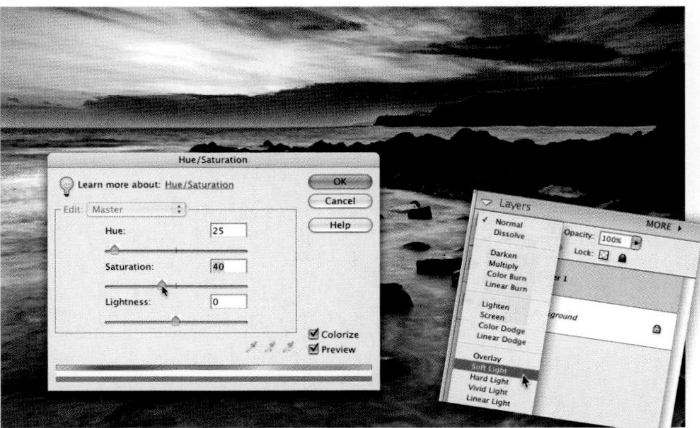

Change the Blend Mode of the new layer to Soft Light, and then go to ***Enhance>Adjust Colour>Adjust Hue/Saturation***. In the window, start by clicking the Colorize box and immediately see the effect in the preview. Finally, adjust the Hue and Saturation sliders until you are happy with the colour, and then click ***OK***.

Monitor calibration

IF YOU PLAN to print your favourite images, whether at home or using a lab, then you should seriously consider buying a monitor calibration device. If you look at the rows of TVs in your local electronics shop, you'll notice that the colours are slightly different, and it's the same with computer monitors. Though your screen may look fine to you, making sure the colours are accurate is very important, as a badly calibrated monitor can have a knock on effect for every other stage of your digital processing. For instance, the adjustments you make to improve your image could in fact making it look worse when viewed on a properly calibrated screen; this means that when you go on to print or share the image, it will appear significantly different on paper or on other users' monitors. Printer calibration is an additional step, but the more advanced devices here have the ability to do this as well. With a range of devices on the market, ranging from £100 to £500+, just how much do you need to spend to get a good result?

1) X-rite Eye-One Display 2

Contact: www.colourconfidence.com
Guide price: £170 / **Street price:** £150

Eye-One Display 2 is a simple, understated device, designed for professional calibration. The Eye-One match software is expandable to include projectors, scanners, printers and cameras but this version works with CRT and LCD screens only. The device works on both Mac and PC, including Vista. The first stage of the calibration detects where the device is on the screen. Once past this stage, it performs an ambient light test that requires a plastic filter cover to be put over the light sensor. Scan time is just under three and a half minutes, but you do have to factor in time to attach and remove the ambient filter. Using the advanced setting, we achieved some great results, though from the basic mode, the screen tended to look slightly cool.

2) Pantone Huey PRO

Contact: www.colourconfidence.com
Guide price: £95 / **Street price:** £90

This pro version of the Huey may be around £30 more than the basic model but the benefits make it worth the extra pounds. In addition to standard calibration, it allows you to check your brightness and contrast settings by showing a series of black and white tones. There's an opportunity at the end of the process to adjust the colour temperature and gamma if required. The scanning process is quick, at just under one minute, and the overall appearance of the screen after calibration is good, with rich colours. It also allows constant light monitoring from its desktop holder. With such a capable specification and a guide price of under £100 this is a truly impressive piece of kit.

3) Datacolor Spyder 3 Elite

Contact: www.colourconfidence.com
Guide price: £153 / **Street price:** £140

This is a more advanced version of the Spyder 3 and is designed for professional use. Within the calibration process, there are options for basic or advanced controls, depending on your level of expertise. The full, advanced mode includes manual adjustment of white and black luminance, and RGB controls, while the basic mode skips straight to the measuring. It features an ambient light meter within the device and can take the reading while on the screen, incorporating it into the measuring process. The overall scan time is under five minutes and can be left alone to get on with it. The finished result looks good, especially if you take the time to use the advanced settings. A good choice if you want pro quality on a budget.

4) X-rite ColorMunki Photo

Contact: www.colourconfidence.com
Guide price: £349 / **Street price:** £300

This device is slightly different to the others here as it can also be used for printer calibration. Also, by using the Digital Pouch application, it can transport colour settings between machines to ensure that your images are viewed in the correct profile wherever you go. The slickly designed software gives a choice of easy and advanced versions, depending on whether you wish to set your own brightness, contrast, luminance and white point. The results are superb and if you really need the very best in colour calibration, this unit is for you, and though the results may not appear £200 better than the Spyder 3 Elite, the inclusion of printer calibration justifies its price.

Graphic tablets

Graphics tablets are not new arrivals to the world of digital imaging, but they do offer a more natural method of editing for the photographer. They allow you to use a pen to control your on-screen cursor, which can be particularly helpful for freehand drawing, dodging and burning, and cutting out. Fine artists who like to paint over their images are the biggest users but tablets can have uses for almost everyone. It can take time to get used to though, as it feels very different to working with a mouse. More recent models have refined their level of control, adding not just pressure sensitivity – to produce a heavier or wider line when the pen is pressed harder against the tablet – but also incorporating the angle of the pen, finer positioning control, and quick keys for scrolling and key function access. If you've never used a graphic tablet before, we'd recommend you start with a budget model as despite their advantages, you may find them too alien to work with. However, persevere and you'll discover how they will improve the speed and precision at which you can manipulate images.

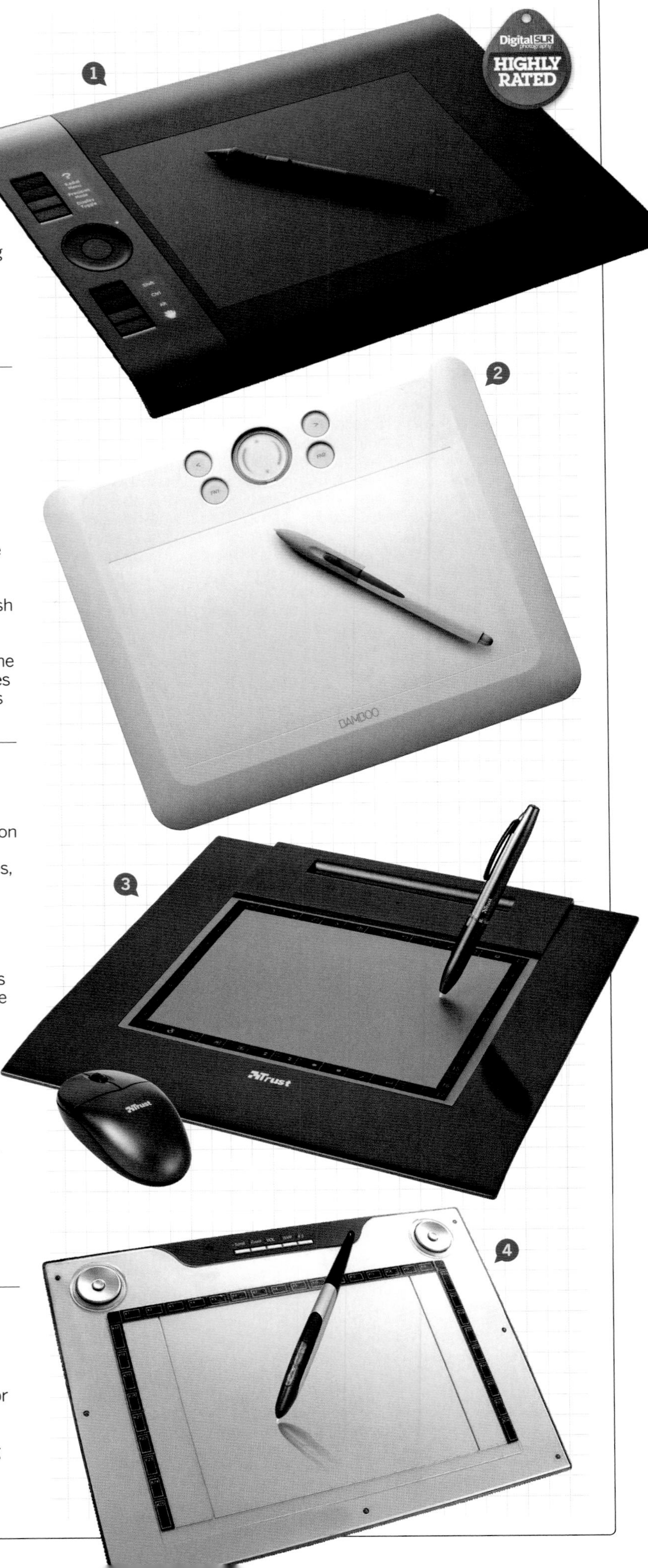

1) Wacom Intuos 4 (Medium)

Contact: www.wacom-europe.com
Guide price: £330 / **Street price:** £290

Wacom's brand new tablet is the fourth version of their professional pen tablet system. The Intuos 4 has a darker, sleeker look and has raised the bar even further in terms of features. It offers 2,048 pressure levels on the pen (double that of most others), improved maximum reading height and 5,080 lines per inch resolution, matching that of their top Cintiq model for a more natural feel. There are eight customisable buttons along the side of the tablet, which feature illuminated displays for easy reference, as well as a touch wheel and centre toggle button for control of zooming, scrolling, brush size, rotation etc. The tablet can also be rotated for left hand use – leaving the function buttons on the right – and can even be powered from most USB ports. The range comes in four sizes, ranging from the small (309x208mm) up to the Extra Large (462x305mm), with prices ranging from £200 to £700. This model, the medium-sized option, is more than ample for most. One of the very best on the market.

2) Wacom Bamboo Fun

Contact: www.wacom-europe.com
Guide price: £90 / **Street price:** £65

The Bamboo range of tablets are designed to be an affordable solution for the creative user, with models starting from just £35 for the Bamboo One. The Bamboo Fun is designed for use with art packages, as opposed to the handwriting bias of the other models, and comes in small and medium sizes. This small model has an active area of 148x92mm (just under 10.5in diagonal), and features four function buttons and a special touch ring for zooming and scrolling. The buttons are designed to be operated with a finger rather than the pen, but work well enough. The pad is tough to fault for the price. It's responsive and smooth, allowing precise control over pressure, angle and positioning. A great tablet for the occasional user or beginner.

3) Trust Slimline Design tablet TB-6300

Contact: www.trust.com
Guide price: £58 / **Street price:** £50

With an 8x6in active area, this mid-range Trust tablet is about as small as you'd want to go for any graphical work. It includes a three-button pen with 512 pressure sensitivity and a wireless three-button scroll mouse, both powered by AAA batteries. Around the edge of the active area are 42 programmable soft buttons for quick function access. It is also fully compatible with Windows Vista's advanced tablet functionality for handwriting recognition, which may come in handy to some users. It proves to be a neat mid-range option.

4) Aiptek Media tablet 1400u

Contact: www.aiptekshop.de
Guide price: £120 / **Street price:** £05

From American technology brand Aiptek, this modern and shiny looking tablet offers a large 304x184mm active area and can be set for widescreen or regular 4:3 displays. It boasts an impressive 4,000dpi resolution and 1,024 pressure levels on the pen. It also features two rolling pads in the top corners, five hot-keys and 34 macro keys along the edge. It comes complete with a full version of Adobe Photoshop Elements 5.0 and was designed to be fully compatible with both PC and Mac operating systems.

External hard drives

BACK IN THE OLD DAYS of film, so long as you put your negatives somewhere safe, you knew you could always reprint a photo should you want to. Essentially this hasn't changed with digital photography. When you download your shots to your computer, you create a folder and store them on your hard drive. However, hard disks have the potential to crash, so invest in additional drives to ensure you never have to face the trauma of losing all your images.

1) LaCie Hard Drive 500GB

Contact: www.lacie.com
Guide price: £70 / **Street price:** £50

This sexy looking black slab has been designed by industry guru, Neil Poulton. When on, it shines a blue strip onto the desk, making it hard to beat on the 'cool' factor. Despite appearances, this is a very functional and affordable unit. On the inside it is a standard 3.5in fan cooled drive – this version is USB 2.0, but a triple interface model is now available, as are larger capacities such as the 1TB version. Though set-up defaults to NTFS, it can be formatted for Mac or made dual format in less than 40 seconds. Transfer times are as quick as any here and at this price you might as well buy two.

2) Freecom 500GB

Contact: www.freecom.com
Guide price: £130 / **Street price:** £75

Freecom's range of external drives used to start at 160GB but this 500GB model is now the smallest capacity in the range. It's a stylish looking piece of kit, with an aluminium surround that acts as a heat sink, the black front features a blue 500GB symbol that lights up when turned on. It can be used vertically as well as horizontally, though there isn't a foot for support. Unlike most here that are formatted to Windows NTFS, this comes in FAT32 format, which is more flexible for PC and Mac use. All devices can be reformatted, and this one can be changed to NTFS if needed.

3) LaCie Rugged Drive 500GB

Contact:www.lacie.com
Guide price: £104 / **Street price:** £90

Designed to be portable (and rugged), this pocket-sized drive is cased in shock-resistant rubber. It takes power from your machine via the USB cable, or iLink, making it ideal for laptop users. The drive requires a format as part of the set-up but this takes less than 40 seconds and allows you to choose the format, including a dual-format mode for PC and Mac use. Despite the smaller drive size and portability, transfer times are still quick, matching any of the desktop models. Though it is one of the more expensive drives, if you're on the move, it's worth every penny to ensure the ultimate protection for your images.

Card readers

While the standard method for transferring images from camera to computer is by connecting both with a lead, the fastest and easiest method is to use a card reader. Here are two models highly recommended by the experts at *Digital SLR Photography* magazine.

4) SanDisk Extreme Firewire reader

Contact: www.uk.sandisk.com
Guide price: £80 / **Street price:** £50

This high-speed card reader is perfect for those transferring large amounts of images. It comes with leads for FireWire 400 and FireWire 800 to allow read and write speeds of up to 40MB/s if you have the FireWire 800 connection (which features on most new Macs). It's a superb choice if you only use CompactFlash cards.

5) Lexar Professional UDMA dual-slot USB reader

Contact: www.lexar.com
Guide price: £40 / **Street price:** £25

This reader is designed for use with the latest high-speed UDMA memory cards but will still read all other SD and CompactFlash card types, thanks to its dual card slots. This model features a USB connection but a CompactFlash-only reader is available with the new fast FireWire 800 connection for Mac users. Fast and very reliable.

Inkjet printers

The process of printing has become easier and, on the whole, cheaper. Better quality sensors and improved inks mean that prints look better, while more intelligent software and colour management make images appear more like they do on screen. With so many printers on the market, the choice is tough. For the enthusiast photographer, A3 printers give the most flexibility, as an A3+ print is more than big enough to hang on a wall, or even exhibit, while smaller prints can still be made in the same way. The drawbacks of an A3 printer are the amount of space it takes up on the desk and the price. If you are only likely to make a few prints larger than A4, it may be more economical to choose an A4 printer and use a lab for larger work. The following are a selection of models that performed extremely well in tests, as well as the Epson 3880, an update of the superb Epson 3800.

1) Epson Stylus Photo R285 (A4)

Contact: www.epson.co.uk
Guide price: £75 / **Street price:** £65

This mid-range printer has been around for a couple of years but still offers a great deal for the money. Being a slightly older model, the installation CD doesn't have quite the glitz of newer versions, but installs just as easily. The R285 uses six single Claria ink cartridges – the same inks used across the majority of their photo printer range. These cost around £9.10 per cartridge or £46.92 for a full set (multipack). This may seem a little steep, however, the results produced by these do justify the extra spend. Colours both in the swatches and main images appear bright and punchy, with strong blacks and good skin tones. Fine detail is resolved well and printing is relatively quiet and gentle The only slight disappointment is in its grayscale (black & white) performance, which could be better.

2) Canon PIXMA iP4600 (A4)

Contact: www.canon.co.uk
Guide price: £109 / **Street price:** £90

This A4 printer from Canon is compact and beautifully designed. It uses five individual ink cartridges, though this is only composed of three colours (Cyan, Magenta, Yellow), a photo black and a pigment black for text. These cost £7.99 per cartridge (£8.09 for the larger pigment black cart) or £38.07 for a full set (C/M/Y multipack). Operation is almost at a whisper and yet print times are lightning fast – taking just two minutes for a standard A4 print, and 20 seconds longer for a borderless print. The results are not a million miles from that of the Epson R285, though they appear less punchy and, in places, more natural and warmer. Grayscale images are good, but are a little on the green side. Fine detail is well resolved.

3) Epson Stylus Photo 3880 (A3+)

Contact: www.epson.co.uk
Guide price: £1,200 / **Street price:** £1,195

If you're really serious about producing prints to a pro standard, whether to display at exhibitions or to sell as fine-art prints, then the latest A2+ photo printer from Epson is one for the shortlist. Using Epson's fourth-generation UltraChrome K3 pigment inks, colour and black & white prints exhibit high levels of sharpness and superb tonal reproduction. The pigment inks also offer excellent colour stability and light fastness so prints can be framed and mounted without fear of colour fading. Prints sizes from 6x4in to 22x17in are possible with three print paths on offer to handle a wide variety of papers.

4) Canon PIXMA iX4000 (A3+)

Contact: www.canon.co.uk
Guide price: £279 / **Street price:** £200

This looks like an enlarged version of Canon's A4 models. The lighter colour doesn't quite look as sleek as the dark grey and black models, but it is well built. It uses four ink cartridges (black/cyan/magenta/yellow) costing £11 each, with a double-sized cartridge for the black at £13, making a total of just £46 for a full refill – though with less cartridges, refills will be more frequent. Image quality is pleasing and natural and black & white images have a very neutral tone. One of its main strengths is its print speed. An A4 print took under two and a half minutes, while an A3+ borderless print was finished in less than seven.

Inkjet Paper

YOUR CHOICE OF INKJET PAPER can have a greater effect on your image than the printer and inks, so choosing the right one for the job is essential. A good starting point is to try out papers from your printer manufacturer, but you'll discover that there are many excellent third-party papers that are worth giving a go. *Digital SLR Photography* magazine has tested an extensive range of papers on a variety of printers, including the Canon Pro 9500 and Epson R2880, to give a balanced view of their performance, but each one may behave slightly differently on your own printer. Here are a small selection covering a variety of finishes from glossy to lustre and satin for you to consider.

1) Ilford Gallerie Smooth Gloss

Contact: www.ilford.com
Price: A4 £13 / A3 £32 / A3+ £40 (25 sheets)
The extra weight in this 290g paper gives a more rigid and photographic feel. The images, in return, have good depth, especially with black & white images, which really suit this paper.

2) Permajet Gloss 271 paper

Contact: www.permajet.com
Price: A4 £12 / A3 £22 / A3+ £40 (25 sheets)
This paper has ICC profiles for most printers, including the R2880 and 9500, allowing them to adapt to the paper. As a result, the images remain natural and very pleasing to the eye.

3) Epson Pro Premium Luster

Contact: www.epson.co.uk
Price: A4 £35 (25 sheets) / A3+ £120 (100)
In Epson's pro range, this 250g paper is designed for wedding and portrait photographers. Though lightweight, the results are truly breathtaking and the lustre finish gives images a pro feel.

4) Hahnemuhle Photo Rag Satin Glossy Fine Art

Contact: www.hahnemuehle.com
Price: A4 £24 / A3 £49 / A3+ £61 (20 sheets)
This is a textured 310g fine-art paper, yet the satin coating gives a detailed and bright image, much like a semi- gloss. The result is absolutely stunning.

5) Permajet FB Royal Fine Art

Contact: www.permajet.com
Price: A4 £28 / A3 £55 / A3+ £68 (25)
This 'digital' fibre-based paper is a weighty 325g and has a smooth gloss coating that has a card-like feel. The gloss is subtle, almost silk-like, working well in both colour and mono prints.

6) Fujifilm Hunt Photo satin

Contact: www.fujifilm.com
Price: A4 £27 / A3+ £65 (50 sheets)
A professional paper from the Fuji Hunt range of large format papers. The Satin finish is slightly less glossy than rival brands and as a result, allows you to really appreciate the texture.

1

2

3
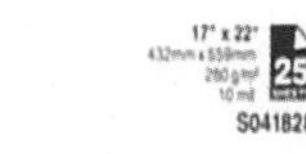

4

5

6

19 Rosebery Avenue, London EC1R 4SP
www.chaudigital.com
020 7833 3938

PRODUCTS

EPSON®
EXCEED YOUR VISION

The NEW Epson SP 3880

The professional A2+ large format printer has 9 pigment inks on board using Epson's Ultrachrome K3 Vivid Magenta ink technology producing a wider colour gamut with excellent lightfastness. Equipped with Epson's Micro-Piezo printhead technology the 3880 can print borderless on a wide variety of media from 4" to 17" with auto-switching between matte and photo black.

Epson Stylus Pro 4880

Produce the highest level of print quality and reliability with Epson's latest ink technlogy in the form of the professional and robust 4880. Create consistent, photo realistic prints on a variety of media that last; the Ultrachrome K3 inkset produces depth in tonal range with subtle shadows and gradations. Enhance your productivity with high speeds, new drivers and simple controls.

Epson SP 7880, 9880 and 11880

Add quality and productivity to in house production printing up to 64" wide and enhance performance in proofing, photography and even fine art reporoductions with Epson's new inkset.See the difference with the advnced Epson 8 colour UltraChrome K3 ink with Vivid Magenta and enhanced image processing technology. The new Vivid Magenta means there is extended colour representation of reds and blues and the 3 black inks means you can achieve the maximum tonal range.

Epson SP7900 and 9900

The next generation of photographic printing technology. Epson's x900 series uses their successful Micro-Piezo TFP printhead technology and Epson Ultrachrome HDR inkset. With the capability of handling ten seperate ink channels with 360 nozzles per channel, and a ten colour screening algorithm, the 900 series gives you high quality prints with superior colour and clarity and a higher production rate. The new inkset, with the addition of Orange and Green, means you are able to achieve a wider colour gamut than ever before.

NEW Wacom Bamboo Touch - the best of both worlds

With Bamboo, Wacom introduces a new, inspiring technology that provides a more intuitive and simple way to work with computers. By combining multi-touch functionality and pen tablet technology in a single device, it provides the best of both worlds – and allows users to express their ideas and thoughts even more spontaneously and immediately.

SERVICES

Fine Art Printing, Retouching and Hi-Res Scanning

Our services cover hi-res film and flatbed scanning, retouching and on-demand giclee printing up to 64" roll widths We print one-offs, short runs and editions for exhibitions, galleries, professional photographers, artists and private individuals. Using the finest machines, with genuine manufacturer's pigment inks on acid-free, museum grade archival papers and canvasses, our high quality work has served the likes of Bob Carlos Clarke, Getty, Chris Levine, National Portrait Gallery and Downing Street. We offer friendly advice to help you achieve the best results possible.

Colour Management

Our on-site and remote colour management services will take the guess work and frustration out of your digital workflow. From putting together equipment solutions to creating proof quality custom ICC paper profiles, let us help you save time and money and achieve consistent output.

SIMPLE STEPS TO BETTER PICTURES

Step-by-step tutorials

BASIC TECHNIQUES

Our favourite Photoshop skills help you make a major difference with minimum effort

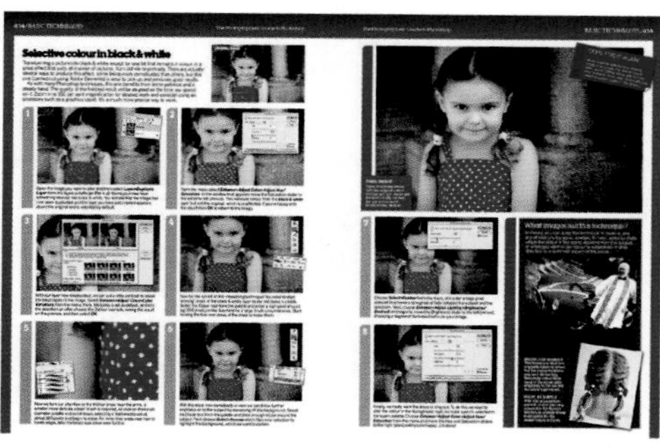

Selective colour in black & white

Transforming a picture into black & white, except for one bit that remains in colour, is a great effect that suits all manner of pictures, from still-life to portraits. There are actually several ways to produce this effect, some being more complicated than others, but this one (carried out using Adobe Elements) is easy to pick up and produces good results.

As with many Photoshop techniques, this one benefits from some patience and a steady hand. The quality of the finished result will be as good as the time you spend on it. Zoom in to 100 per cent magnification for detailed work and consider using an accessory such as a graphics tablet. It's a much more precise way to work.

1

Open the image you want to alter and then select ***Layer>Duplicate Layer*** from the layers palette ***(or Ctrl + J)***. Name your new layer something obvious like black & white. You will see that the image has now been duplicated and the layer you have just created appears above the original and is selected by default.

2

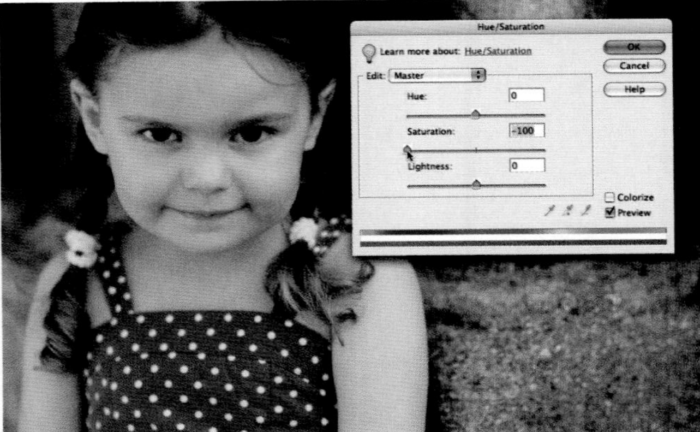

From the menu select ***Enhance>Adjust Color>Adjust Hue/ Saturation***. In the window that appears move the Saturation slider to the extreme left (minus). This removes colour from the ***black & white*** layer but not the original, which is unaffected. If you're happy with the result click ***OK*** to return to the image.

3

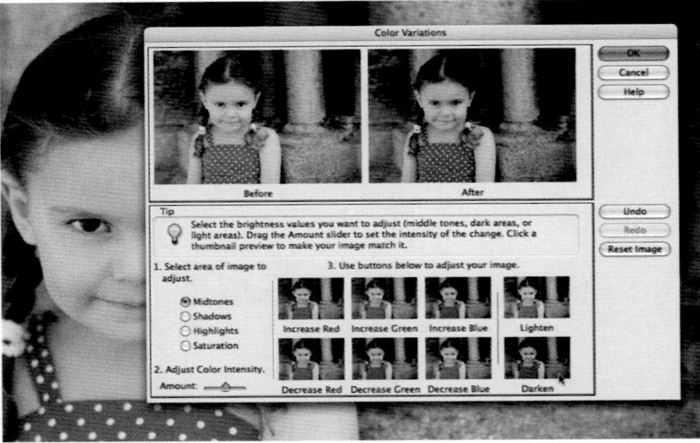

With our layer now desaturated, we can put a little contrast to boost the tonal depth of the image. Select ***Enhance>Adjust Color>Color Variations*** from the menu. Here, Midtones is set as default, so from the selection on offer, choose the Darken example, noting the result on the preview, and then select ***OK***.

4

Now for the fun bit of this interesting technique! You need to start 'erasing' areas of the black & white layer so the red dress is visible. Select the Eraser tool from the palette and enter a high pixel amount (eg 300 pixels) in the Size field for a large brush circumference. Start moving the tool over areas of the dress to erase them.

5

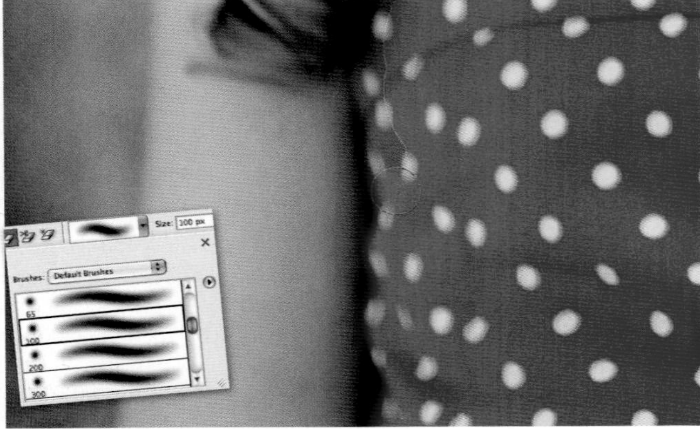

Now we turn our attention to the trickier areas near the arms, a smaller more delicate eraser brush is required, so click on the brush diameter palette and scroll down, selecting a feathered brush at about 100 pixels and begin to erase. For even finer areas near hair or harsh edges, take the brush size down even further.

6

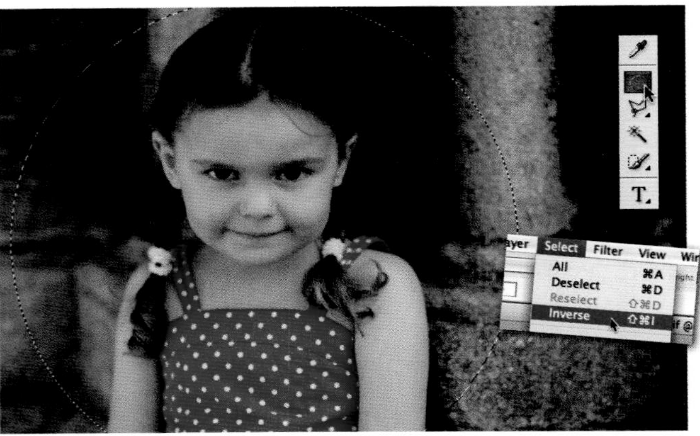

With the dress now completely in view we can throw further emphasis on to the subject by darkening off the background. Select the Elipse tool from the palette and draw a rough elipse around the subject. Next choose ***Select>Inverse*** which flips your selection to highlight the background, which we want to darken.

PRO TIPS

OOPS, I DID IT AGAIN!

When making selections or erasing areas of an image, the odd error will often occur. **Ctrl+Z** allows you to undo any mistakes made, and History lets you revisit previous stages of the project

FINAL IMAGE
There is nothing wrong with the original colour photograph, but the bright red dress really catches the eye in this semi-monochrome version.

7

Choose ***Select>Feather*** from the menu and enter a large pixel amount to achieve a nice gradual fade between the subject and the selection. Next, choose ***Enhance>Adjust Lighting>Brightness/Contrast*** and begin to move the Brightness slider to the left (minus), choosing a degree of darkness that suits your image.

8

Finally, we really want the dress to sing out. To do this we need to alter the colour in the Background layer, so make sure it's selected in the layers palette. Choose ***Enhance>Adjust Color>Adjust Hue/Saturation*** from the menu and move the Hue and Saturation sliders to the right (plus) until you're happy. Job done!

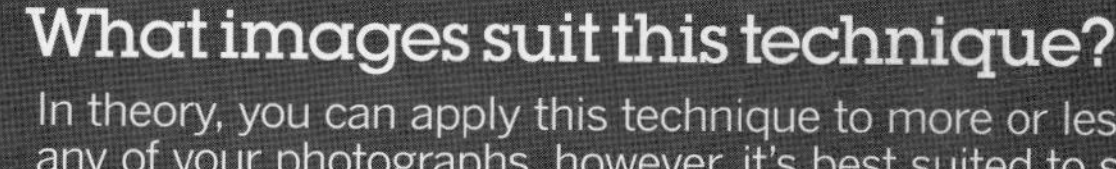

What images suit this technique?

In theory, you can apply this technique to more or less any of your photographs, however, it's best suited to shots where the colour in the scene distracts from the subject, or when you want to use colour to emphasise or draw attention to a particular aspect of the scene.

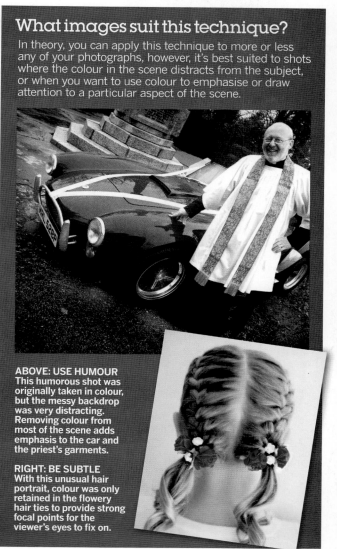

ABOVE: USE HUMOUR
This humorous shot was originally taken in colour, but the messy backdrop was very distracting. Removing colour from most of the scene adds emphasis to the car and the priest's garments.

RIGHT: BE SUBTLE
With this unusual hair portrait, colour was only retained in the flowery hair ties to provide strong focal points for the viewer's eyes to fix on.

Add motion to a static subject

Automotive photographers go to great lengths to get those stylised pictures of cars speeding through country lanes that we see in the motoring press. They lean out of cars, clamp their cameras to bumpers and take all manner of risks to get the shot. Thankfully, you can achieve similar effects by some less risky work in Photoshop.

The motion blur filter can be used to simulate the streaks made by panning your camera along while following a moving subject. The trick is to cut out the car so that you are only applying the effect to the background. It's easy to do with Photoshop's range of selection tools. Then you'll need to pay attention to the small details: are those wheels still sharp? Should they be? Some radial blur will help fix that.

1

We're going to inject some pace into this rather static image using a variety of feathers and blur techniques. First things first, we need to cut out a copy of the car and have it sit in a new layer. Use the Polygonal Lasso tool and work around the edge of the subject, in this case the car, until you reach the point back where you started.

2

On every selection made throughout this guide we want to avoid nasty harsh edges, so remember to always feather selections. Go to ***Select>Feather***, enter a preferred Feather Radius. For a nice tidy edge, choose 5 pixels. To place into a new layer choose ***Edit>Copy*** then ***Edit>Paste***. By default, this will become the active layer.

3

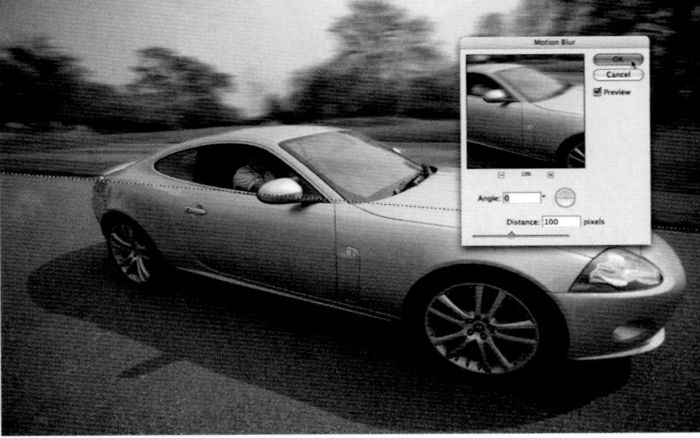

We want to play with the background layer, so make sure it's selected in the Layers panel. Next, select the grass and treeline area using the curb as a good cut-off point. Feather the selection, using a large pixel count of around 10. Choose ***Filter>Blur>MotionBlur***. Then we need to enter an angle of 0° and blur at 100pixels.

4

Note the effect the blurring has on the background without affecting the 'cut-out' layer. A sense of speed is already evident. Repeat the previous step, this time selecting the ground area from the kerb down. This time, when in the Motion Blur window, alter the blur angle to around -10 to reflect the grain in the road.

5

Leaving the background layer a moment, you need to select the 'cut-out' layer in order to put some movement into the wheels. Using the polygonal lasso, draw a rough selection around the front wheel and feather the selection at 5 pixels. Go to ***Filters>Blur>RadialBlur*** and enter an amount of 25 pixels and then click ***OK.***

6

The results are very effective for this kind of technique and the wheel now appears to be moving at great speed. Repeat for the rear wheel, using a smaller blur amount this time to avoid distortion, as this wheel is less face-on. Once completed, the car now really appears to be moving, but this effect can be enhanced further.

PRO TIPS

WORKING IN LAYERS

It can often prove wise to save additional versions of your project whenever you flatten or merge layers together, as once you've flattened, saved and closed your image, all layers are then lost!

FINAL IMAGE

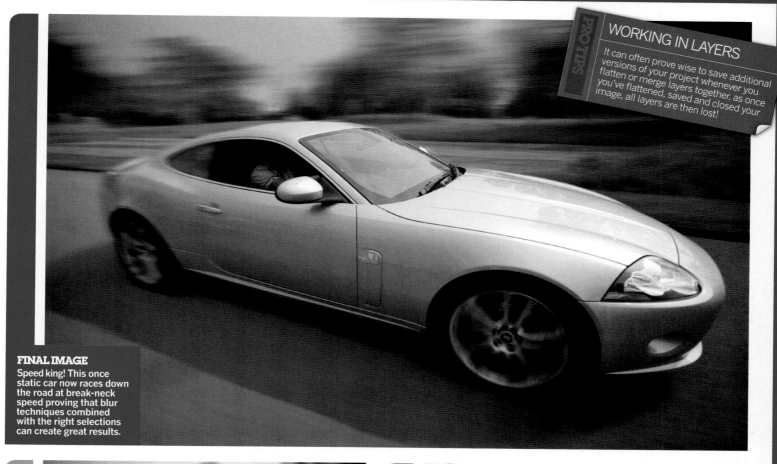

Speed king! This once static car now races down the road at break-neck speed proving that blur techniques combined with the right selections can create great results.

7

At this stage our eye is drawn to the driver. You may find him slightly distracting and want to make him less distinctive. To do this, use the Polygonal Lasso again and select the area inside the window frame and feather the selection. Go to **Enhance>Adjust Lighting> Brightness/Contrast**, then adjust to darken the area down.

8

There is a halo apparent around the bonnet and bumper, caused by blurring the background layer earlier on. With the Background Layer selected use the Clone Stamp tool with a large, soft brush to remove the halo by selecting reference points from the surrounding road areas for the tool to clone from.

9

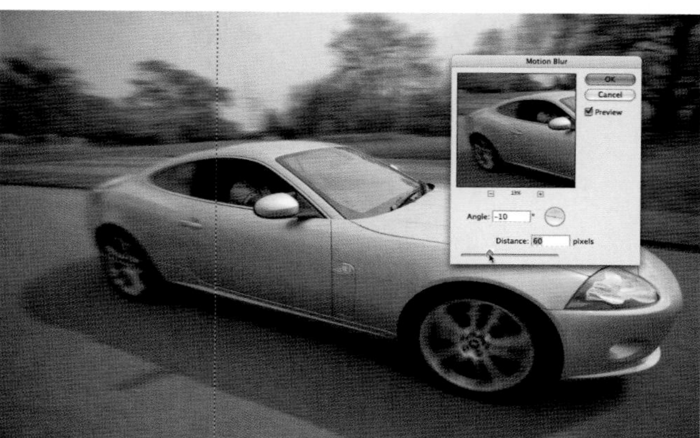

We want to throw the rear of the car out even more. To do this you need to affect all layers and choose **Layer>Flatten Image** to flatten the image. Using the Rectangular Marquee make a large selection, including the car's rear. Now give the selection a large feathering (200 pixels), and increase the blur amount until satisfied.

10

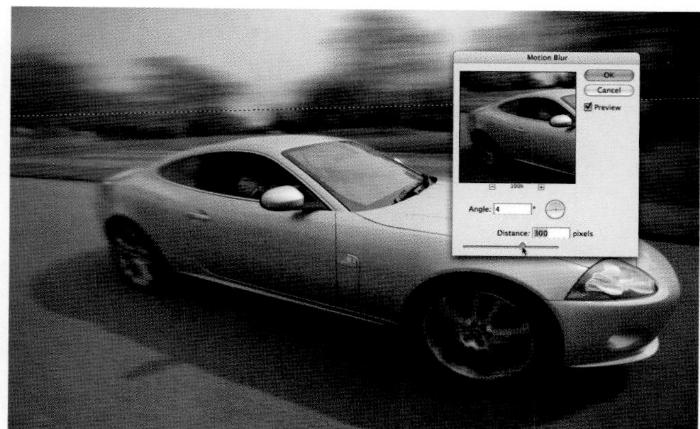

Using the Polygonal Lasso, make a diagonal select to the tree area and add a large feather (100 pixels) and really blur this time (300 pixels)! When you're happy with the effect, repeat this process to the road from the shadow to the edge of frame. Use the same feather and blur amounts but angle the blur to the road grain.

Create a studio-quality still-life image

You could be forgiven for thinking that professional-looking still life pictures require an extensive studio lighting kit and background equipment, but if you have Adobe Photoshop at your fingertips, then you'll be fine with your dining table and a white wall. We've shot a vase of flowers using this kind of set-up, lit with light from a nearby window, and taken the result onto a computer for some post-shoot editing that will give it the edge.

As well as brightening up the colours of the tulips, and cleaning up the background, we've added a reflection that makes the vase look like it's sitting on a glass surface. We've also introduced some careful mood lighting to draw the eye into the middle of the frame. Each of these effects sit in its own layer, and all of the layers build up to give the final result. Don't be put off if you haven't used layers before in Photoshop, though, this is an ideal time to give it a go. It's not as complicated as you might think.

1

This still-life is dull and uninspiring so first we need to liven up the colours of the tulips and whiten up the background to aid in making a clean selection for cutting out. You can do this in one action by using ***Enhance>Adjust Lighting>Levels***, moving the white slider in the Input Levels field to the left, which brightens up all areas.

2

Now we need to make a selection around the tulips and vase to isolate them from the background layer. To do this, use the Magic Wand and click the white of the background. Tidy any stray areas up with the Polygonal Lasso, holding **Shift** to add to and **Alt** to remove from the selection, then go to ***Select>Invert***.

3

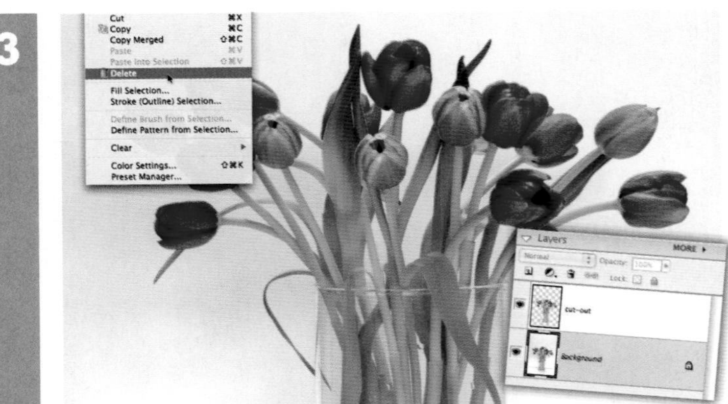

Go to ***Select>Feather*** and enter 1 pixel to soften the selection's edge, then go ***Edit>Cut*** followed by ***Edit>Paste*** to place the tulips in a new layer above the background, which we name *'cut-out'*. Tidy the background layer by clicking it in the Layers palette, then go to ***Select>All*** and ***Edit>Delete***, which effectively deletes all content.

4

To add a sense of dimension we need to create a reflection. Ensuring the *'cut-out'* layer is active, select ***Layer>Duplicate Layer*** and name the new layer *'reflection'*, then go to ***Image>Transform>Rotate>Flip Horizontal***, then repeat, this time choosing the ***Flip Vertical*** option to create a mirror image of the tulips and vase.

5

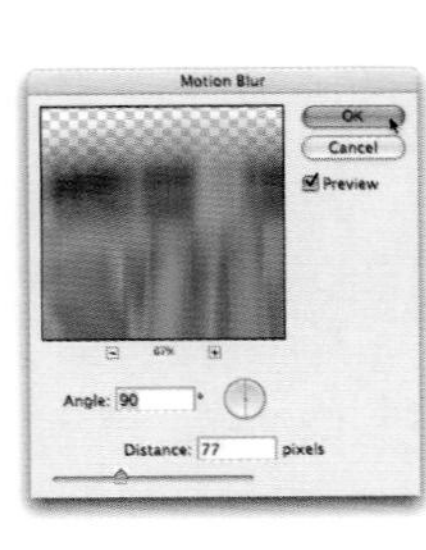

To move the *'reflection'* layer to the base of the vase, hold ***Alt*** (Option on the Mac) and drag. Now in the Layers palette, drag the *'reflection'* layer so it sits underneath *'cut-out'*. Reduce the Opacity, situated at the top of the layers palette, to about 40%, then use ***Filter>Blur>Motion Blur*** at 90° to distort the reflection slightly.

6

A subtle shadow will make the vase seem as though it's sitting on a solid surface. Create another layer, (***Layer>New layer***), and using the Elliptical Marquee, draw a selection at the base of the vase. Now use a Feather at 10 pixels to create a soft edge, then go to ***Edit>Fill***, choosing black and finish by setting the Opacity to 25%.

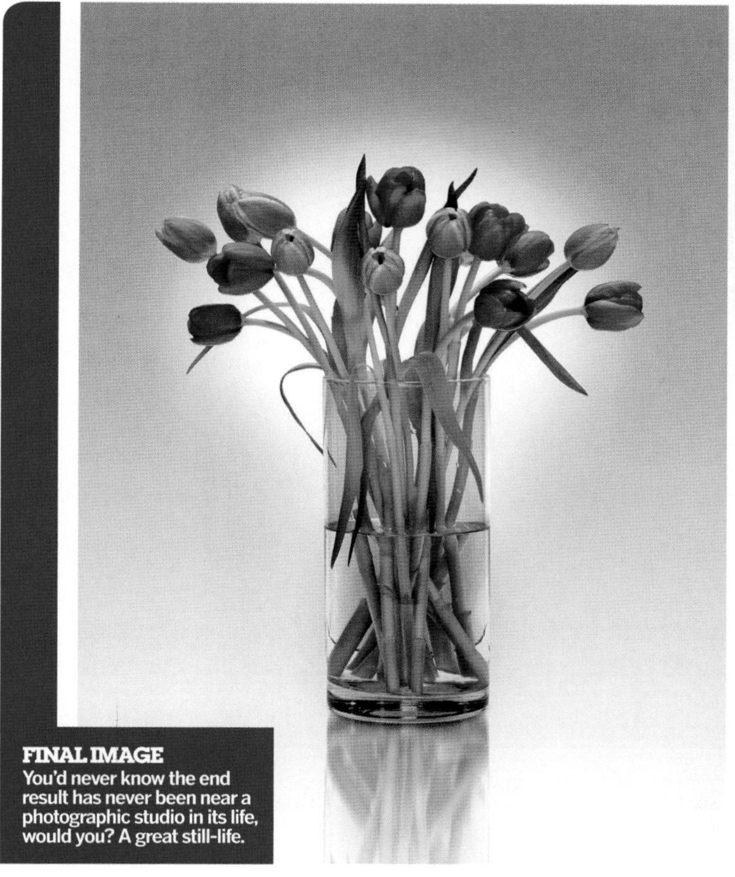

FINAL IMAGE
You'd never know the end result has never been near a photographic studio in its life, would you? A great still-life.

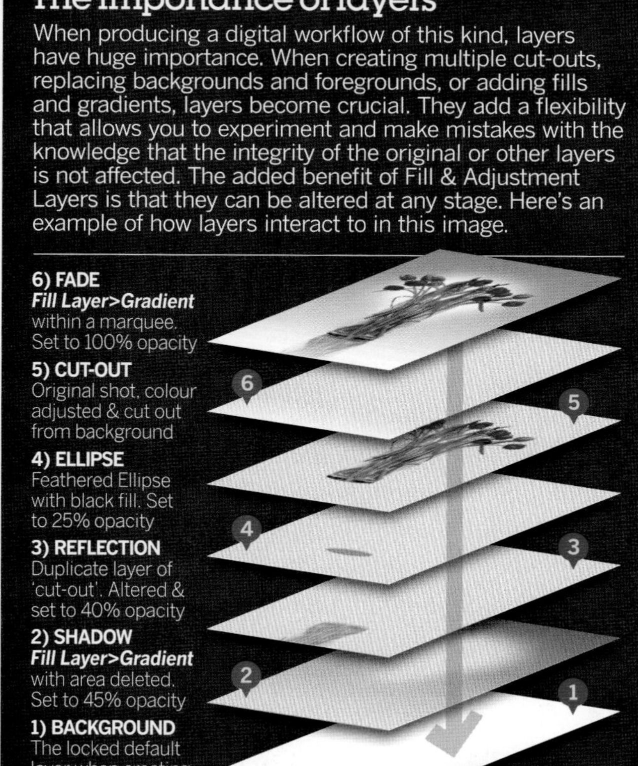

The importance of layers

When producing a digital workflow of this kind, layers have huge importance. When creating multiple cut-outs, replacing backgrounds and foregrounds, or adding fills and gradients, layers become crucial. They add a flexibility that allows you to experiment and make mistakes with the knowledge that the integrity of the original or other layers is not affected. The added benefit of Fill & Adjustment Layers is that they can be altered at any stage. Here's an example of how layers interact to in this image.

6) FADE
Fill Layer>Gradient within a marquee. Set to 100% opacity

5) CUT-OUT
Original shot, colour adjusted & cut out from background

4) ELLIPSE
Feathered Ellipse with black fill. Set to 25% opacity

3) REFLECTION
Duplicate layer of 'cut-out'. Altered & set to 40% opacity

2) SHADOW
Fill Layer>Gradient with area deleted. Set to 45% opacity

1) BACKGROUND
The locked default layer when creating a new document.

7

The background now needs some depth and for this we need to use ***Layer>New Fill Layer>Gradient***. Simply tick Reverse to flip the gradient so it runs from top to bottom and click ***OK***, creating a new layer with a gradient fill that we call 'shadow'. Move the layer in the Layers palette so it sits just above the 'background' layer.

8

Now change the *'shadow'* layer Opacity to 45% so the gradient is less harsh. It's now ready for a false spot-light to be added, using the Elliptical Marquee. Make a large selection around the tulips, then holding ***Shift***, add another selection at the neck of the vase. Next, you need to add a large Feather amount of 150 pixels.

9

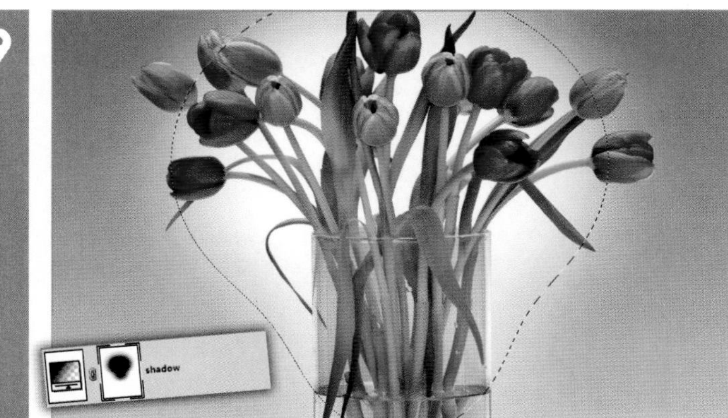

It's time to delete the selected area of the gradient and reveal the white of the *'background'* layer in this area, to create a spot-light effect. Go to ***Edit>Delete*** and note the effect this action has on the gradient, and the layer, by viewing the preview in the Layers palette (inset), the black being the affected area.

10

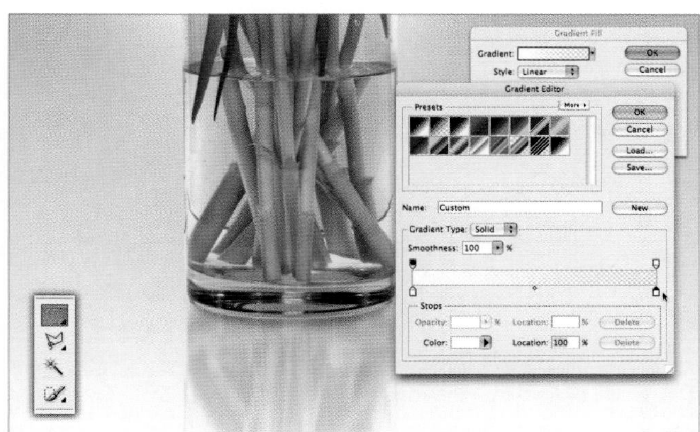

Make a Rectangular Marquee selection to the base of the vase, to hold a gradient. Then create a ***New Fill Layer>Gradient*** and open the Gradient swatches. Selecting the bottom sliders on either side, change the colour from black to white. The result is a white to transparent gradient within the marquee area.

Replace the sky

One of the best things about digital photography is taking parts of one picture and inserting them into another. For the landscape photographer, this is a great way of ensuring that both sky and foreground are correctly exposed. Shoot one frame for the sky and another for the foreground, then splice them together in Photoshop. It's simple to do; here's a method that takes no more than five minutes to master.

1

Start by opening the image with the foreground you require. Select the entire image using ***Select>All then Edit>Copy***, which will copy the image to the pasteboard. Next, open the image with the sky you want to use. Use ***Edit>Paste*** and the foreground image will be placed on a layer above, which should be labelled foreground for ease.

2

Firstly, we want to work on the foreground layer, which is active by default, so we can remove the overexposed sky. Using either the Lasso or Magic Wand tools, select the sky ensuring all areas required to be remove are clearly selected. You can add to your initial selection by holding shift, noting the + symbol that appears over the icon.

3

To refine the selection further you can expand the selection accurately using ***Select>Modify>Expand***, entering a small amount as required – in this case 1 pixel was used. Next we need to feather the selection to avoid harsh edges when we finally delete the selection. Go to ***Select>Feather*** and enter 1 or 2 pixels.

4

With our selection perfected it's time to remove the unwanted bleached sky. Go to ***Edit>Delete*** noting that the sky on the layer below becomes visible. Refer to the Layers palette to see how the layers interact. To proceed we need to ensure the sky marquee selection is removed – use ***Select>Deselect*** to achieve this.

5

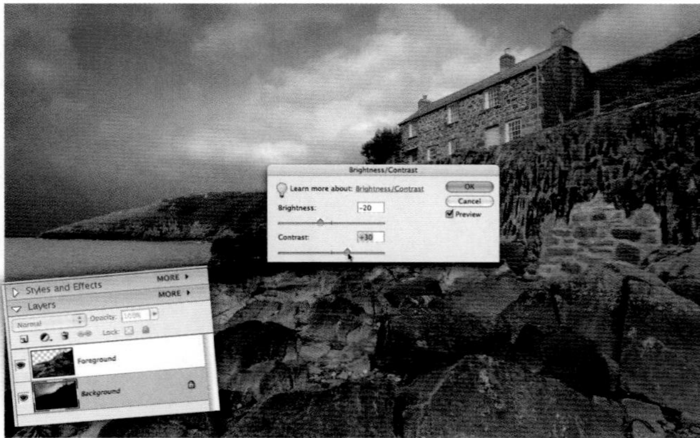

To work with the sky ensure the Background layer is selected in the layers palette. The sky is a huge improvement but can be improved further. Go to ***Enhance>Adjust Lighting>Brightness/Contrast***, adding contrast (plus) and removing a little brightness (minus) to add a bit of depth to the sky and clouds.

6

You can also graduate the sky to introduce some mood. Using the Marquee tool to select the top half of the sky, go to ***Select>Feather***. This effect needs to be very gradual so enter a large pixel amount – for this image 150 pixel has been used. As before, in ***Brightness/Contrast***, reduce brightness and increase contrast.

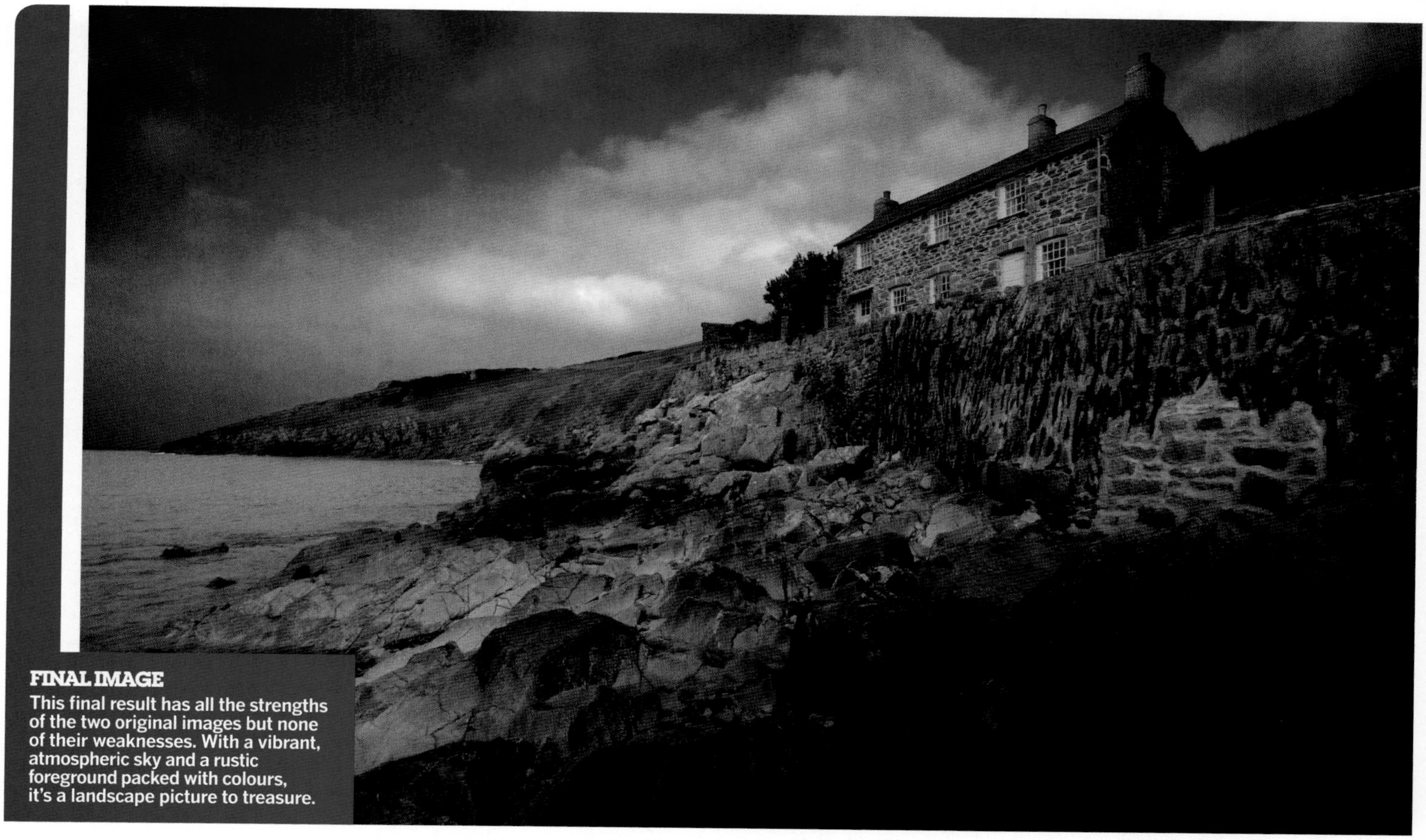

FINAL IMAGE

This final result has all the strengths of the two original images but none of their weaknesses. With a vibrant, atmospheric sky and a rustic foreground packed with colours, it's a landscape picture to treasure.

7

It's time to start improving the foreground layer in a few areas, so ensure it's selected in the Layers palette. Start by knocking back the foreground rocks a little. Using the Lasso tool draw a diagonal selection and feather to around 100 pixels for a gradual effect. Go to ***Brightness/Contrast***, darken and remove some contrast.

8

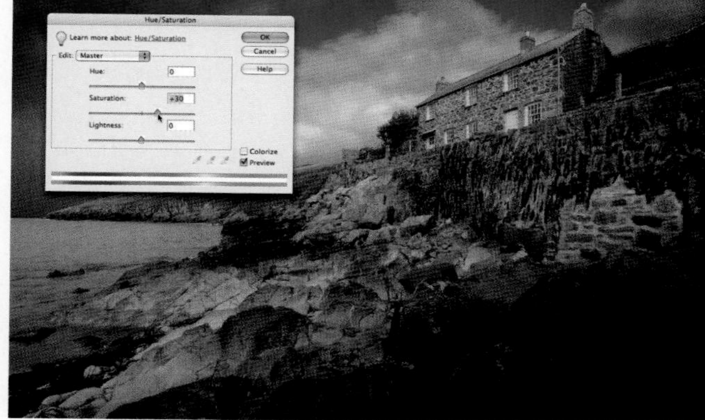

It's getting closer to a final image but still lacks a little colour. Go to ***Enhance>Adjust Colour>Hue/Saturation*** and move the Saturation slider to the right (plus) until you're happy with the result –but be careful not to overdo things! If required you could isolate individual areas of colour, such as the doors, and repeat the step.

9

With close inspection you may note a halo appears on the deleted edge of the foreground layer, which can be easily removed. Select the Eraser tool with a soft brush of around 130 pixels, setting the brush Opacity to around 30%, and begin to erase the halo. Note the reduced opacity lowers the harshness of removed areas.

10

Once you're happy with the result, it's time to flatten the image so we can perform any task we want to affect the entire image, such as sharpening or colour tweaks. First, it's always a good idea to save a copy with layers intact should you want to access them later, then go to ***Layers>Flatten***, saving the final flattened image.

Creating autumnal landscapes

Digital editing of landscapes in Photoshop or Elements gives photographers the chance to inject more mood into their images, or change the feeling of their pictures completely. In this easy-to-follow, step-by-step tutorial, you will learn the value of the Adjustment Layer in post-processing and, more specifically, how to adjust Hue/Saturation and Gradient Fill. We'll show you not only how to create a misty look in a picture, but also how to make the mist appear as if it's floating behind the tree, for a really three-dimensional look.

The advantage of using adjustment layers is that each adjustment can be edited independently, meaning that if you change your mind about something you did a few stages ago, you can go back and change it without affecting anything else in the picture.

1

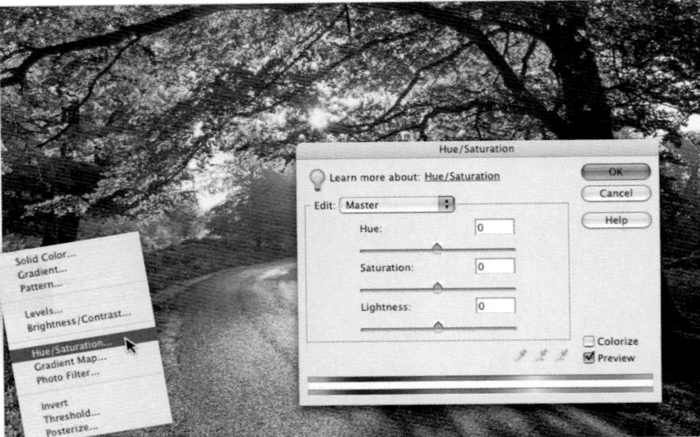

The best way to alter the hue of an image is with Hue/Saturation through the ***Adjustment Layers*** menu. Adjustment layers are good because they allow you to edit and re-edit your image without actually altering the original. So, go to the Adjustment Layer symbol ( ) in the Layers palette (inset) and scroll to Hue/Saturation.

2

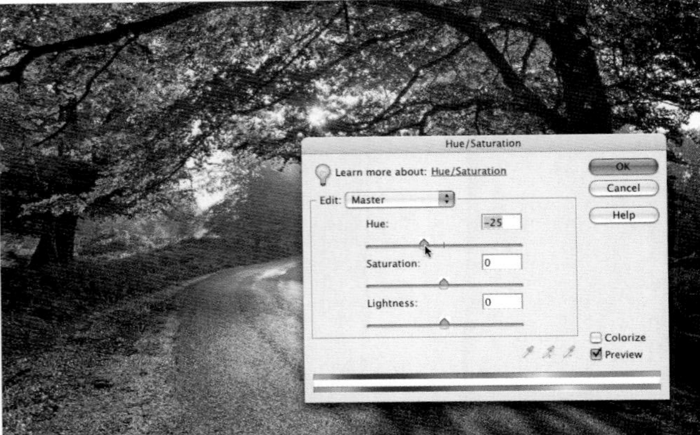

In the Hue/Saturation window, we drag the Hue slider left (–), changing the hue of the image. Stop when you reach the desired autumnal mood and click ***OK***. Because this command affects the entire image, certain areas may look a little odd, such as the road. This is where Photoshop's Adjustment Layer comes in handy.

3

Selecting the Eraser tool (inset) and with a large soft brush, begin to 'paint' out the areas of the foreground that look odd due to the change in hue, allowing the original image to be seen from beneath. The thumbnail preview in the Layers palette allows you to check your progress, with the erased areas indicated in black (inset).

4

To create the fog effect, you can use a Gradient Adjustment Layer. The gradient will be based on the foreground colour, which by default is black, so to change it to white click the ***Switch Foreground Color*** icon at the base of the tool palette (inset). Next, select Gradient through the Adjustment Layer ( ) and name it.

5

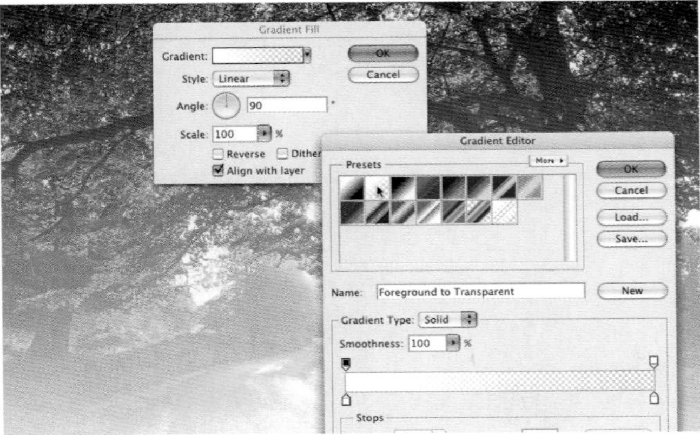

The Gradient Fill window appears and the gradient is previewed live on the image. Click in the Gradient Field and the Gradient Editor opens. You must ensure that Color to Transparent is active, the colour being white as set in step four, then click ***OK*** to close and return to the canvas, complete with gradient.

6

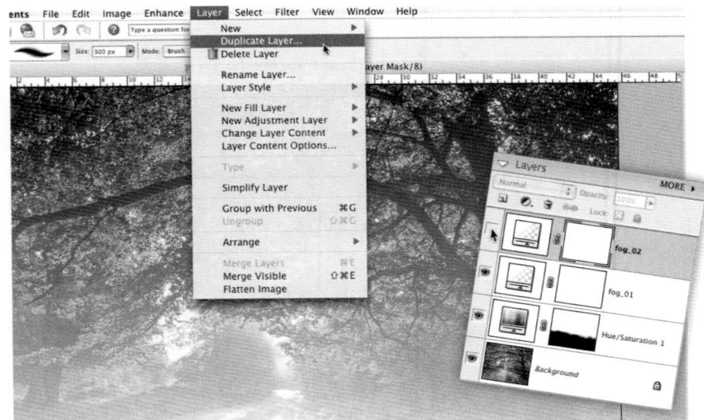

You now need another identical gradient to build some depth to the fog effect, so go to ***Layer>Duplicate Layer***, naming the new layer accordingly. You won't be using the new layer yet so we'll hide it. To do this, click the Layer Visibility icon – note that the eye disappears (inset) to indicate that the layer is no longer visible.

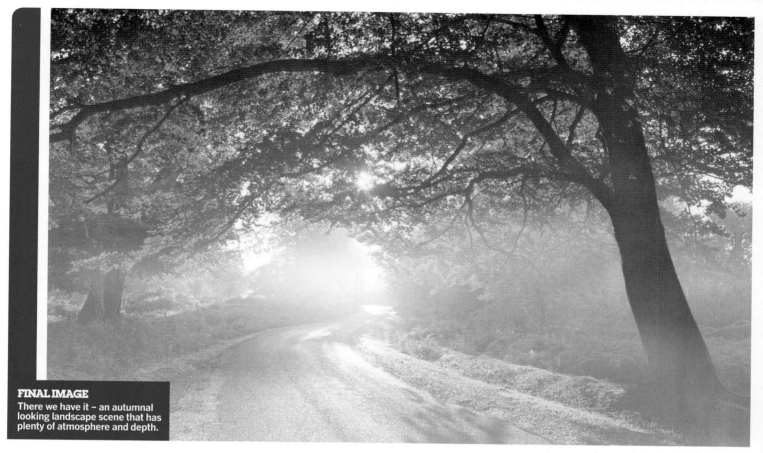

FINAL IMAGE
There we have it – an autumnal looking landscape scene that has plenty of atmosphere and depth.

7

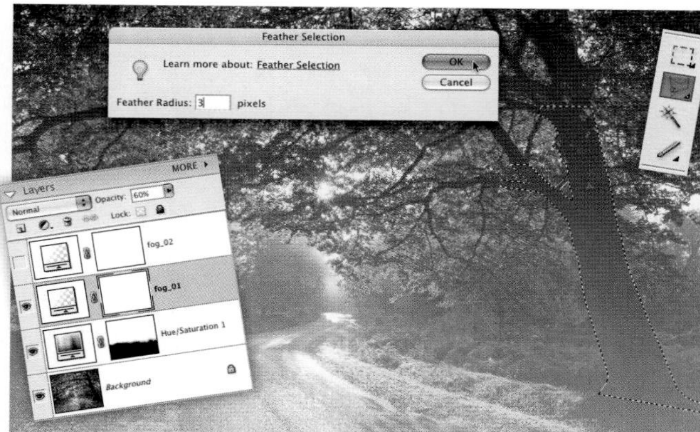

Before moving on, ensure that the original gradient layer you create is active by clicking on its thumbnail in the Layers palette (inset). With the Polygonal Lasso selected from the tool palette, draw an accurate selection around the trunk of the foreground tree using ***Select>Feather*** at three pixels to soften the selection.

8

Back to the Eraser tool, this time with a smaller soft brush and the Opacity to 25%, which allows for a gradual removal and so offers more control. Begin to 'paint' out the 'fog' from the gradient layer, the polygonal selection ensuring only the trunk is affected, giving the illusion that the tree is in front of the layers of fog.

9

We're going to use the Brush tool to add some depth to the fog behind the tree, so click ***Select>Inverse*** to select the background. We now need a new layer as Adjustment Layers only allow for application of specific tasks, in this case, gradients. Click ***Layer>New Layer*** and with the brush set to 20% opacity, create denser fog areas.

10

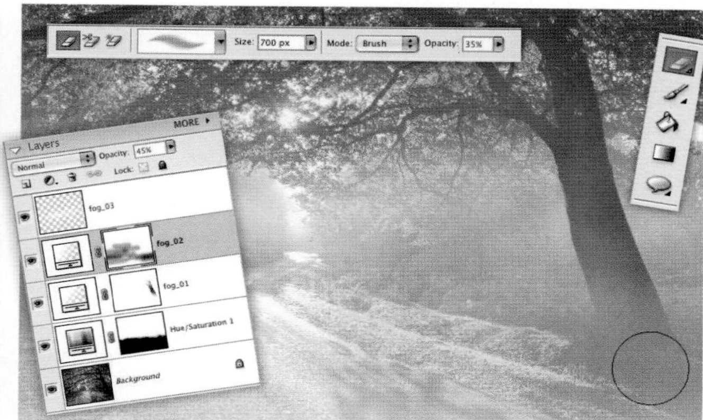

Now use ***Select>Deselect*** to remove the trunk selection, then activate a second gradient in the layers palette, clicking the empty box opposite to make it visible. This gives a denser fog effect, which you can tone down by setting the opacity to 45%. Using the Eraser with opacity at 35%, erase creatively to complete the effect.

Composite shots

You've spent the day taking pictures only to get home and find that no one image from the session stands out. Well, there's no need to panic! More often than not, there will be attributes from various images that, if combined, would solve your problem. In a portrait, for instance, you might have one shot where you subject has just the right body position, but another where their expression is absolutely perfect. Why not combine the two?

1

Start by opening your images in Adobe Elements. The first thing you'll want to do is to replace the arm and coat on the background image with a nicer version from another shot. Now use the Rectangular Marquee to select the half of the image containing the shoulder and go to ***Edit>Copy***, adding it into the clipboard.

2

Close the 'shoulder' image and select the background shot, before clicking ***Edit>Paste***, placing the section from the clipboard into a new layer on top of this image. Now change the layer Blend Mode to Difference in the Layers palette (inset) creating a temporary effect that will aid in aligning the two layers accurately.

3

Zoom out a bit using the magnification field at the bottom left corner of the workspace (inset), as you will need full access to the scaling pointers once activated. Click on ***Image>Transform>Free Transform***. Now use the pointers to align the layers, holding *Shift* to maintain the proportions, and double-clicking to apply the changes.

4

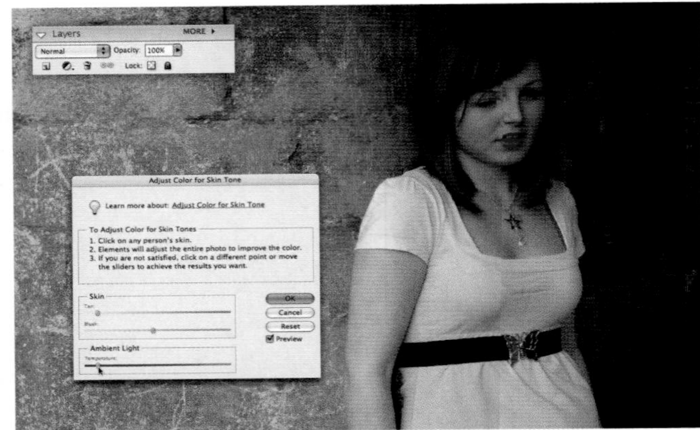

Next, change the layer Blend Mode back to Normal (inset) as you now need to match the colour of the layers. For this, use ***Enhance>Adjust Colour>Adjust Color for Skin Tone.*** Click the Eyedropper on the model's skin, and adjust the three sliders that appear, to get the tones to match as closely as possible, then click ***OK***.

5

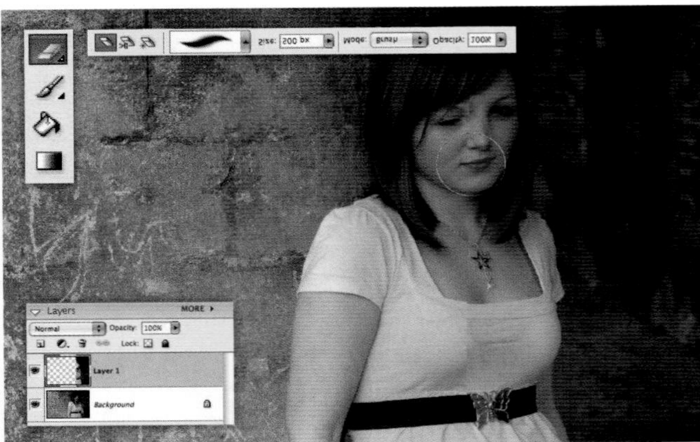

With the layers aligned and matched, all you need to do now is erase areas of the top layer to make the merge. With the Erase tool set to a medium brush, erase down the left edge of the layer. Alterations to alignment can still be made and you can use ***Edit>Undo*** (***Ctrl+Z***) or the Undo History panel to go back in your workflow if required.

6

Now open the file with the best facial expression and using an Elliptical Marquee, make an oval selection around the head. Select ***Edit>Copy***, then ***Edit>Paste*** this selection onto the background file creating a new layer. Next, repeat the actions from steps 2 to 4 to match the new head with the scale and tone of the background.

FINAL IMAGE
Although it's always best to set out to achieve the best results in-camera, this technique shows that if you take enough pictures you can always salvage something from a session that hasn't gone as well as planned.

7

Now follow the process from step five. Selecting the Erase tool (this time with a smaller brush), and setting the Opacity to 85% for greater control, begin to gradually erase from the outside of the hairline until the layers begin to merge convincingly. Once again, use ***Edit>Undo*** (***Ctrl+Z***) to go back a stage or two if you think it's necessary.

8

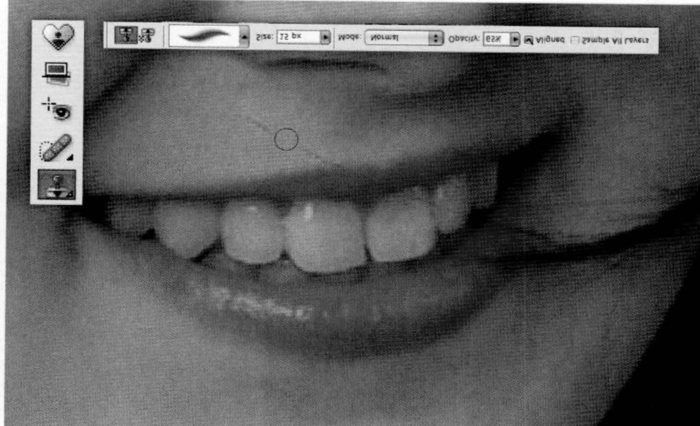

Although this expression was by far the best from the set, there's an annoying section of hair blowing across the model's face. So, with the Clone tool set to a small brush and Opacity at 65% to allow a gradual build-up, begin removing the hair by holding the ***Alt*** key to select the source points from the face, lips and teeth.

9

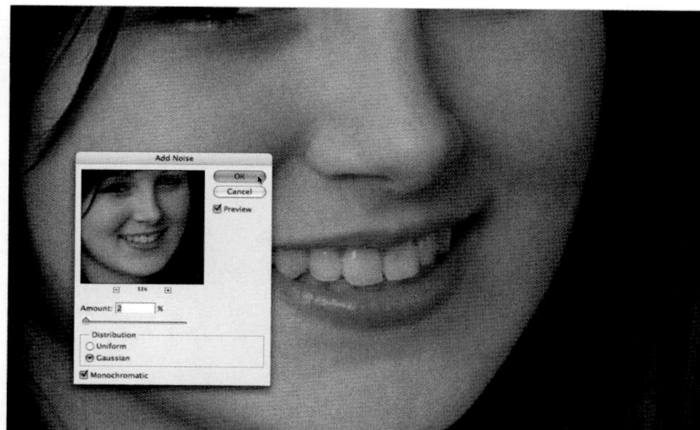

Before moving on, save a copy of your work as a Photoshop file *(.psd)* to preserve all layer work. Then go ***Layer>Flatten Image*** to allow for some overall alterations. Now use ***Noise>Add Noise*** to help reduce the visibility of any cloning. We suggest never going beyond 3 pixels, and always ensure you have Monochromatic ticked.

10

Make a Polygonal Lasso selection around the model and Feather to 250 pixels for a gradual effect. Then go to ***Enhance>Adjust Lighting>Levels,*** using the sliders to boost the model, and click OK. Finally, flip the selection with ***Select>Inverse*** to select the background and use Levels again to darken and reduce contrast. Remember to save your file again.

Add drama to dull portraits

Ever wondered how portraits shot by professionals for magazines and books always look so stylish? Well, the answer often lies in the retouching! Half an hour in Creative Suite or Elements will transform a favourite portrait, and most likely have lots more people queuing up to have their pictures taken! So if you've any images that you really like but wish you could inject a little more mood and atmosphere into, here's a great technique to try. Let's see how this children's portrait can be improved by taking some of the colour out of it, putting the subject on to a new background and adding some carefully designed shading effects. We'll also see how slightly blurring part of the image can draw attention to the most important part of any portrait – the eyes.

1

The photographer had focused their attention on getting the lighting right on the child's face and had given less consideration to the composition. So, as is often the case when improving an image, the first thing to do is improve composition with the Crop tool, by intentionally placing our subject to the right of the frame.

2

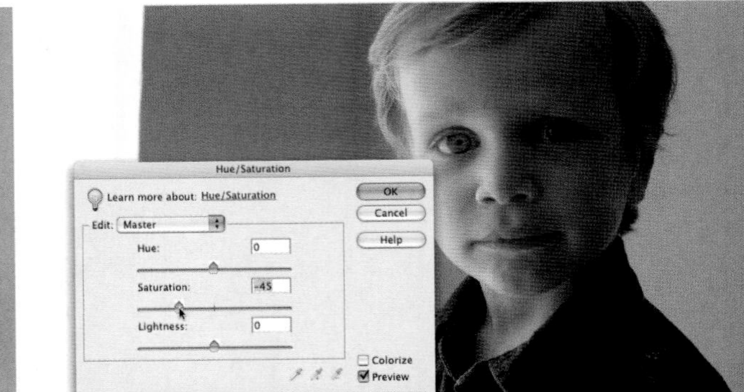

We need to add a slightly cool mood to match the child's direct stare, further increasing the drama of the shot. To do this use ***Enhance>Adjust Lighting>Adjust Hue/Saturation*** and move the Saturation slider to the left (–) until you're happy that there is the right balance of colour remaining in the image, then click ***OK***.

3

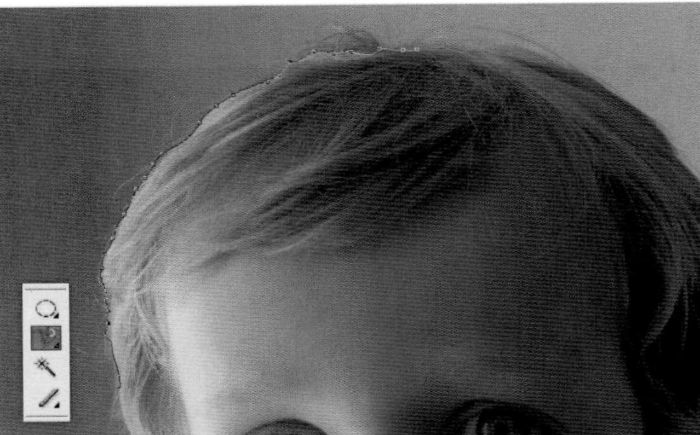

The next step is to cut our subject out and place him on a new layer. To speed up the selection process use the ***Magnetic Lasso*** tool, which is best used when there is good contrast between subject and background. Move the tool's pointer along the edge of the subject and it automatically creates the selection.

4

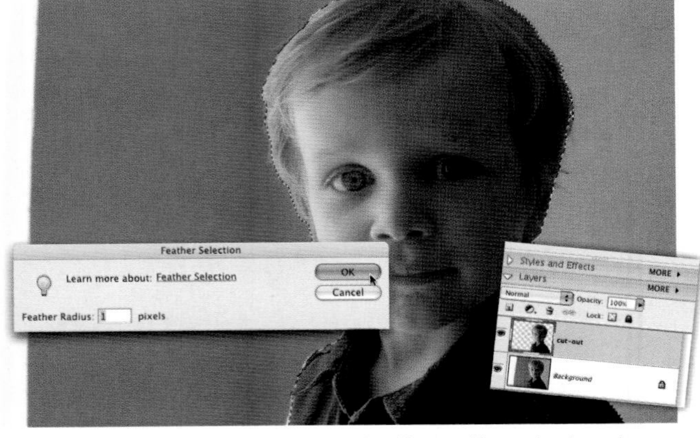

Touch up the selection using the standard Lasso if required, and with the selection complete it's always a good plan to use ***Select>Feather*** and apply around 1 or 2 pixels to soften the selection a little. Now click ***Edit>Copy*** then by ***Edit>Paste*** and note that a new layer appears containing the 'cut-out' subject (inset).

5

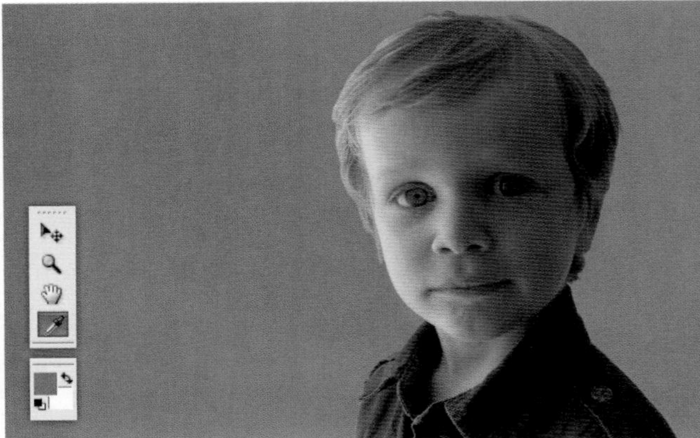

Make sure you click the 'background' layer before continuing to activate it, then with the Eyedropper tool selected, take a colour selection from the background and this appears in the Foreground Color swatch at the bottom of the tool bar (inset). Now click ***Edit>Fill Layer*** to apply this colour to the entire background.

6

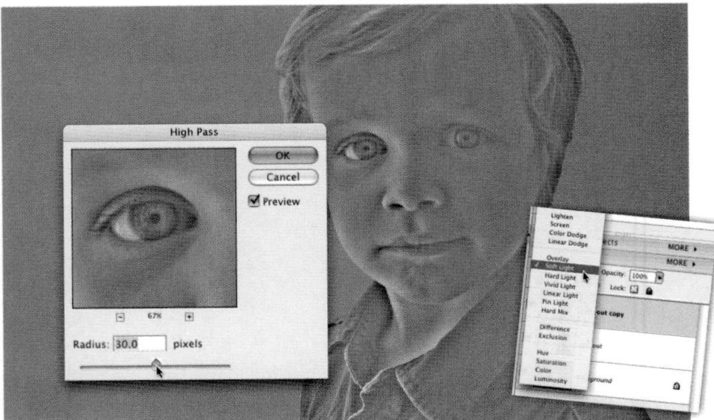

We want to add depth and a surreal mood to the subjec, so we need to use the High Pass filter. Go to ***Layer>Duplicate Layer*** to create a duplicate of the subject's cut-out and select ***Filter>Other>High Pass***, enter a Radius of around 30 pixels and click ***OK***. Select Soft light in the Blending Mode menu (inset) to see the layers interact.

FINAL IMAGE
By seeing the promise in an ordinary portrait, you can create dramatic results with your Photoshop skills. The secret is not to go too far, and remain true to the original.

7

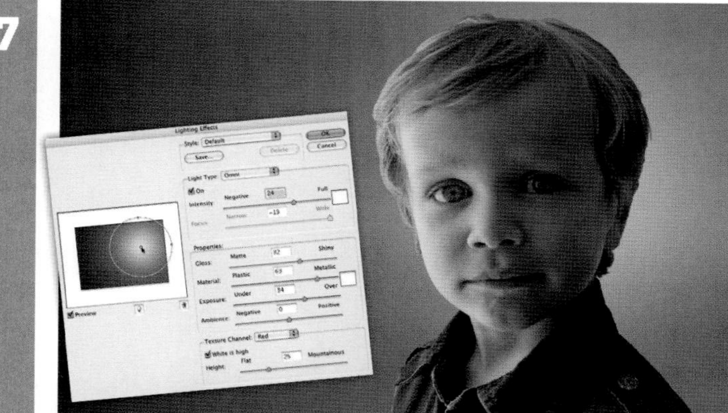

Now it's time to light the backdrop. With the 'background' layer active, go to ***Filter>Render>Lighting Effects*** and you're presented with a window packed with sliders and menus. Switch to Omni in the Light Type menu then, in the preview window, move the light position to where the head sits by dragging the white 'dot'.

8

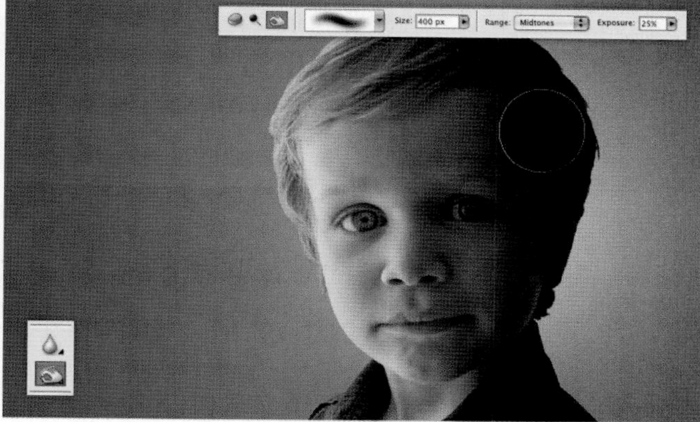

With the background light altered, the child's shadow now looks a little unnatural, so select the **Burn tool** (inset) with a large brush (400 pixels) and set the **Exposure** to 25%, which will allow you to build up a gradual effect. Then 'hand-paint' the shadow into the picture moving the pointer down the left side of his face.

9

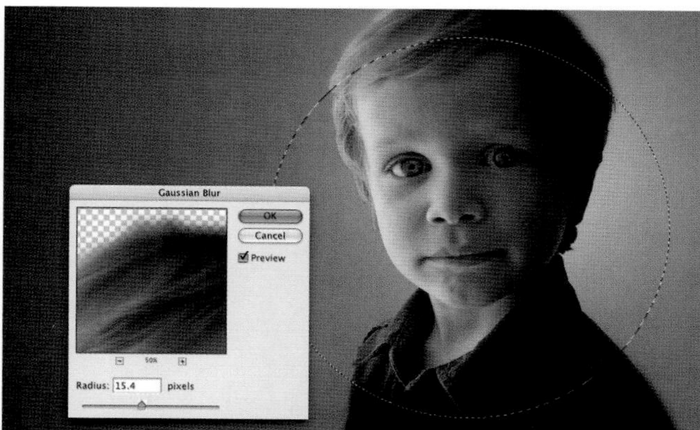

The picture is almost done, but the plan is to emphasise the stare further. We'll throw the top of the hair and the shirt slightly out of focus to draw the viewer in centrally. Use the Elliptical Marquee and make a large selection, with the areas you want to effect on the outside. Click ***Select>Inverse*** then ***Filter>Blur>Gaussian Blur*** to about 15 pixels.

10

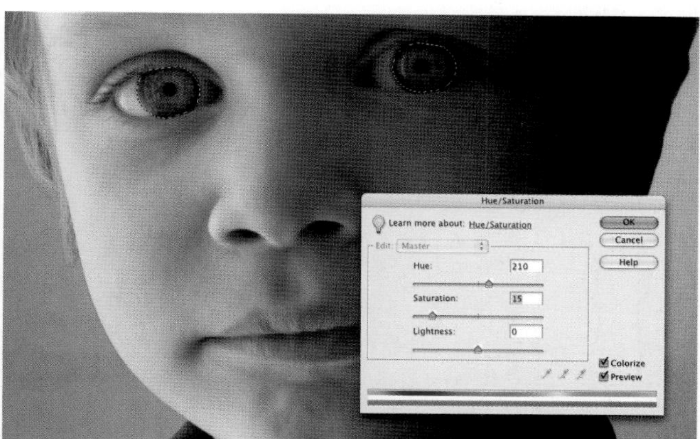

The eyes lost some impact in the desaturation process (Step 2) and they would benefit from a colour boost. Select them with the Lasso tool, feather to one pixel, then go to ***Enhance>Adjust Lighting>Adjust Hue/Saturation***. Click the colorize box, move the Hue slider into the Blue field, then adjust the Saturation so the effect is realistic.

Create a high-key portrait

The high-key portrait has been the mainstay of high street portraiture chains, such as Venture, for a good few years now. These high street chains can be rather expensive though, so it's good to know how to reproduce the effect yourself.

The effect works best on pictures that have been shot against a white backdrop. We'll use a mixture of Photoshop filters to make the subject 'pop off' the background and retouch any spots or pimples with the Healing Brush and Clone Stamp tools. High-key portraits are supposed to be very bright, consisting predominantly of tones that are lighter than 50 per cent grey. For this reason, you shouldn't be afraid of pushing the brightness up to levels where you might normally consider it to be overexposed.

1

This effect tends to work best on images shot against a white background or with a shallow depth-of-field. Open up your image and hit ***Ctrl+L*** to bring up the levels palette. Select the White Point eyedropper and click on the background or the whitest point of the image.

2

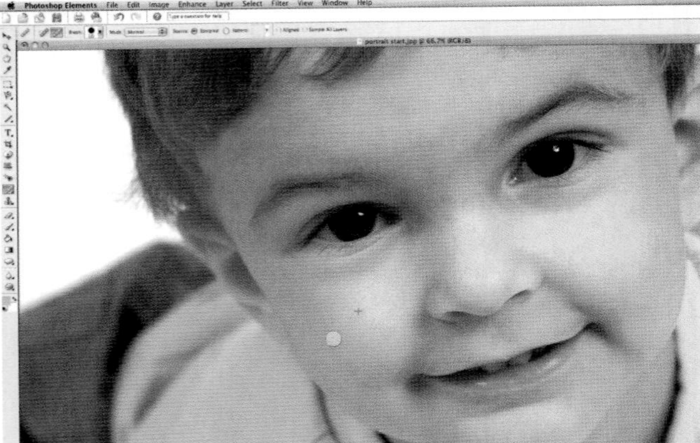

From the tool palette, select the Magnifying Glass and click to Zoom in. Select the Healing Brush and then hold down the ***Alt*** key and click on a suitable source point. Now click and drag to paint over any blemishes, re-selecting the source point if needed.

3

Select the Lasso tool from the tool palette or press ***L*** on the keyboard to cycle through the modes. Holding down the mouse button, draw a rough oval around the first eye area, then hold down shift (to add to the selection) and draw around the second eye in your image.

4

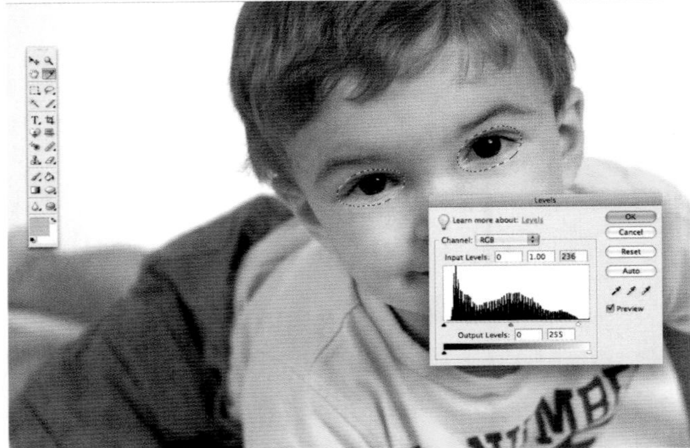

From the menu bar, go to ***Select>Feather*** and select around 30 pixels. Then bring up the Levels palette (***Ctrl+L***) and drag the far right handle (under the histogram) slightly in to the left to lighten the eye area in the selection you just made in step three.

5

Select ***Layer>Duplicate layer***. Do this three times. Now bring up the Layers palette (***F7***) and you should see four layers. With the top layer selected, go to ***Filter>Other>High Pass***. Set to around 30-50 pixels or until you can just see the outline and the eyes.

6

Back in the Layers palette, click the drop-down menu and change the mode from Normal to Vivid Light and reduce the Opacity if the effect looks too harsh. Now select the next layer down in the stack and change the Blending mode from Normal to Overlay.

PRO TIPS

LESSENING THE EFFECT

As each step is performed on a separate layer, if the effect is too harsh you can simply select the individual layers in the Layers palette and reduce the opacity to reduce the harshness of the effect

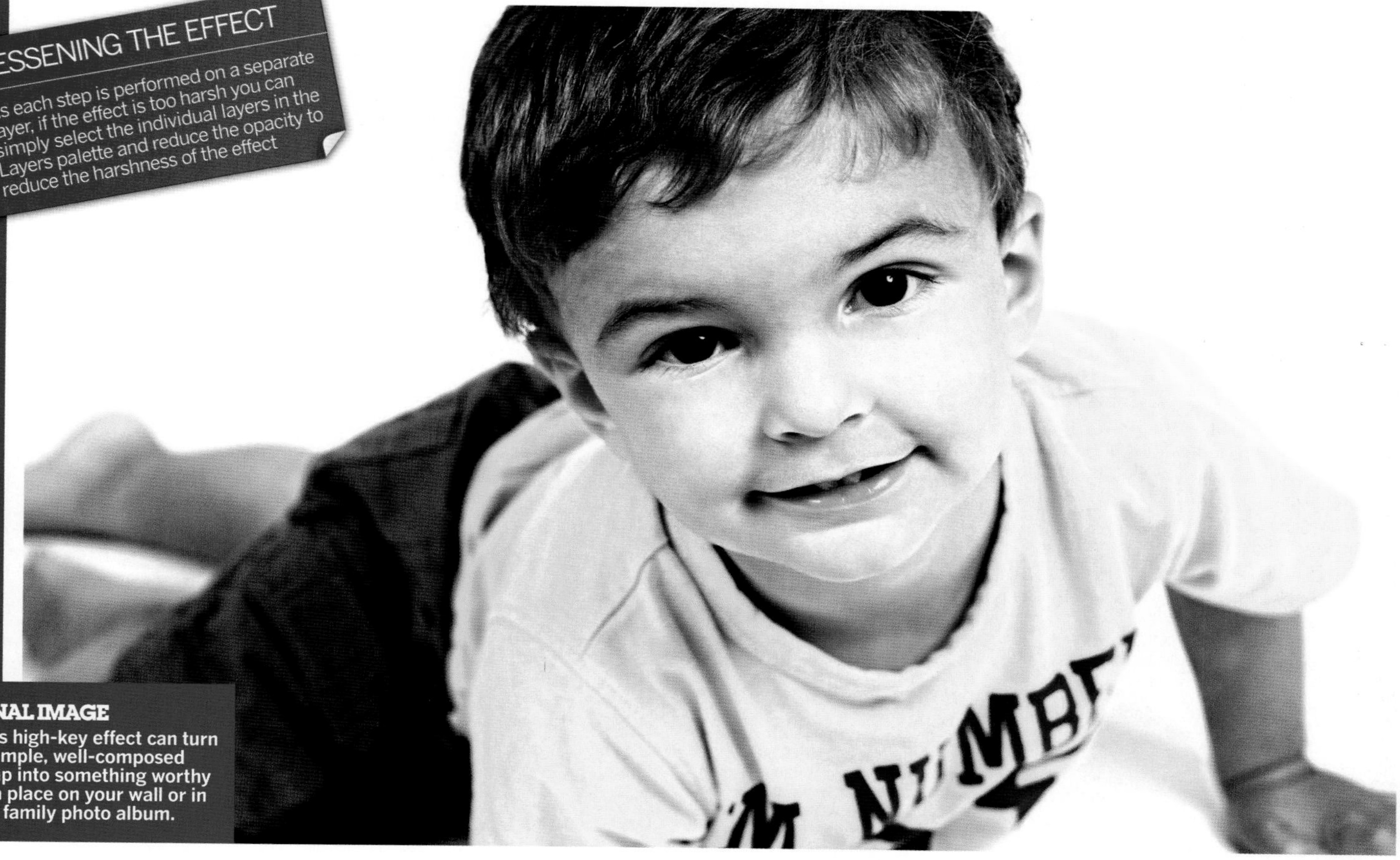

FINAL IMAGE
This high-key effect can turn a simple, well-composed snap into something worthy of a place on your wall or in the family photo album.

7

The next step is to select the next layer down (Background copy 2) and go to ***Filter>Distort>Diffuse Glow***. Reduce the Graininess to around 1 and adjust the Glow and Clear Amounts to suit. Now try a Glow Amount of 4 and Clear Amount of 13 to begin with.

8

If you want to begin the editing process again, then your bottom layer is still the original image. Just delete the other layers and start from the beginning. If you are happy with the result, though, you can go to ***Layer>Flatten image*** and save the file with a new name.

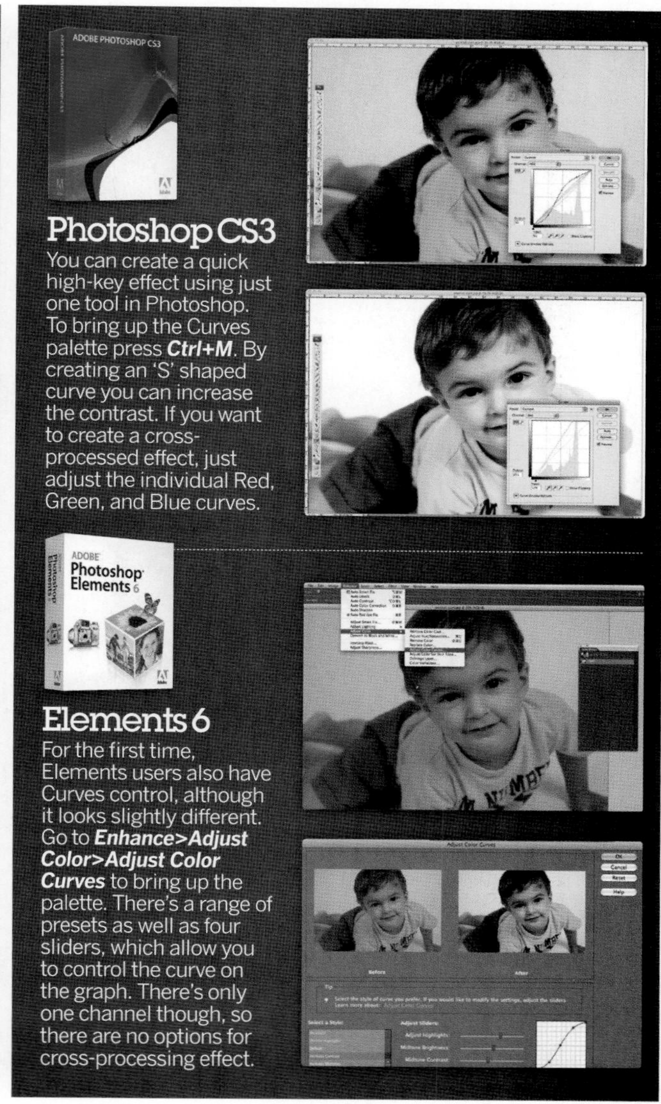

Photoshop CS3

You can create a quick high-key effect using just one tool in Photoshop. To bring up the Curves palette press ***Ctrl+M***. By creating an 'S' shaped curve you can increase the contrast. If you want to create a cross-processed effect, just adjust the individual Red, Green, and Blue curves.

Elements 6

For the first time, Elements users also have Curves control, although it looks slightly different. Go to ***Enhance>Adjust Color>Adjust Color Curves*** to bring up the palette. There's a range of presets as well as four sliders, which allow you to control the curve on the graph. There's only one channel though, so there are no options for cross-processing effect.

Add a HDR effect

No other technique polarises opinion as much as HDR photography. Some people think such post-processing is the epitome of photographic cheating, while others embrace this technique and love its results. Whatever your opinion, there's no denying that HDR can produce some stunning results. HDR works by merging the image's highlights and shadows and, as a result, the photo becomes a lot more dynamic. After all, that's what HDR stands for: High Dynamic Range.

What's more, the Photoshop process is a lot easier than you may think. All you need to get going is at least three images of the same subject, shot exactly in the same position and at the same focal length, although you tend to get better results using upwards of five files. Your images should be bracketed for exposure – ideally one image would be correctly exposed, while the other two would be exposed for highlights and shadows respectively. Along with your images, the easiest way to use HDR is through software program such as Photomatix or Photoshop. We've opted to use Photoshop as it's the more popular program, but you may want to check which version you have, as CS2 was the first version to offer the HDR option.

1/5sec at f/18

ORIGINAL EXPOSURES

As you can see, there are three original shots taken from the same position. One is correctly exposed, but the shutter speeds of the other two have been altered to under and overexpose the scene. These shots will help produce the extremes of tone in the final HDR image.

0.8 secs at f/18

1/30sec at f/18

1

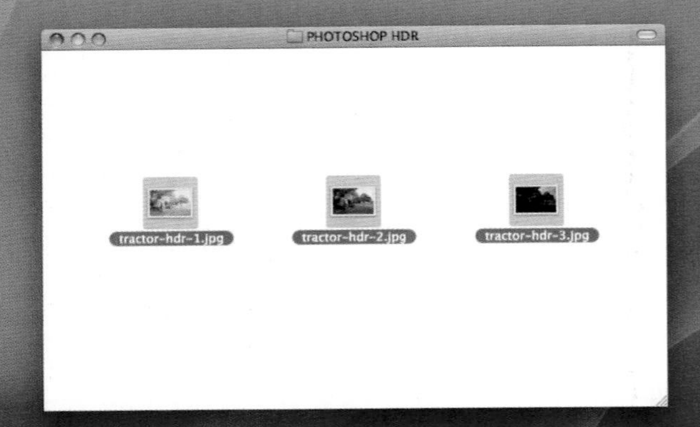

Before you open your Photoshop program, make sure that all the files you wish to use are grouped together in a folder. Photoshop can access these files if they're lying about on your desktop, but it's always good working practice to keep your images in organised folders.

2

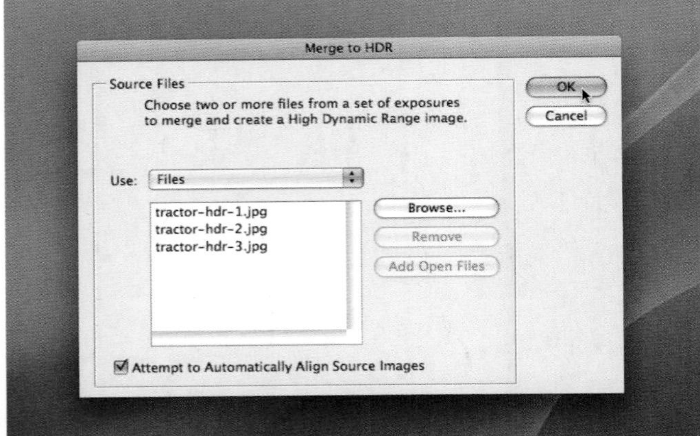

Now your images are ready and accessible, click ***File>Automate>Merge To HDR***. This will then display a pop-up box and allow you to select the files you want to use for your HDR image from your computer. Once you have selected the files you want to use, just click ***OK***.

3

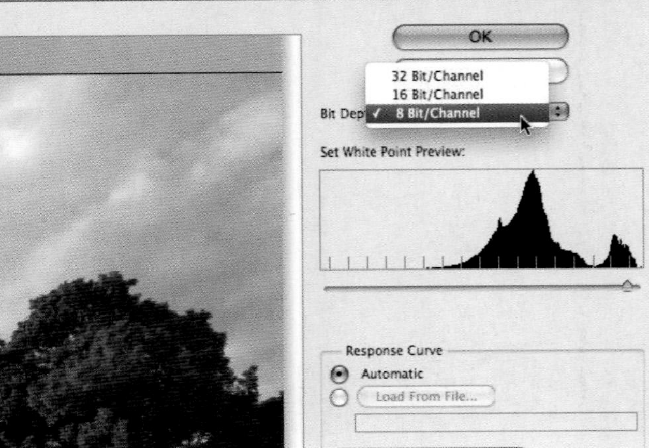

The files may take a bit of time to merge, depending on how fast your computer runs, but you'll eventually be presented with a preview image. Your image will automatically be in 32-bit mode, but this needs to be changed in the Bit Depth box to 16-bit or 8-bit. Select an option and click ***OK***.

4

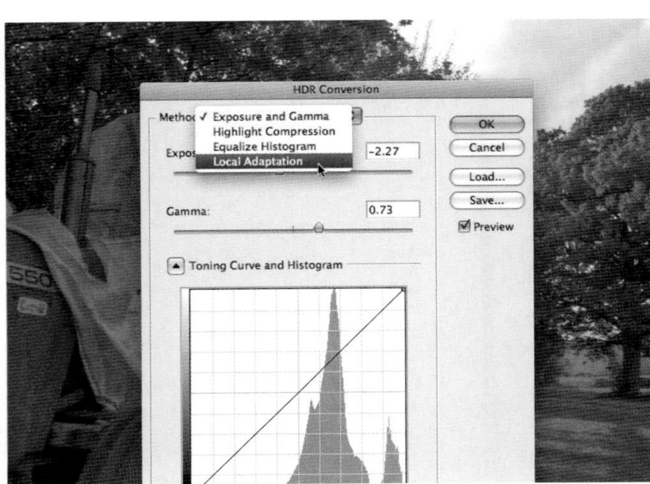

You will now be presented with four options to tweak and customise your HDR image. Feel free to try all of them, but we found the easiest one to work with was Local Adaptation, because you can adjust a histogram curve. You can find this option on the drop-down menu. Select it, then click ***OK***.

FINAL IMAGE
The HDR process has enhanced the image's shadows and highlights, adding a dynamic feel to the photo.

5

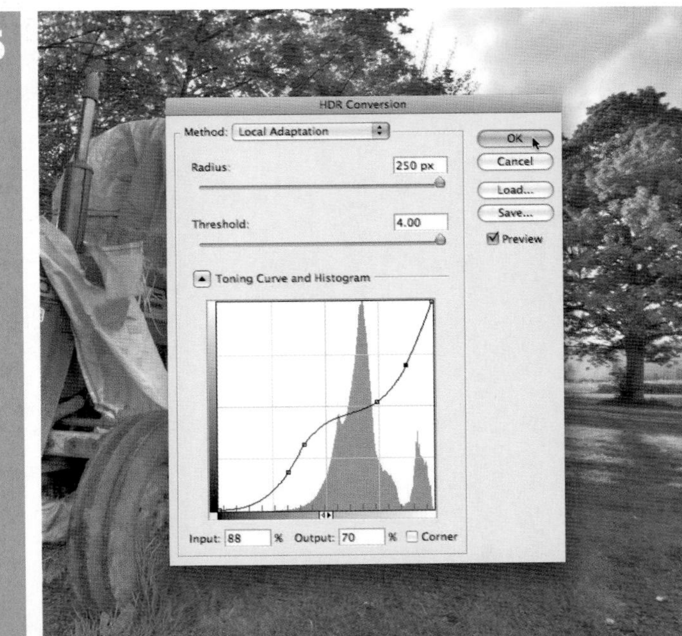

You're nearly there! All you have to do now is to adjust the Radius and Threshold sliders, along with the Toning Curve Histogram, until the image is to your taste. One useful tip to help enhance the image is to manipulate the curve into an inverted 'S' shape. Once you're happy, click ***OK***.

6

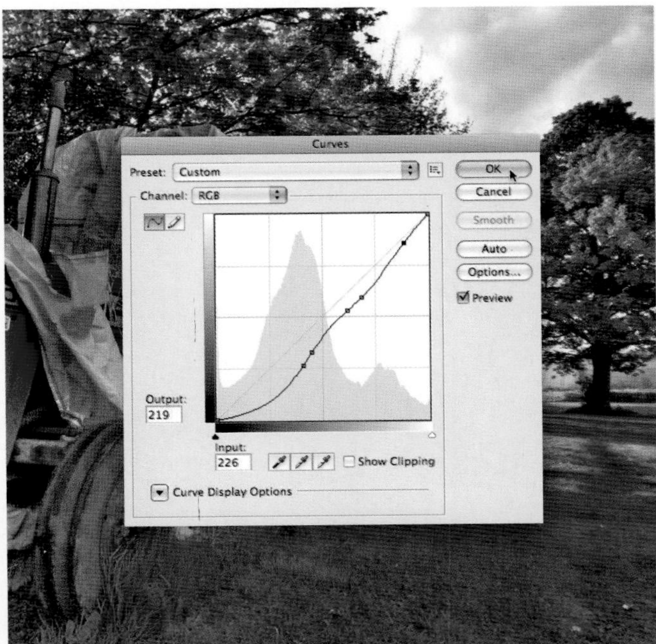

As you can see from the image, the HDR effect has transformed the photo. However, the image in this case remains a little flat – this is common in some HDR images. To get around this problem, tweak the Curves and try adding some contrast until the image is satisfactory.

Cross-processing in Photoshop

Photoshop has allowed us to create all sorts of wonderful effects, but many photographers who grew up in the film age still hanker for some of the old favourites. The portrait enthusiasts amongst you may remember cross-processing, which involved developing a film in the 'wrong' chemistry, (i.e. running a slide film through chemicals meant for negatives, or developing print films in slide film chemistry). This would lead to some unpredictably and very unusual results, such as particularly punchy colours and pale and tinted skin tones in your image.

This technique was popular with fashion and 'lifestyle' photographers in the nineties and many digital photographers now successfully mimic the effect. Cross-processing was very unpredictable and varied according to film brands and film type – slide films gave very different results to cross-processed print films .

Outlined here is a simple, yet effective, technique for recreating the cross-processed look digitally in Photoshop. It makes use of the Curves adjustment, which means you'll need the full version of Photoshop, or a Curves plug-in for Adobe Elements.

1

Choose a portrait image you like, but one you feel would benefit from more visual impact. Select ***Window>Layers*** to reveal the Layers palette. Select the half white/half black icon that allows you to create a new Adjustment Layer and choose Curves from the drop-down menu. Note a new layer called Curves 1 appears above the background layer (original image).

2

A Curves box appears, which displays a histogram of the image, with a straight diagonal line running from bottom left (pure black) to top right (pure highlight). Above the histogram is an option tab called Channel that will currently read RGB. You'll use the Channel tab to select the individual channels in the following order: Red, Blue, then Green.

3

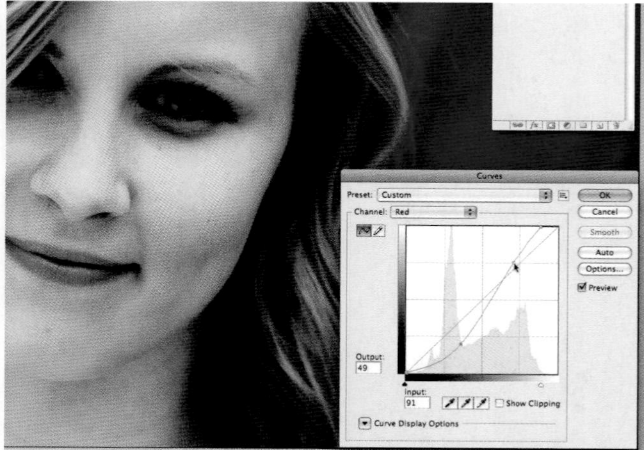

Select Red and drag the top right of the curve a little to the left. Then click two points around a third of the way from the top and bottom and drag them to create a gentle S-curve (i.e. drag the top point slightly to the left and the bottom point to the right). This gives deeper shadows and brighter highlights in the Red channel – check the Preview button to see the effect.

4

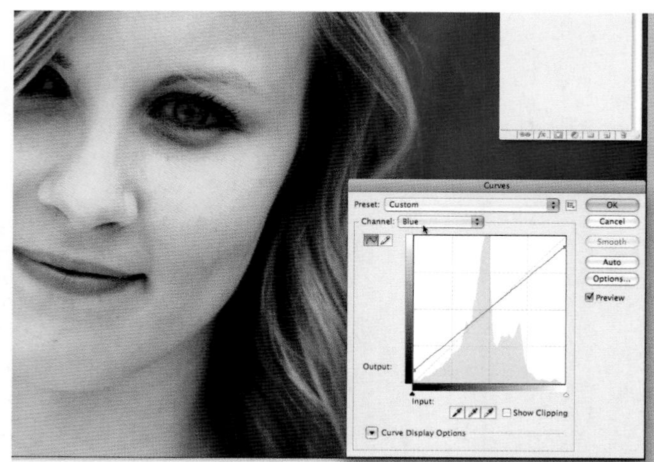

Once you've adjusted the Red channel, click on the Channel drop-down menu and select the Blue channel. Pull the top right end of the curve downwards to remove some blue from the highlights. When you've done this, pull up the bottom of the curve by no more than half a square, to make the shadows in the blue channel a bit more solid. The line should remain straight.

PRO TIPS: COLOUR EXPERIMENTS

Cross-processing films often gave very unpredictable results, so when you're working on the colour channels, don't be afraid to experiment with your channel tweaks to see what effects occur

FINAL IMAGE
Compare this image to the original and the effect speaks for itself: an image that holds far more visual impact thanks to the extra colour and contrast.

5

You can now click on the Channel tab and select Green. With the Green channel, you need to select two points as you did with the Red channel, and drag them to create another gentle S-curve. However, there is no need to drag the top end of the curve. You can then fine-tune the adjustments to your satisfaction. Once you are happy with the resulting image, click ***OK***.

6

You should now have an effect that's reminiscent of cross-processed film, with more solid, bold colours and skin tones taking on a yellow/green tinge. However, you can also create other adjustment layers to further enhance your image – in particular the Hue/Saturation and Brightness/Contrast layers, which can be selected to fine-tune the effect to your liking.

Alternative cross-processing technique

While our main step-by-step mimics the effects of cross-processing print film in slide chemistry, many film photographers favoured experimenting with processing slide film in print (C-41) chemistry. This produced extremely high contrast images, with near-bleached white skin tones, bright red lips and very strong colours. It's a relatively easy effect to mimic by making adjustments to the Hue/Saturation and Brightness/Contrast controls in Photoshop.

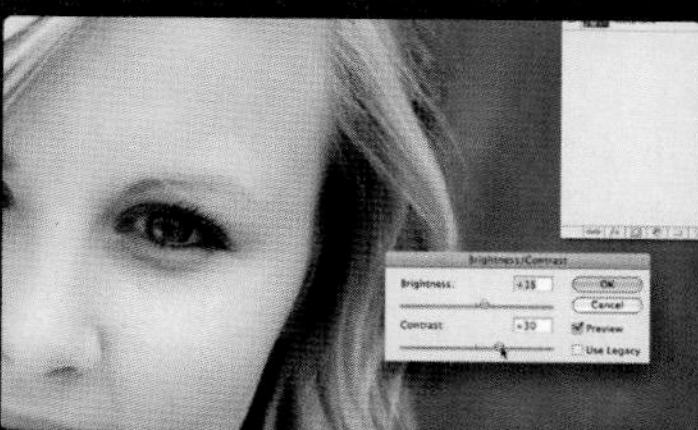

1) Open the image and select *Window>Layers* to reveal the Layers palette. Select a new Adjustment Layer and choose Hue/ Saturation from the drop-down menu. Boost the saturation and adjust the hue to your liking (but make sure that you don't overdo the effect!).

2) Now select a new adjustment layer for Brightness/Contrast and increase the contrast (and brightness if you so wish). You'll find that you'll start to lose detail in the highlights and shadows and the colours become far more punchy. Again, don't overdo it.

Create shallow depth-of-field

It's not always easy to isolate subjects against a blurred background. Professional photographers use very expensive wide aperture lenses to do this, but the kit lenses that come bundled with DSLRs aren't always up to the job. Fear not though – there is a good way of creating the effect digitally in Adobe Photoshop instead and it's not too difficult.

The idea is to duplicate the image into two layers and make one of these blurred using one of Photoshop's many blur filters. We can then cut holes in the non-blurred layer, positioned on top, and let the blurred one show through the gaps. The principle is easy, and the reality isn't too difficult either. As ever, a steady hand and enough patience to take your time will yield the best results in the final image.

1

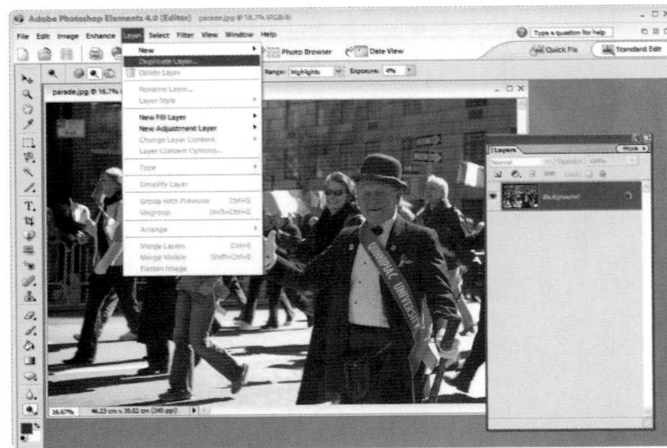

Select an image with a subject that needs pulling out of a busy background – a person in a crowd is often a good example. First create a duplicate layer by selecting ***Layer>Duplicate layer*** in the menu bar. This will appear as background copy in the Layers palette.

2

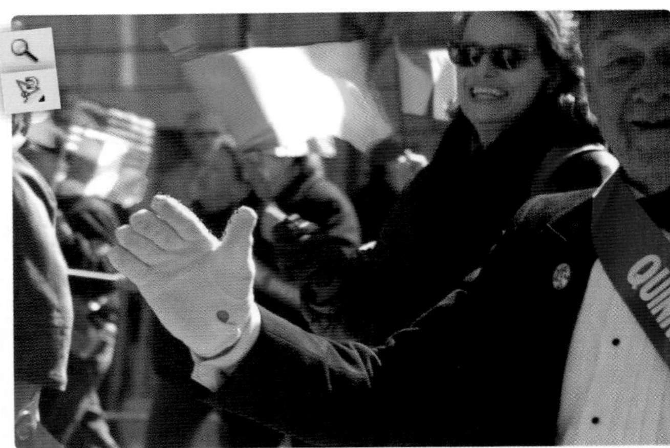

Choose the Zoom tool and click to enlarge the area that you want to stay in focus. To cut out the area you want in focus, select the Magnetic Lasso tool from the tool palette or by pressing the ***L*** key (pressing ***L*** again will scroll through the different lasso modes).

3

Click on your starting point and guide your mouse around the edge of the area to cut out. It will automatically follow the edge of a well-defined shape and you can guide it by clicking at regular points. Press ***Backspace*** to remove a point if you make a mistake.

4

To scroll during the selection process, hold down the ***Space bar,*** click and drag the image. You may need to remove the last few anchor points by hitting ***Backspace***. Once you return to the starting point, click on its anchor point to complete the selection.

5

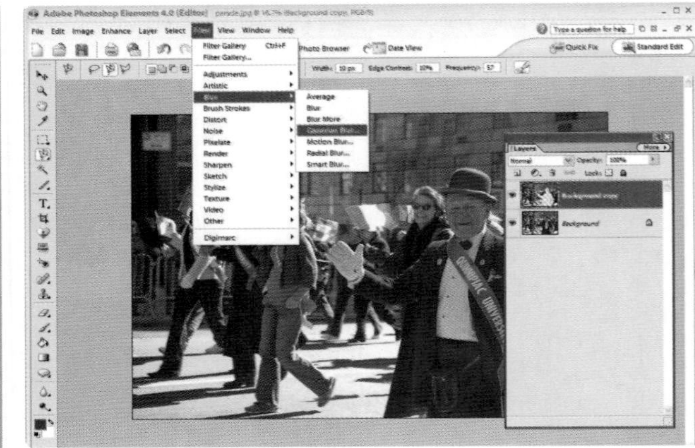

Having made your selection, hit ***Backspace***, or ***Edit>Delete*** in the menu bar. This will leave you with just the area you want to throw out of focus on the Background copy layer. So now go to ***Filter>Blur>Gaussian Blur*** to bring up the Gaussian Blur palette.

6

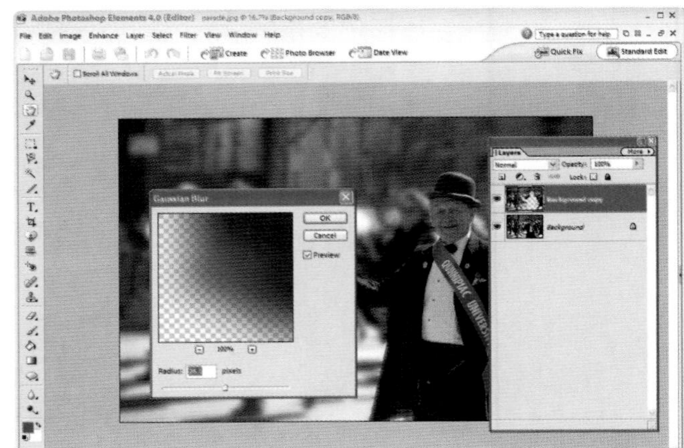

The Gaussian blur creates a lens blur effect, and can be varied in strength. Too much blur will give previously sharp areas of the image harsh edges, so for this image we've chosen a value of around 25 pixels. Adjust the slider until you're happy, and click ***OK***.

FINAL IMAGE
Creating the effect of a shallow depth-of-field gives the impression that a powerful telephoto lens was used to shoot this scene, and helps the subject stand out from the busy background.

7

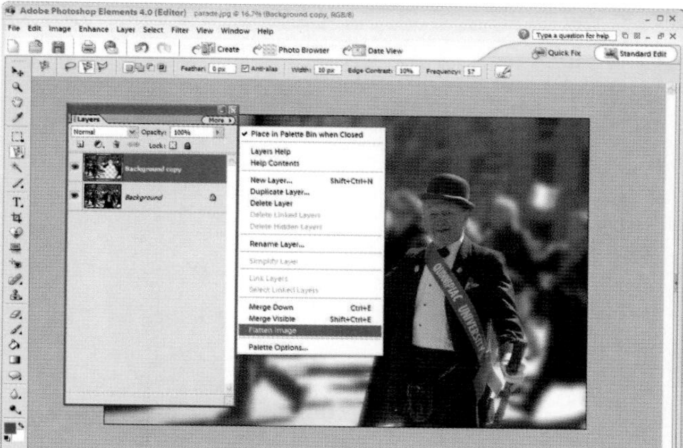

Your image should now look as though it was taken with a very wide aperture. The blurred part is still on a separate layer, so you can try again if desired. If you like the result, click ***More*** in the Layers palette and select Flatten image, or choose ***Layer>Flatten image***.

8

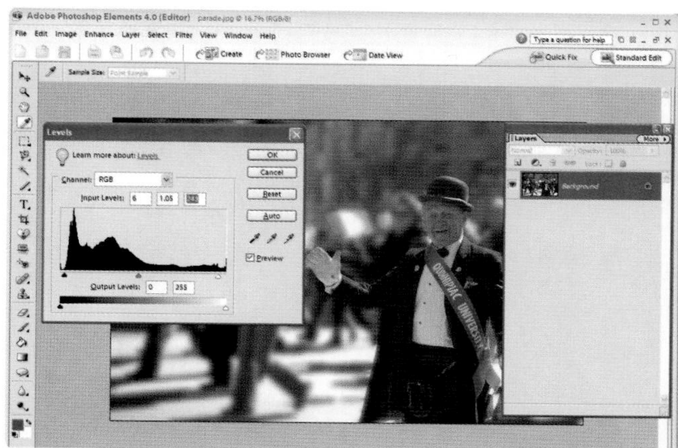

Finally, to brighten your subject and make the image stand out, press ***Ctrl+L*** to adjust the levels. Move the right and centre triangles slightly to the left, to add brightness, and the left triangle to the right slightly, darkening the shadows and adding contrast.

Using layer masks in Photoshop CS3 & CS4

If you have the full version of Photoshop you can make use of the layer masks to create your selection. Layer masks are created within a layer, like an adjustable selection. You can create a mask from the Layers palette either by converting a selection or bringing up a blank mask and painting on to it. A quicker method though, is to use the Quick Mask from the Tool palette (or by pressing Q on the keyboard). You can then use the paintbrush with black selected to paint over your selection. This will appear in red to highlight the masked area. To remove the mask from an area, change your brush colour to white and paint over. Once you have the area selected, return to normal mode (by hitting Q or repressing the option on the Tool palette). This will convert your quick mask back into a selection, allowing you to delete it and carry on from step five in the tutorial.

Give your subject a digital make-over

Ever wondered how those celebrities and models look so good in the glossy mags and fashion adverts? Well, the secret is, they don't. In fact, we are confident you won't find a single non-retouched picture in the magazine press these days. 'Virtual make-up' treatments are absolutely the norm in the 21st Century fashion and glamour world. You can learn a trick or two from these industries that can help in your own portraiture. Everyone has an off day, so it's good to be able to assure your subject that you'll be able to shoot a great picture of them even if they have just developed a spot or blemish over night. Be aware though: it's often said that digital imaging is only as good as the amount of time spent on it, and this is never more true than with skin retouching.

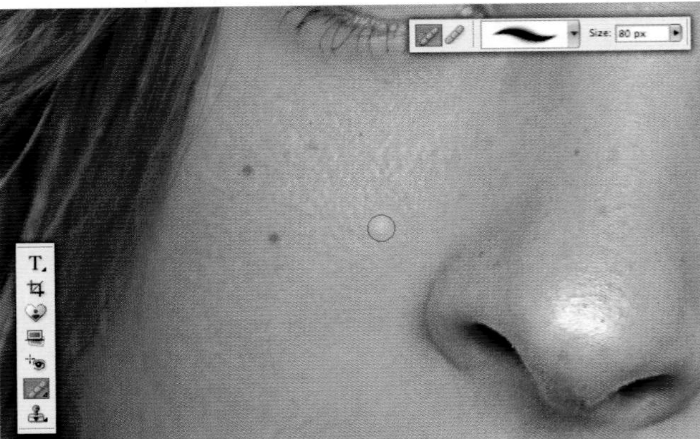

To remove skin blemishes, moles and pimples, try using the Spot Healing Brush (inset left) with a soft brush (inset top). This tool works by looking at pixels surrounding your selection, and using these to calculate new pixels to 'heal' those inside. To use either click once over the desired area or, for larger areas, click, drag and release.

2

Next, it's time to prepare the face for skin 'smoothing', which is a standard technique used throughout the fashion and glamour industry to retouch images. We need to isolate the face so as not to affect the surrounding areas, and to do this use the Polygonal Lasso (inset) to make a rough selection, then ***Select>Feather*** this selection.

To start 'smoothing' any pores, wrinkles and scars, first use the Eyedropper (inset), which when clicked will select a colour from your image and show it as the active colour in the swatch visible at the bottom of the tool bar (inset). When 'smoothing', always choose a close tonal match to the area you're working on.

4

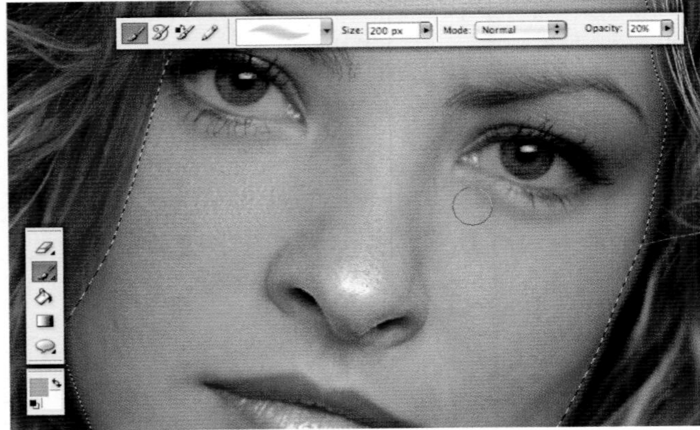

The art of 'smoothing' quickly is to switch between the Eyedropper and the Brush tool (inset). Once both have been used, switch between them by pressing the 'alt' key. Starting with the bags under the eyes, choose a medium brush size and set the Opacity (inset top) down to 20%, to allow a natural paint effect.

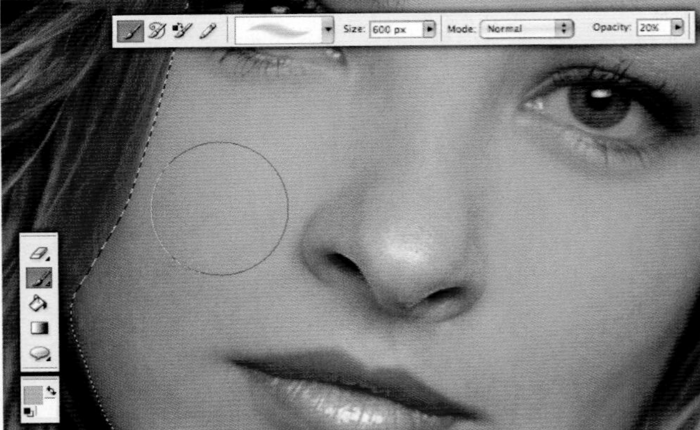

It will soon become apparent why the Opacity is set low, as it allows for a controlled and gradual build up of strokes, allowing for original skin texture to remain visible. Work your way over the face, switching to the Eyedropper to update tonal selections, then back to the Brush, adjusting the size to accommodate the area.

6

Edit>Undo (Ctrl-Z) and ***Window>Undo History*** are essential for controlling the 'smoothing' process, as there is a large margin for error due to the amount of manual brush strokes involved. To soften burnt-out highlights, such as the tip of the nose and the bottom lip, use exactly the same method of Eyedropper and Brush.

PRO TIPS

GET DOLLED UP!

Once you've mastered skin 'smoothing', apply the same technique to create colourful eye-shadow or cheek-blusher, this time using the ***Colour Picker*** rather than the ***Eyedropper*** as reference

FINAL IMAGE

A healthy complexion, bright eyes and full sumptuous lips, you can hardly tell our model had been up partying until 3am the night before!

7

Next we want to add a hint of colour to the lips so select them with the Polygonal Lasso (inset), then add a small feather to the selection with ***Select>Feather*** to avoid any harsh colour effects. Use ***Enhance>Adjust Colour>Adjust Hue/Saturation*** raising the Hue slightly, but not too much, to create a subtle 'lipstick' effect.

8

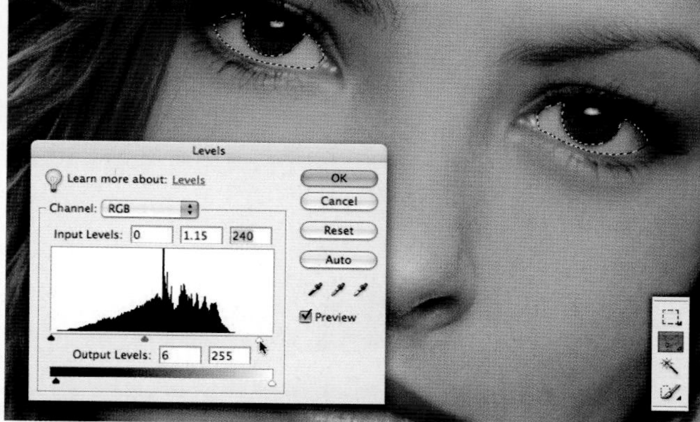

Now it's time to work on the eyes by first making a rough selection of the eye whites with the Polygonal Lasso and then Feather the selection as previously. Go to ***Enhance>Adjust Lighting>Levels*** and move the mid-tone (grey) and highlights (white) sliders of the Input levels until visibly happy with the Preview results.

9

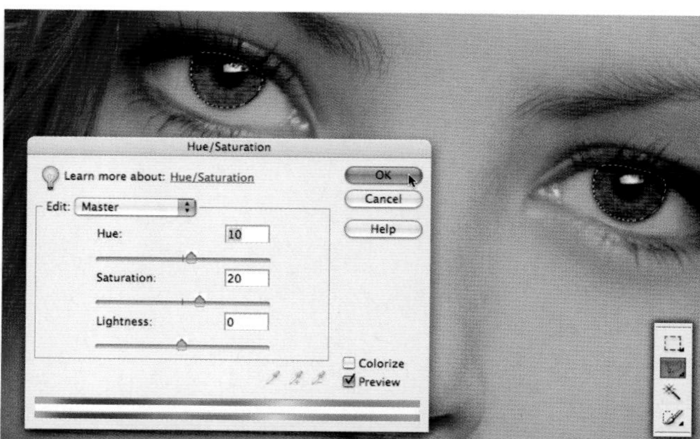

Turning my attention to the inner eye, make a selection with the Polygonal Lasso, this time of the pupil area and, as before, Feather the selection. We used ***Filter>Sharpen>Unsharp Mask*** with an Amount of 100% and Radius of 5 pixels to sharpen, then Hue/Saturation, as in step seven, to add a subtle hint of colour.

10

With all the facial processes complete, we use one final technique to soften the outlining areas of the image, throwing even more focus into the subject's face. First, we made a rough selection with the Polygonal Lasso then Feather with a large amount (150 pixels), and finally used a small amount of ***Filter>Gaussian Blur***.

Add a digital graduated filter effect

Using Photoshop to recreate the effect of a graduate filter allows a variety of effects to be created in minutes. This easy-to-follow tutorial will show you how to create stunning graduated effects using adjustment layers, so the effects can be repeated and adjusted until the combination of layers and original image is perfect.

Over the following steps, we'll introduce you to Adjustment Layers, Gradient Fill, Gradient Editor, Color Picker, Blending Mode and Photo Filter for mood. Photoshop isn't an alternative to optical filters, it's a complementary skill. Use it to produce images that are not possible on location or when you've forgot your graduate filter. Photoshop Elements 4.0 was used here, but more recent versions are suitable too.

1

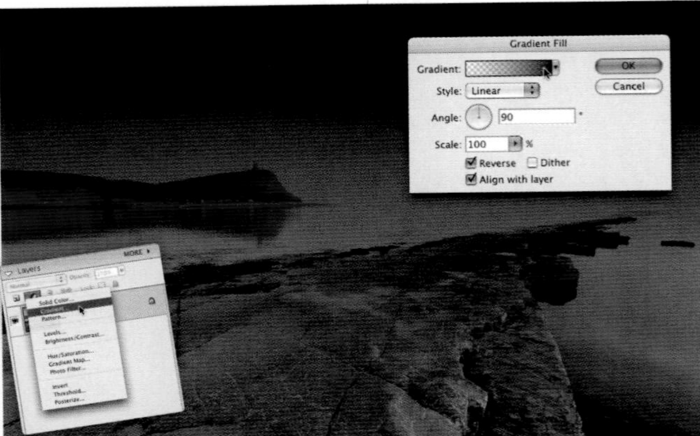

The aim is to create a similar effect to a conventional grad filter, but using a series of digital graduated layers instead. Create the first gradient by clicking the ***Create Adjustment Layer*** icon ( ), situated at the top of the Layers palette, and scrolling to Gradient, which opens the Gradient Fill window.

2

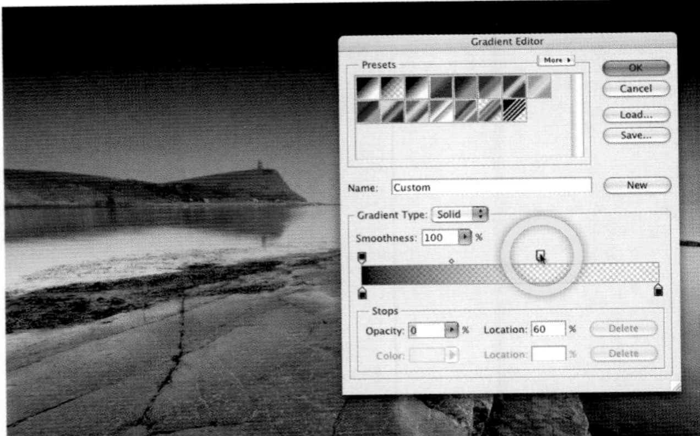

In the Gradient Fill window, tick ***Reverse*** so the gradient runs top to bottom, then click anywhere within the Gradient field (situated top) to open the Gradient Editor sub-window. The sliders at the top of the visible gradient control opacity, and moving the White slider will increase the transparent ratio of the gradient.

3

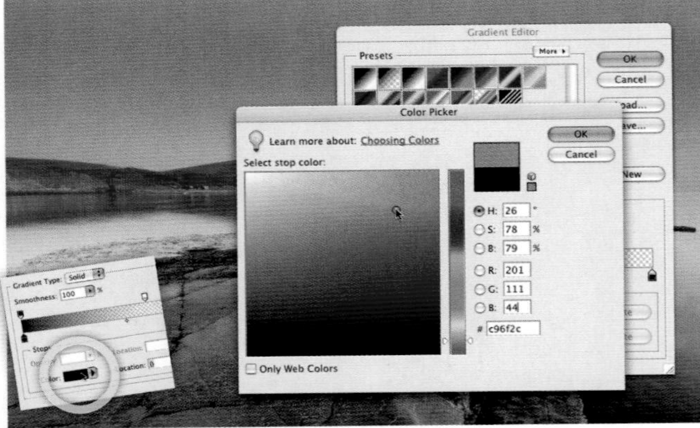

The sliders at the bottom of the gradient control colour, the left representing black. Click the black slider and note that the colour now appears in the field below, clicking here opens the Color Picker sub-window. Use the vertical spectrum (centre) and the main window (left) to select the desired colour then click ***OK***.

4

Click ***OK*** in the subsequent windows to apply the gradient, then choose ***Multiply*** from the Blending Mode menu situated to the top of the Layers palette (inset) to create a more natural merging of the gradient to the original image. This Adjustment Layer Gradient can be tweaked at any time by selecting it in the Layers palette.

5

It's quite often necessary to create more than one gradient layer to build up the filter effect. Here, duplicate steps 1 and 2 creating a gradient that is black to transparent, then, choosing Soft Light in the Blending Mode menu and reducing the layer Opacity (inset) creating a natural darkening effect that can easily be adjusted.

6

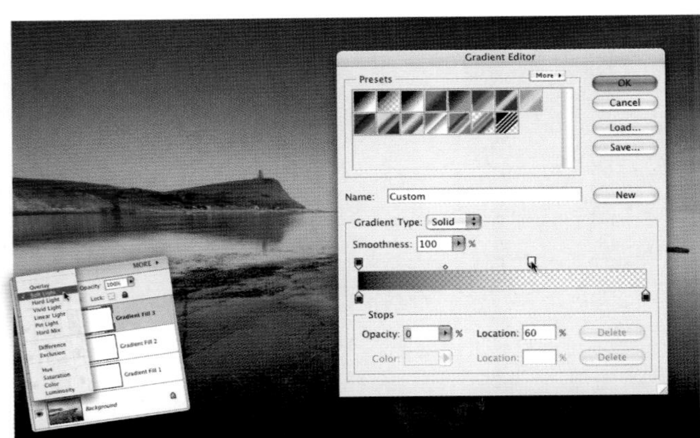

The final gradient layer is going to add a subtle fall-off to the rocks leading out of the image to the bottom of the frame. Again, repeat steps 1 and 2, this time leaving the Reverse box unticked so the gradient runs from bottom to top. Once again, you need to set the Blending Mode to Soft Light and reduce the Opacity.

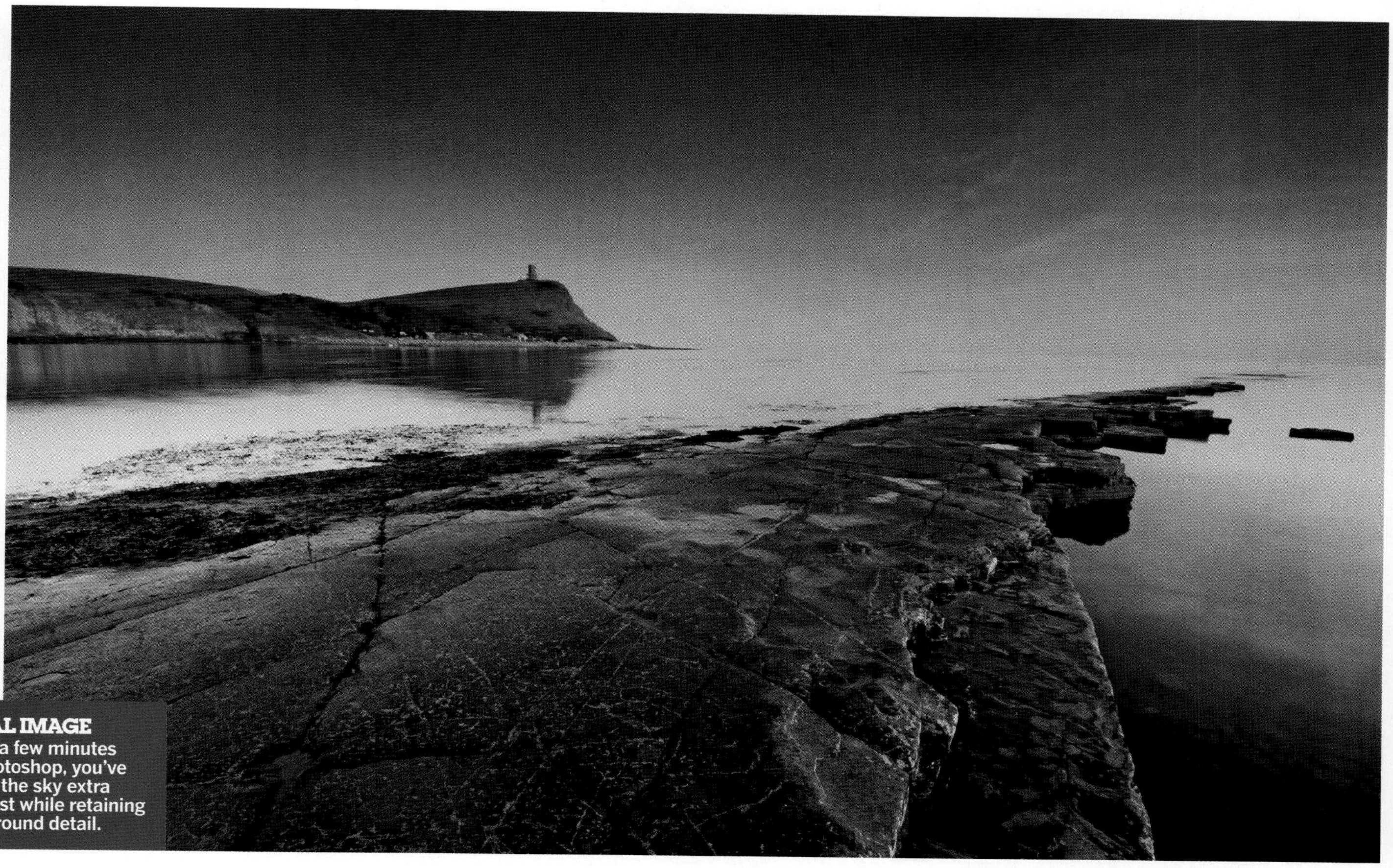

FINAL IMAGE
After a few minutes in Photoshop, you've given the sky extra interest while retaining foreground detail.

7 Adding the final touch with Filter>Adjustments>Photo Filter

Photoshop Elements and CS have mood filters that can be used to change the overall tone of your image, much like using a coloured gel or filter on your digital SLR. This handy action, found in the top menu under ***Filter>Adjustments>PhotoFilter***, has several preset filters including Warming, Cooling and Sepia or you can choose to manually filter through the Color Picker. The intensity of the selected tone can then be adjusted with the Density slider to allow for some very subtle effects, giving far greater control than that of optical lens filters. When you've finished adding a grad effect to an image, it's well worth the time trying some of these out to see if the image can be improved upon further.

COOLING

WARMING

VIOLET

EMERALD

FINAL COLOUR

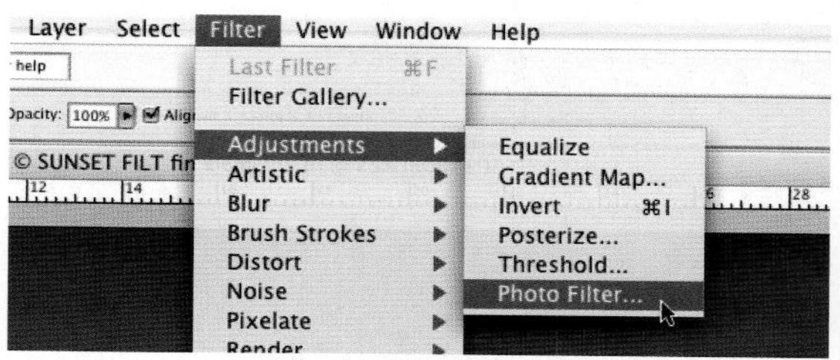

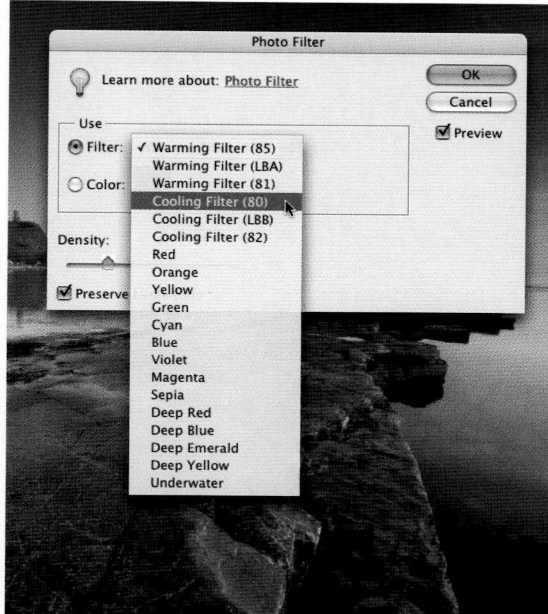

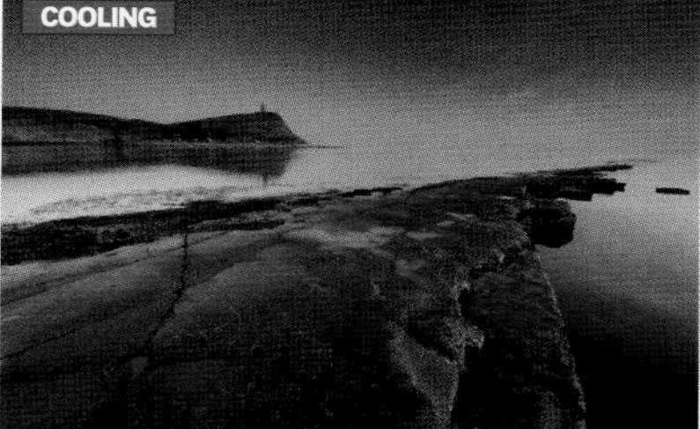

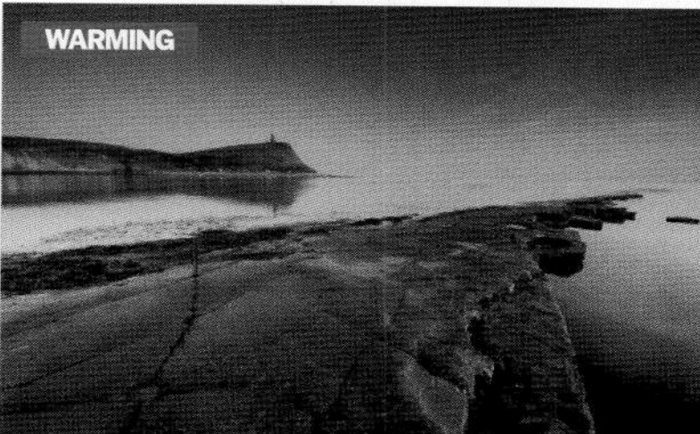

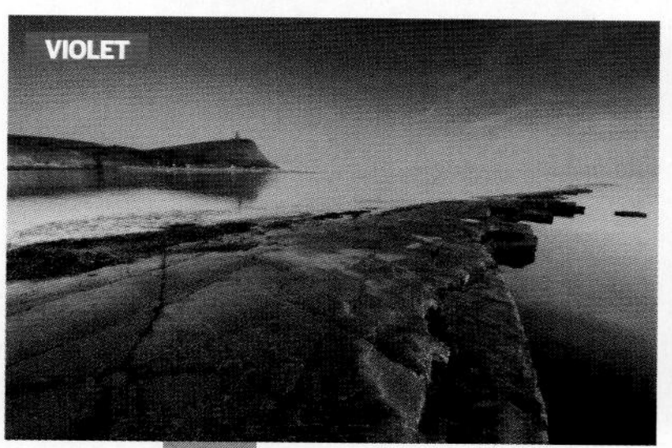

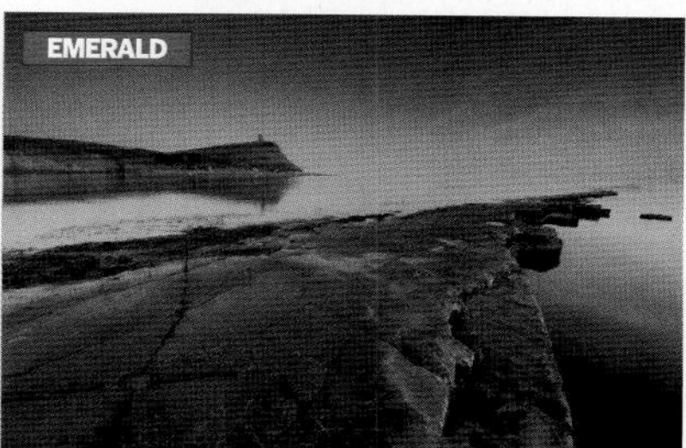

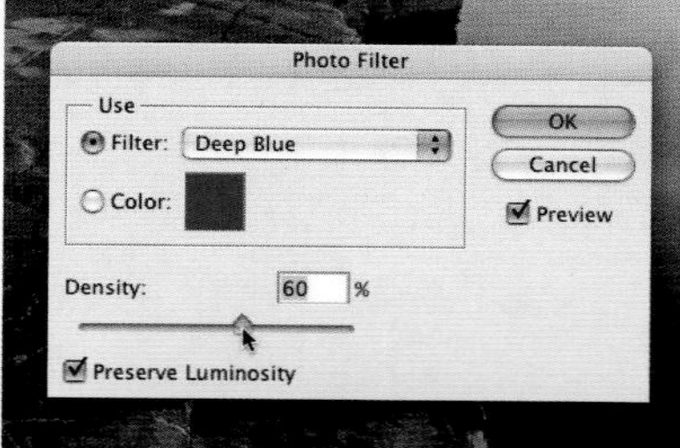

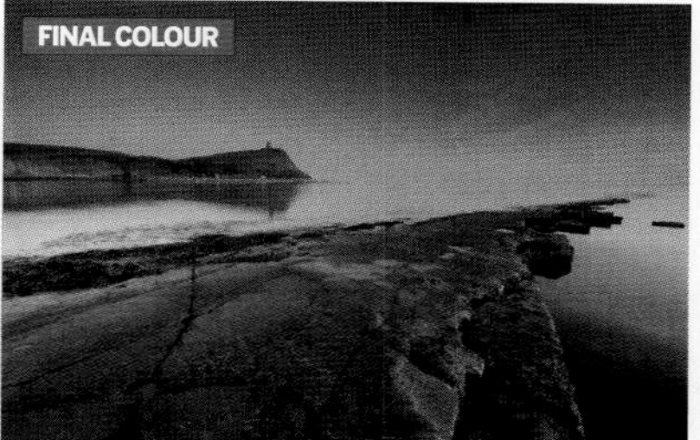

ABOVE: Choose from a range of preset filters available in the Photo Filter function or use the Color Picker to customise.

RIGHT: FINAL COLOUR SELECTION Although happy with the results of the grad filter effect, the image could be improved upon further with the use of the Photo Filter action. After a little experimenting, the Deep Blue proved to be the most appropriate preset filter at about 60% Density, making the overall mood of the image slightly cooler, which works better with the coastal subject matter of the rock formation.

ORIGINAL PRINT

Restore old photos to their former glory

People often say that digital photos don't provide the same lasting memory as traditional prints, but in reality, the opposite is true. Your digital files, if properly backed up, will look as good, in 20 or 30 years as the day they were taken, while your prints will have faded, turned yellow and may be creased. Thanks to the digital imaging process though, we can now rescue these images with a little patience and creativity, repairing the damage that years of oxidisation and careless storage have caused.

Firstly, you'll need to get the print onto your computer, so you'll need a flatbed scanner. Scan it at a higher resolution than you need to get maximum detail; we'd suggest around 600dpi for an A4 print. This will create a huge file, but you can then resize it. You can use most editing software, although a version of Photoshop or Photoshop Elements is ideal. Unless you are a highly talented illustrator, you're never going to make the photo look modern, so leave in the border or rough edge, if it has one. Work in layers when possible, and keep checking back against the original picture as it's very easy to go over-the-top and ruin it. If your photo is in quite a state, like this one, the process can take a long time, so do it in stages, returning to it at different times. Where detail is lost completely you may need to be slightly inventive, darkening down an area to black, or brightening it up to white. It's very rewarding work, and a very handy technique to learn. Be warned though – doing too good a job could land you with requests from friends and family to restore their old pictures too!

Essential tool

HEALING BRUSH

This is an extremely powerful editing tool that is ideal for portraits. It works by blending the pixels from a selected sample point to the chosen area and will match the colour and luminosity values to make the join look seemless. It's very handy for removing spots and blemishes, or even dust particles, and can work with scratches too.

1

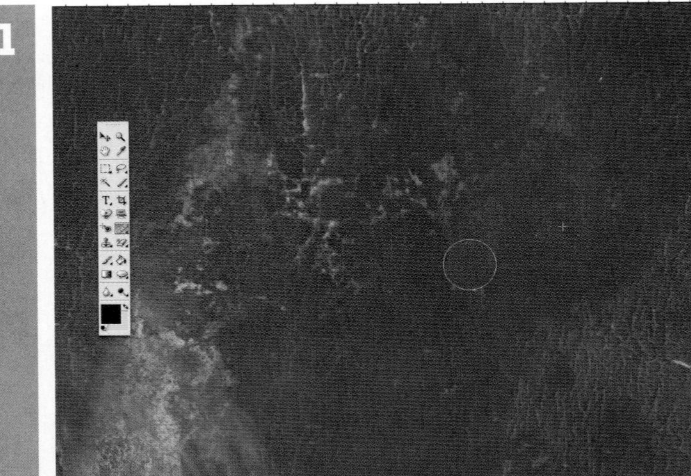

First make a copy of the image, by creating a duplicate layer (***Ctrl+J***). Then look for the most obvious problems, such as scratches and stains. The Healing brush is perfect for fixing these, as it will blend back into the area you're healing. Select a plain area as your source by holding down the ***Alt*** key and clicking; then carefully paint over the area you want to heal.

2

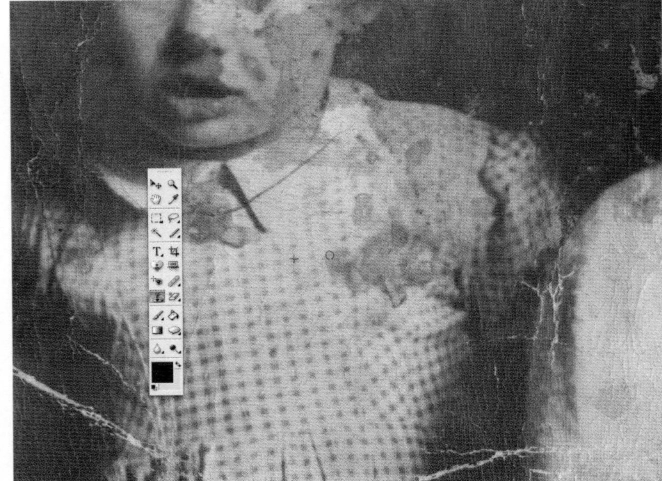

For the more difficult areas, such as patterns or defined edges, switch to the Clone tool. This will allow you to replace areas by copying exact sections of the image, without the blur that can be caused by the Healing brush. Select your source point, as you did in step 1 (by ***Alt***-clicking), and use a small brush. For realistic results, you'll need to keep changing the source point.

FINAL IMAGE
Memories are meant to last a lifetime. Restoring old prints from yesteryear could make someone's day. Plus, they are a great birthday or Christmas present.

3

Once you've done as much as you can with those two tools, you can use the Paint Brush to smooth over areas with unwanted paper texture. When using this tool, you can hold ***Alt*** and click to select the brush colour from the image. Pick the colour in the place you are painting, and select a large brush set to a low opacity (around 20%), so as not to over-paint a section.

4

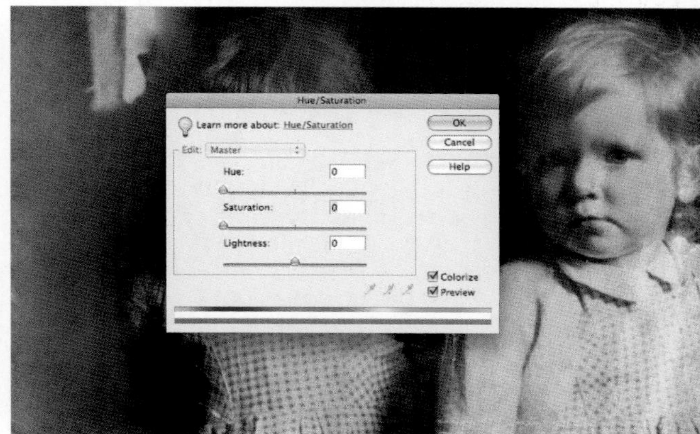

To remove any unnatural colouration that has resulted from the ageing process, hit ***Ctrl+U*** to bring up the Hue/Saturation palette and drag the Saturation slider back to zero, converting the image to black & white. If your software allows, use an adjustment layer by going to ***Layer>New Adjustment layer***. Alternatively you can use a black & white filter.

5

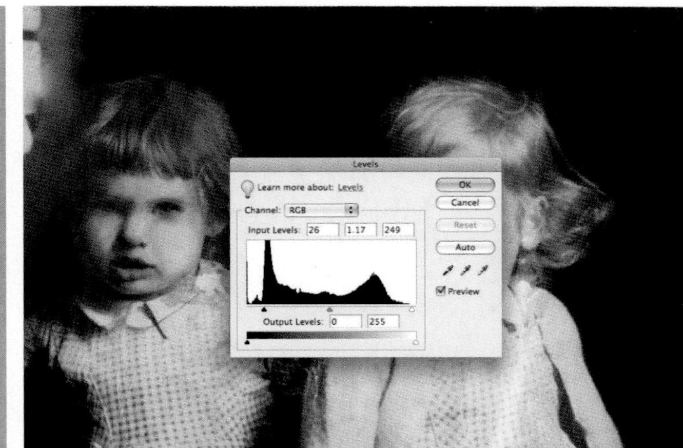

The chances are that your picture will look a little 'flat' by modern standards, so hit ***Ctrl+L*** on the keyboard, to bring up the Levels palette. Then, drag the far left marker (triangle under the histogram) slightly to the right to boost the blacks; drag the far right marker slightly to the left to boost the whites, and move the centre slider slightly, to adjust the contrast.

6

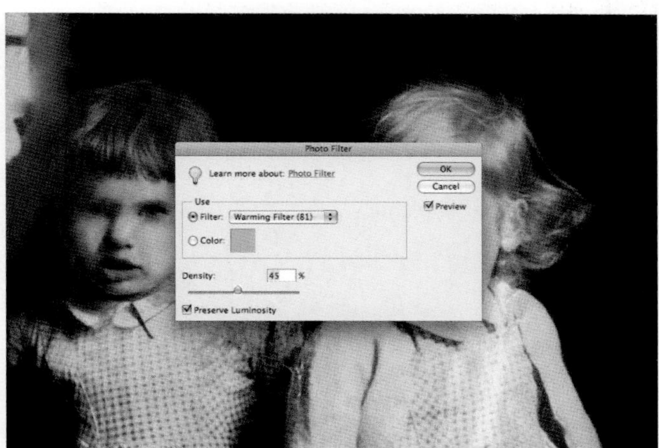

The final step isn't essential, but as you're not trying to hide the fact that the picture is old, it can help add a little authenticity. Open the Photo Filter menu by going to ***Filter>Adjustments>Photo Filter***, and select Warming Filter (81), then adjust the density slider below to give a slight sepia tone to your image. Now print it out, frame it and give it to someone special.

Correcting for lens distortion

Buy an entry-level or mid-range DSLR and, chances are, it will come in kit form with a standard zoom lens included. That's all very nice, but the reality of these 'kit zooms' is that they often aren't the best optically. To get the most detail from your sensor you really need to upgrade that chunk of glass to something a bit better, which can cost a bit of money to do.

So what's the problem with the humble kit zoom? Well in the middle of the frame, not much, but go further towards the edges and you'll encounter distortion of straight lines, a darkening of the corners (also known as light fall-off), chromatic aberrations (manifested as coloured fringing) and a drop in sharpness. It's not all bad news though: while sharpness is hard to tackle digitally, distortion, chromatic aberrations and vignetting can all be addressed through Photoshop or Elements, using the excellent Lens Correction filter ('Correct Camera Distortion' in Elements).

This brilliant filter is a kind of 'one-stop shop' for fixing not only lens faults, but also perspective problems, like converging verticals and sloping horizons. You can also save groups of settings for a specific lens, enabling you to recall them more quickly later on.

You'll find the Lens Correction filter in Photoshop, from version CS2 onwards, located under **Filters>Distort**. In Elements versions 5.0 and above, it's called the 'Correct Camera Distortion' filter, and lacks the chromatic aberration correction options. Let's have a look how it works on this picture of this Cambridge pub, The Pickerel Inn. It was shot with a Nikon D80 and 18-55mm kit lens, which means it displays pronounced barrel distortion at the top and bottom of the picture, a tiny bit of purple fringing, and significant darkening towards the corners of the frame. It's also got a wonky horizon – typical of much quickly grabbed street photography – and suffers from 'converging verticals' as the lens was angled upwards slightly.

1

Bring up the Lens Correction dialogue by choosing ***Filters>Distort>Lens Correction***. Our first job is to correct the wonky horizon. You can do this in a couple of ways, but the easiest is to choose the Straighten tool from the toolbox at the top-left of the screen and draw a line along something in the picture that is meant to be either horizontal or vertical. Opt for something that's central; lines near the edges are about to be changed.

2

With the picture level we can get to work on the other problems. It's obvious the lens suffers from barrel distortion. We can apply distortion correction in one of two ways in order to remedy this: either drag the Remove Distortion slider left (to correct for pin-cushion) or right (to correct for barrel). Alternatively, use the Remove Distortion Tool and click and drag the picture inwards to correct barrel or outwards to correct pin-cushion distortion.

3

The edges of the building are angled inwards, which is a natural consequence of perspective, called 'converging verticals'. Unfortunately it doesn't look that natural, so we'll get rid of it with the Vertical Perspective control, moving the slider to the right. The Horizontal Perspective slider is good for those occasions when you've tried to photograph something square-on, but haven't quite managed to get parallel with your subject.

4

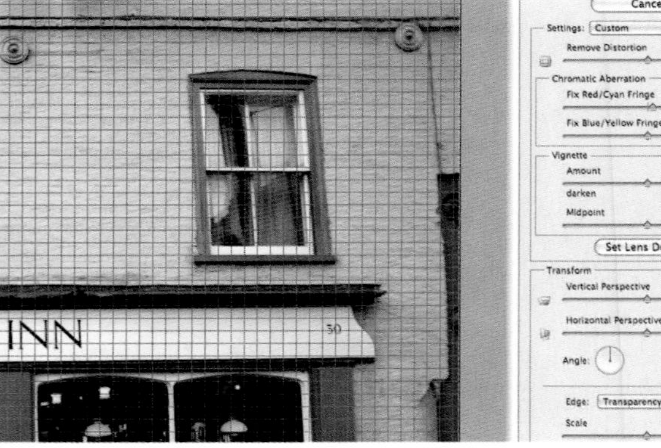

The coloured fringing isn't too bad in this example and thankfully, this is one particular nasty that camera manufacturers have worked hard to reduce, and in some cases eliminate altogether. A little tweak of the Fix Red/Cyan Fringe slider has done the job. Chromatic aberrations such as this are most prevalent along high-contrast edges, such as silhouetted trees or the tops of buildings when shot against a bright sky.

Technique watch

TYPES OF DISTORTION
Lens distortion generally comes in two flavours: barrel and pin-cushion, the former being when parallel lines at the edges of the frame bow outward, the latter being when they bow inward. Barrel distortion is most commonly exhibited by wide-angle lenses, while pin-cushion is more symptomatic of telephoto lenses.

BARREL

PIN-CUSHION

BELOW: FINAL IMAGE
The corrections we've made using the Lens Distortion filter have given this shot a more structured look. We've also used the Clone Stamp and Healing Brush to remove some of the modern looking signs in the windows.

PRO TIPS

SPEEDING THINGS UP
Lens faults are constant at specific zoom settings, so once you've worked out your various correction values, save them as a preset by clicking the triangle next to the Settings drop-down menu

5

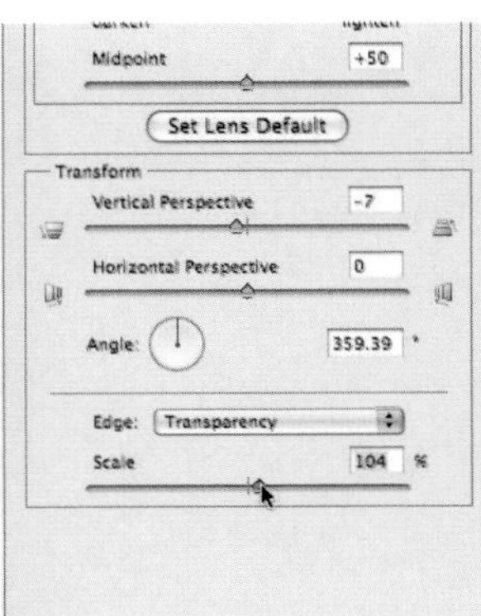

All this mucking about has led to a few gaps at the edge of the canvas. You can deal with this later by cropping the image in the main application, or you can sort it out here with the Scale slider. This control does more or less the same thing as the Crop tool, by zooming in on the image. We've done this up to a point, and then selected Edge Extension from the Edge drop-down menu, to fill-in the last bit of the gap by repeating pixels.

6

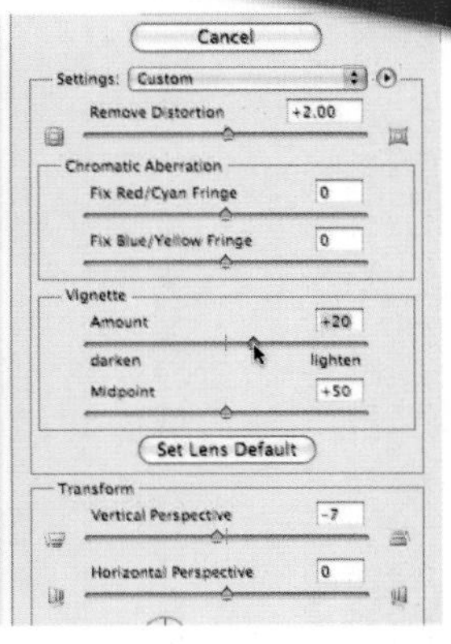

Lastly, we correct the corner darkening with the Vignette slider, dragging it to the right to lighten the edges of the frames. We can choose how far this correction extends into the frame by playing with the Midpoint slider. It's often hard to judge when you've got the vignette correction right, but as it's always the same value (at a specific zoom setting) you can work out the correct setting by photographing a blank white wall.

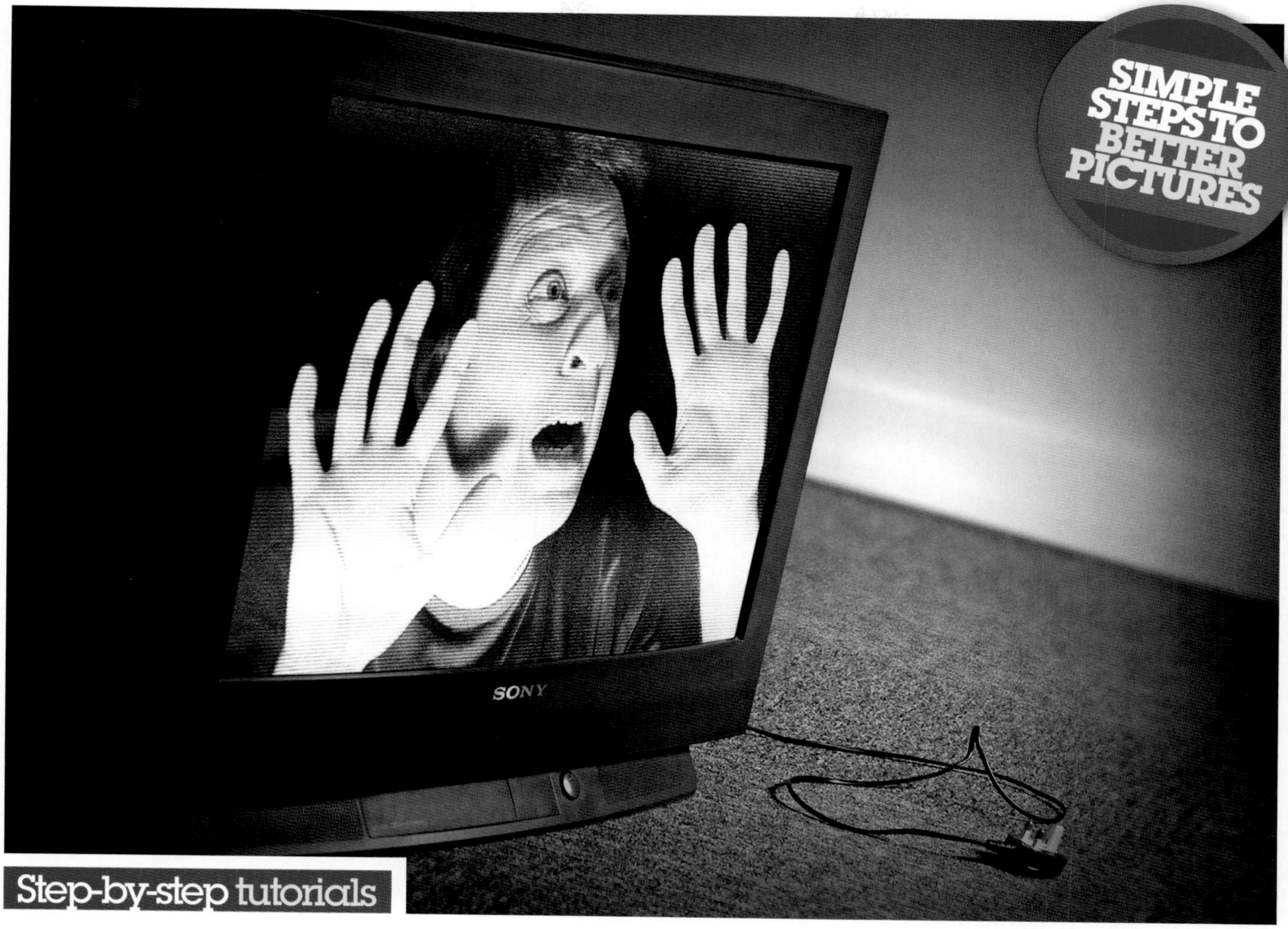

SIMPLE
STEPS TO
BETTER
PICTURES
SONY

Step-by-step tutorials

FUN TECHNIQUES

We take you through a variety of skills that help you to create weird and wacky images

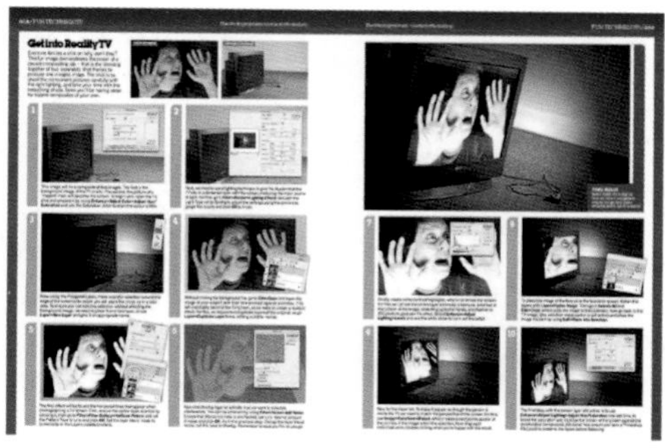

Get into Reality TV

SIMPLY
PUNK ROCK
FEMALE HUMAN
PERFECTLY PRESERVED

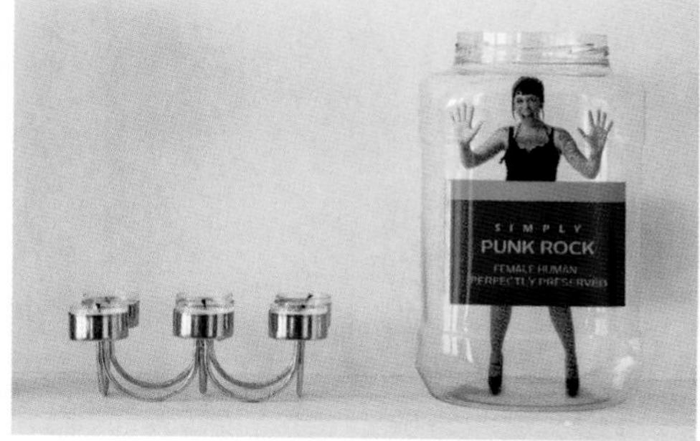

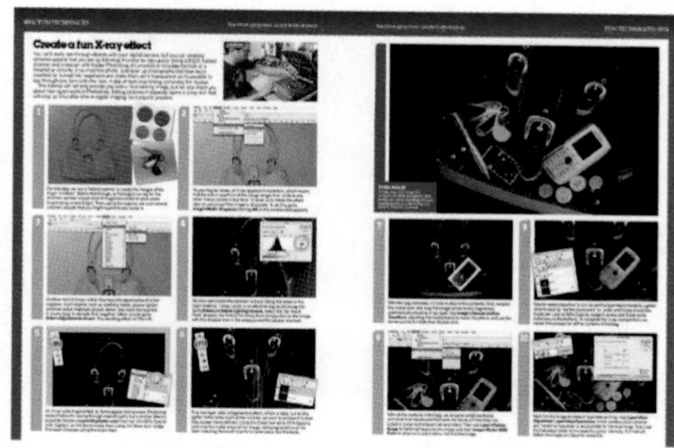

Create a fun X-ray effect

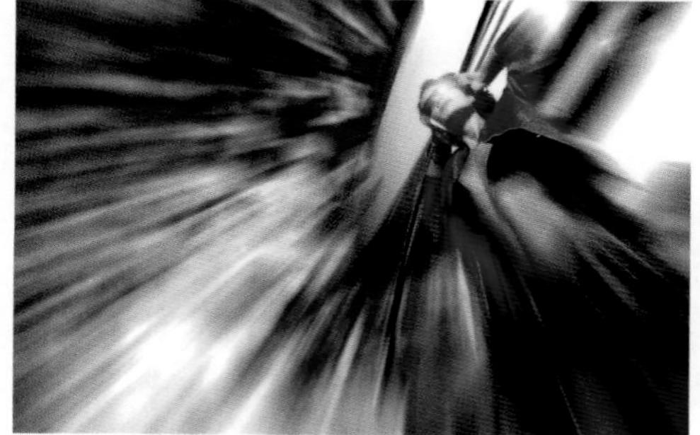

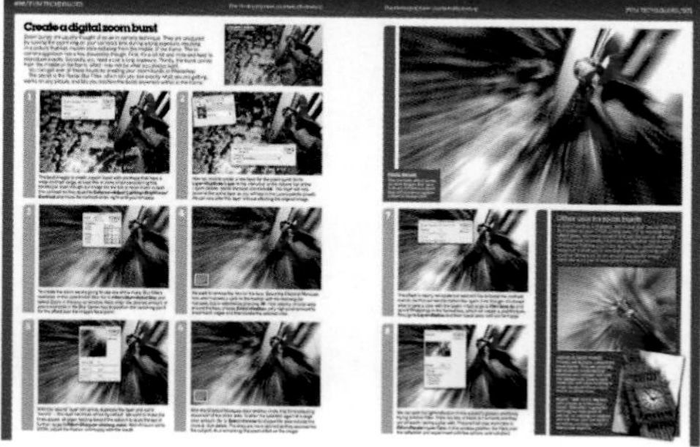

Create a digital zoom burst

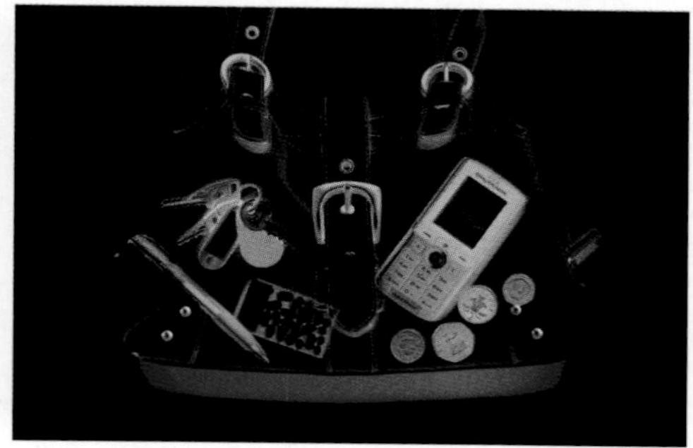

Create a Photoshop prison!

Kitchen cupboards are full of jars and bottles containing all sorts of spices, sauces and herbs, but imagine what it would be like if someone bottled humans! Using some very simple Photoshop techniques, we can create an image that looks like someone has done just that. The technique is simple. Take two shots, the first of your shelf with a range of props, including one empty jar or bottle, then a second of your human subject. If possible, try and shoot them against a plain white background, as this will make the later steps easier. We also used a sheet of Perspex in front of the model for her to press her hands against, making the effect look more authentic. You can always just get your model to mime this, or shoot them from behind a patio window.

Light continuity is one thing that is often neglected in composites. It's important that the lighting of your still-life image matches that of the model. So, if the light comes in from the left-hand side in the jar shot, make sure it does when you shoot the model too. Shooting both images in Raw will allow you to match the colours and exposures too. Get this right, and you'll have a fun image that will amaze your friends.

1

First you need your jar. Find a clean, empty one, ideally with a label on the front of it to add interest. We used this large popcorn jar, as we liked its shape and label. Once cleaned out, place it on a shelf along with a few other items. We'd recommend you tripod mount the camera, as you should set a low ISO rating and mid-aperture for high image quality, but this gives a slow shutter speed.

Shoot your jar first so you can then work out what type of person and pose works best with it. Here, we chose a 'punky' model to add extra interest to the picture. She was placed her against a white background and we used a studio light to mimic the lighting position of the first shot. We then introduced a sheet of Perspex in front of the model, asking her to press her hands against it, as though it were the jar's side.

Essential tool

BLENDING MODES

Blending modes are nothing new to digital imaging, and have featured on the Layers palette since the early days (1994's Photoshop 3, to be exact). You may not have noticed them before, as the only clue to their existence is the word Normal, sat at the top of the palette. They essentially allow pixels on different layers to interact, and are often used to add textures to images. In this technique, we use the Multiply mode, which blends the pixels, much like placing two slides together on a lightbox. The beauty of this mode is that any white in the top layer disappears, so it is really effective for adding people to images, without the hassle of cutting them out. All that you need to do is ensure that they are shot on a white background.

Layers

✓ Normal
Dissolve

Darken
Multiply
Color Burn
Linear Burn
Darker Color

Lighten
Screen
Color Dodge
Linear Dodge (Add)
Lighter Color

Overlay
Soft Light
Hard Light
Vivid Light
Linear Light
Pin Light
Hard Mix

Difference
Exclusion

Hue
Saturation
Color
Luminosity

2

After downloading the shots and choosing our favourite, we opened them in Elements' Raw converter and matched the White Balance of both before boosting the exposure on the image of the model, ensuring it had a really white background. We then opened both images in the main editing screen. Using the Move Tool from the tool palette we dragged the model shot onto the background image of the jar, thereby creating a second layer.

3

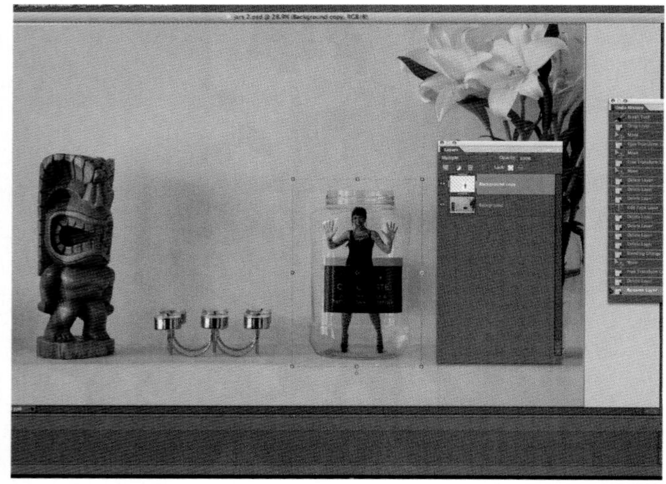

With the Free Transform Tool, we resized the model to fit the jar. Then, in the Layers palette, with the 'model' layer selected, we changed the blending mode to Multiply. This blended the model into the jar, allowing just enough reflection to show through to make it look believable (apart from the label). To tidy things up, we used the Eraser Tool, with a soft-edged brush, around the edge of her to remove any dark patches where light had dropped off.

FINAL IMAGE

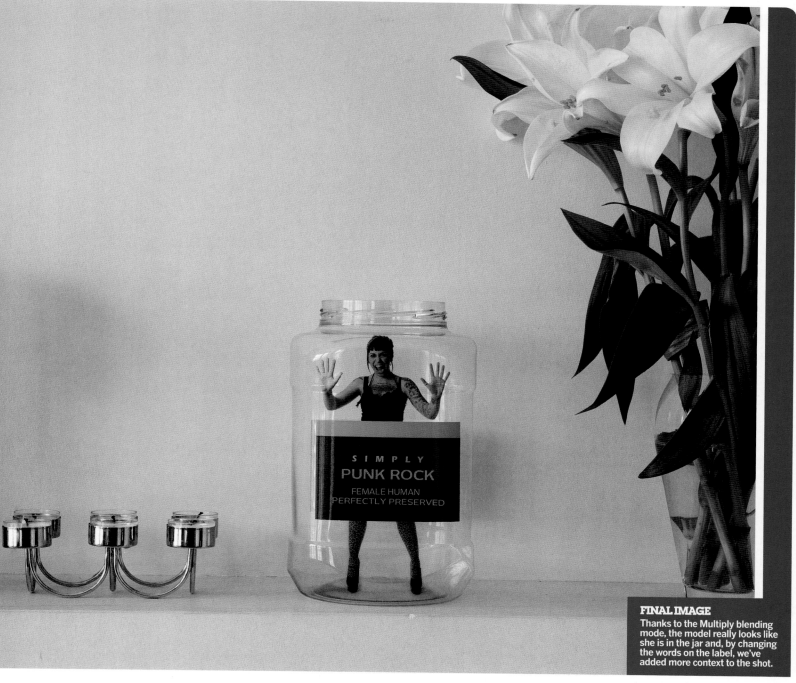

Thanks to the Multiply blending mode, the model really looks like she is in the jar and, by changing the words on the label, we've added more context to the shot.

4

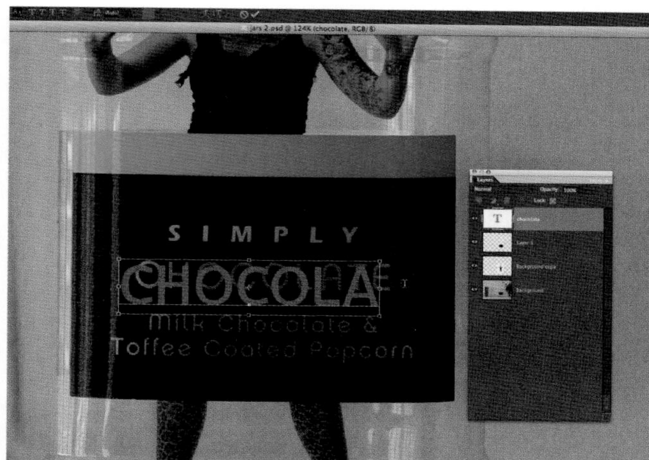

To place the label back in front of the model, select it with the Polygonal Lasso. Then hit ***Ctrl+J*** to copy it to a new layer and move it on top of the layer containing the model. You can then use Photoshop's Text Tool to reproduce the words on the label, changing the font until it is similar to the original lettering. You can change its colour by clicking the colour box and using the Eyedropper Tool to pick from the existing text.

5

Once we'd copied each line of the text, we selected the new label layer and removed the original text with the Clone tool. This just left the new text on the label. We could now alter the words by clicking on them with the Text tool selected, or double-clicking the relevant layer. Finally, the layers were flattened to a single layer and we added some dodging and burning over the letters to help them blend in and look more natural.

Get into Reality TV

Everyone fancies a stint on telly, don't they? This fun image demonstrates the power of a decent compositing job – that is the blending together of two separately shot frames to produce one merged image. The trick is to shoot the component pictures carefully with the right lighting, and take your time with the retouching phase. Soon you'll be having ideas for bizarre composites of your own.

1

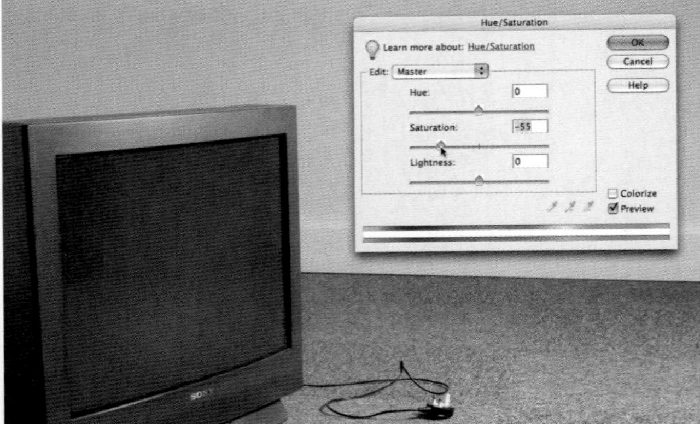

This image will be a composite of two images. The first is the background image of the TV in situ. The second, the picture of a 'trapped' man, will become the screen. To begin with, open the TV shot and prepare it by using ***Enhance>Adjust Color>Adjust Hue/ Saturation*** and use the Saturation slider to drain the colour a little.

2

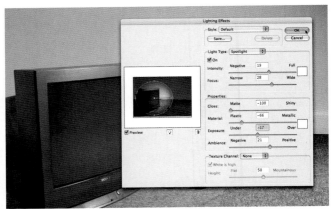

Next, we need to use a lighting technique to give the illusion that the TV sits in a darkened room with the screen producing the main source of light. For this, go to ***Filter>Render>Lighting Effects*** and with the Light Type set to Spotlight, adjust the settings using the preview to gauge the results and click ***OK*** to finish.

3

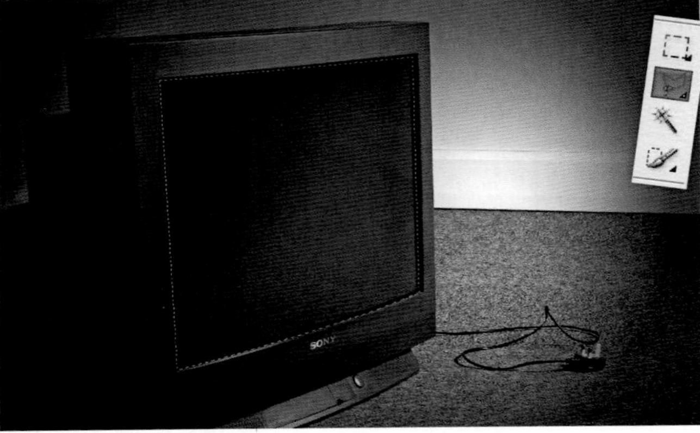

Now, using the Polygonal Lasso, make a careful selection around the edge of the screen onto which you will place the photo on in a later step. To ensure you can edit this selection without affecting the background image, we need to place it on a new layer, so use ***Layer>New Layer*** and give it an appropriate name.

4

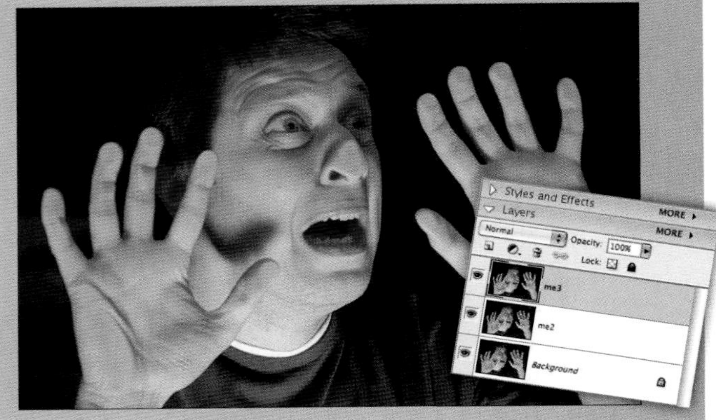

Without closing the background file, go to ***Edit>Open*** and open the image of your subject with their face pressed against a window. This will eventually become the TV screen, so we need to create a realistic effect. For this, we require two duplicate layers of the original, so go ***Layer>Duplicate Layer*** twice, adding suitable names.

5

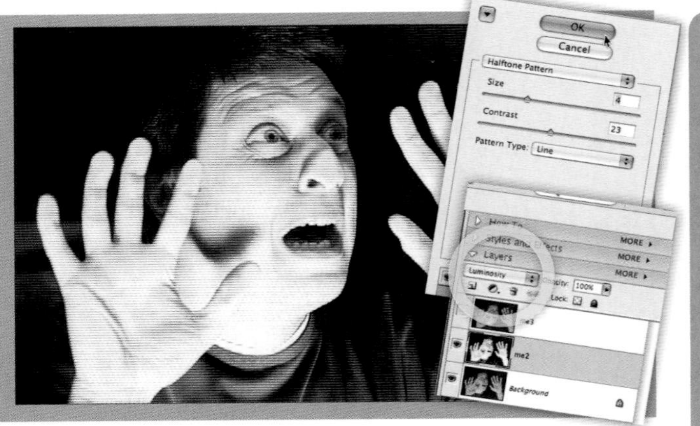

The first effect will be to add the horizontal lines that appear when photographing a TV screen. First, ensure the centre layer is active by clicking it, then go to ***Filter>Filter Gallery>Halftone Pattern*** and set the Pattern Type to Line and click ***OK***. Set the layer blend mode to Luminosity in the Layers palette (circled).

6

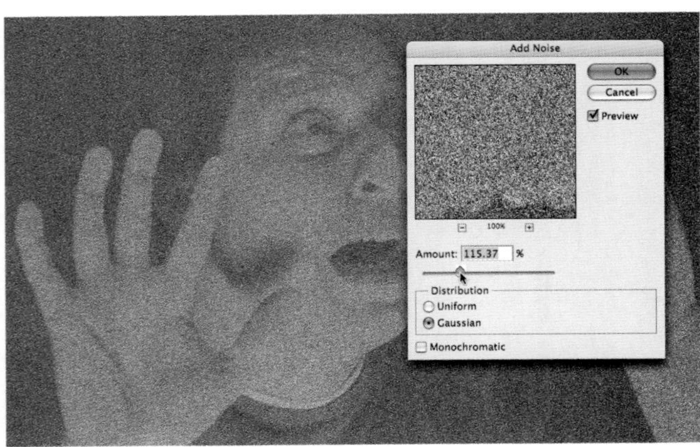

Now click the top layer to activate it as we want to simulate interference. This can be achieved by using ***Filter>Noise>Add Noise***. Ensure that Monochromatic is unchecked, set your desired amount of noise and click ***OK***. As in the previous step, change the layer blend mode, but this time to Overlay. Remember to save you file as you go.

FINAL IMAGE
MAKE SURE TO TUNE IN!
Now we have a completely original image that looks amazing and is fun to achieve!

7

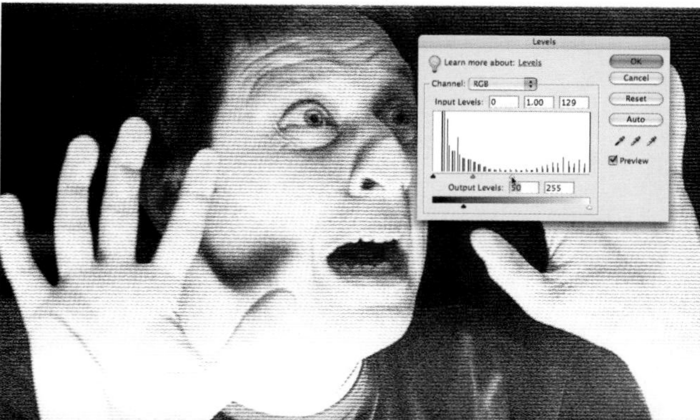

Finally, create some contrast highlights, which run across the screen. For this we can use the centre layer and make a Marquee selection at the bottom of the image, stretching up to the hands, and Feather to 100 pixels to graduate the effect. Select ***Enhance>Adjust Lighting>Levels*** and use the white slider to burn out the detail.

8

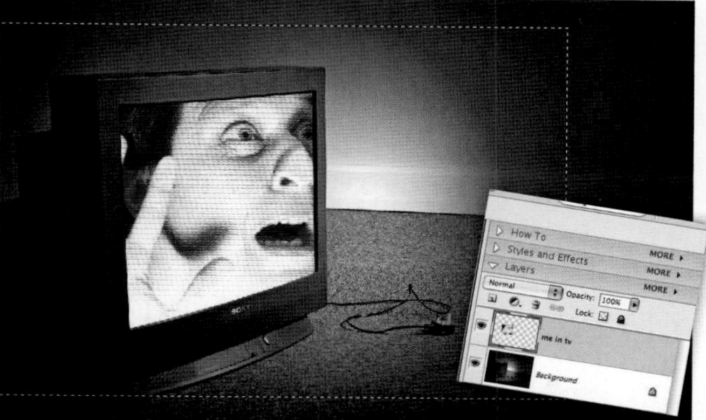

To place the image of the face on to the television screen, flatten the layers with **Layer>Flatten Image.** Then go to **Select>All** and **Edit>Copy**, which adds the image to the clipboard. Now go back to the TV image, (the selection made earlier is still active) and place the image inside it by using **Edit>Paste into Selection**.

9

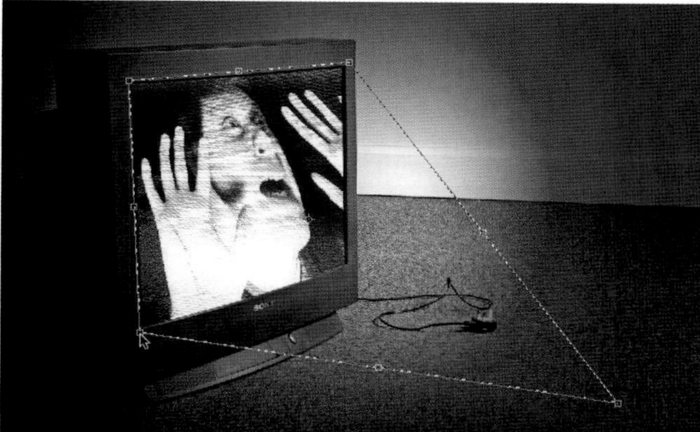

Now for the clever bit. To make it appear as though the person is inside the TV, we need to match the perspective of the screen. For this, use ***Image>Transform>Distort***, which makes boxed points appear at the corners of the image within the selection. Now drag each individual point, double-clicking when you're happy with the result.

10

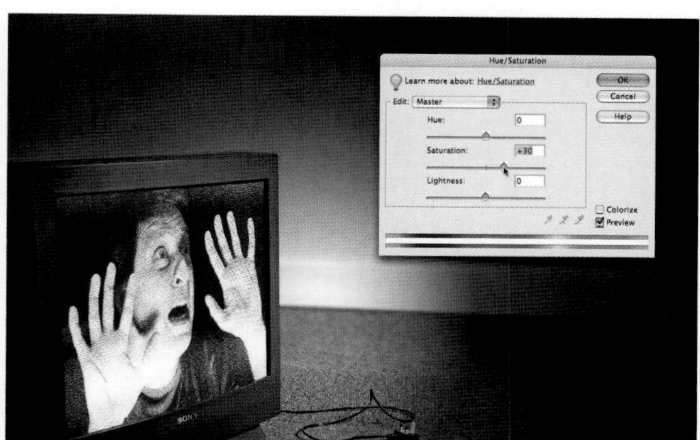

The final step, with the screen layer still active, is to use **Enhance>Adjust Lighting>Adjust Hue/Saturation** one last time, to boost the saturation and increase the impact of the screen against the desaturated background. Job done! Now ensure you save a Photoshop file (.psd) to preserve the layers before flattening.

Create a digital zoom burst

Zoom bursts are usually thought of as an in-camera technique. They are produced by turning the zoom ring on your camera's lens during a long exposure, resulting in a picture that has motion trails radiating from the middle of the frame. The in-camera approach has a few drawbacks though. First, it's a bit hit and miss and hard to reproduce exactly. Secondly, you need a use a long exposure. Thirdly, the burst comes from the middle of the frame, which may not be what you always want.

You can get over all these issues by creating your zoom bursts in Photoshop.

The secret is the Radial Blur Filter, which lets you see exactly what you are getting, works on any picture and lets you position the burst anywhere within in the frame.

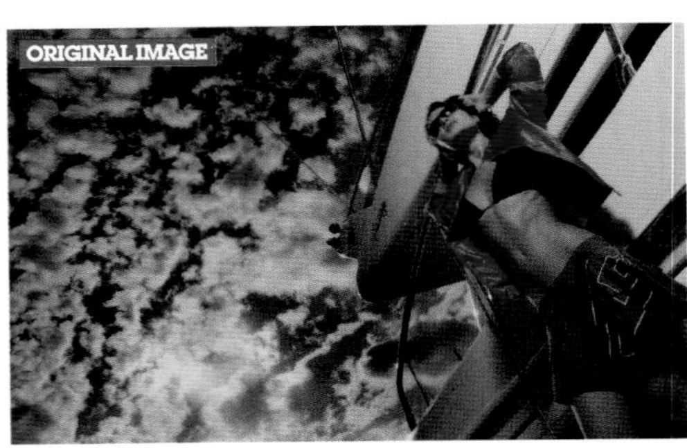

1

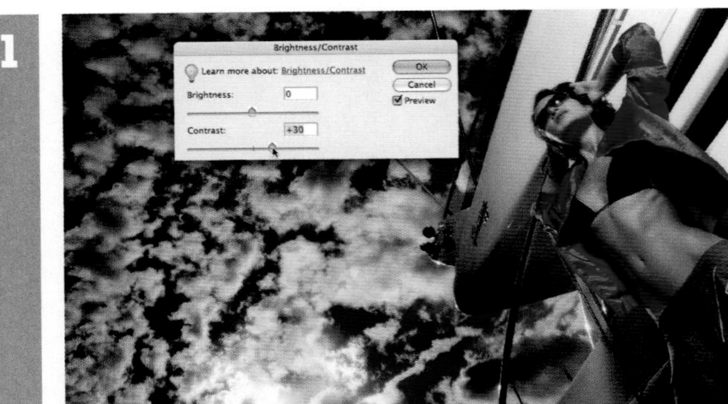

The best images to create a zoom burst with are those that have a wide contrast range, so bear this in mind when considering this technique. Even though our image fits the bill, it never hurts to beef the contrast further, so got to ***Enhance>Adjust Lighting>Brightness/ Contrast*** and move the contrast slider right until you're happy.

2

Now we need to create a new layer for the zoom burst. Go to ***Layer>Duplicate Layer*** in the menu bar or the options bar of the Layers palette. Name the layer and click ***OK***. This layer will now become the active layer as you will see in the Layers palette (inset). We can now alter this layer without affecting the original image.

3

To create the zoom we are going to use one of the many Blur filters available, in this case Radial Blur. Go to ***Filter>Blur>Radial Blur*** and select Zoom in the pop-up window. Next, enter the desired amount of zoom and click in the Blur Center box to position the vanishing point for the effect over the image's focal point.

4

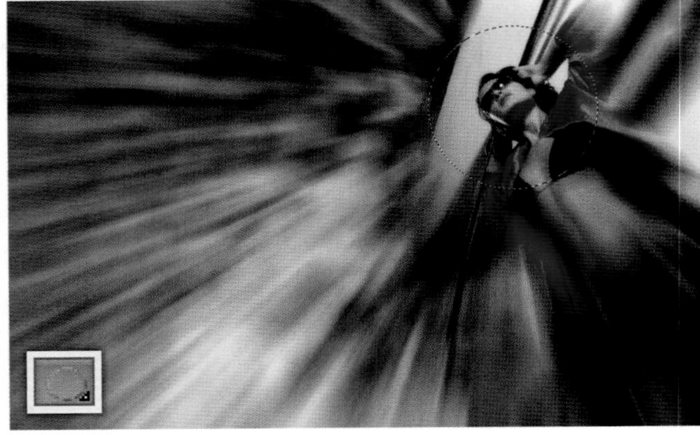

We want to remove the blur on the face. Select the Elliptical Marquee tool, which shares a spot on the toolbar with the Rectangular marquee, but is selected by pressing '***M***'. Now select a circular area around the face, choose ***Select>Feather,*** set a high pixel amount to avoid harsh edges and then delete the selected area.

5

With the 'zoom1' layer still active, duplicate the layer and call it 'zoom2' – this layer becomes active by default. We want to make the lines appear stronger, leading toward the subject to draw the eye in further, so go to ***Filter>Sharpen>Unsharp mask***. With Amount set to 100%, adjust the Radius until happy with the result.

6

With the Elliptical Marquee draw another circle, this time selecting about half of the zoom area. Feather the selection again at a large pixel amount. Go to ***Select>Inverse*** to choose the area outside the circle & click delete. The lines are more defined as they approaches the subject, thus enhancing the zoom effect on the image.

FINAL IMAGE
This dramatic effect works on most images that have a clearly definable subject that will stand out against a blurred background.

7

The effect is nearly complete but we'd still like to boost the contrast overall, for this we need to flatten the layers. First though, it's always wise to save a copy with the layers intact so go to ***File>Save As*** and select Photoshop in the format box, which will create a .psd file type. Now go to ***Layer>Flatten*** and then tweak away until you're happy.

8

We can spot the light reflection in the subject's glasses and fancy trying another filter. There are lots of filters in Elements and they are all worth having a play with. The one that may work here is ***Filter>Render>Lens Flare***. In the window, position the Flare over the reflection and experiment with the options until satisfied.

Other uses for zoom bursts

A zoom burst is a dramatic technique that can be difficult to master on your DSLR. Using your PC to recreate the effect gives you more control and can be just as effective. Zooms work on pretty much any image that has a point of interest that the zoom can lead to. You could use it to resurrect a shot you're not that pleased with or to add another dimension to an already successful image. Here are a couple of examples to inspire you...

ABOVE: FLOWER POWER
Flowers are fantastic subjects for zoom bursts. They are generally full of colour, create natural shadows and contrast well with the background. Zooms work especially well when isolating a single focal point from a busy bunch as shown here.

RIGHT: TIME FLIES! Big Ben with a twist, or in this case a zoom! This effect is great for defining the main point of interest on buildings or statues and will draw your eye right in, as well as creating a sense of drama and urgency.

Create a fun X-ray effect

You can't really see through objects with your digital camera, but you can certainly convince people that you can by following this step-by-step guide. Using a DSLR, flatbed scanner and a session with Adobe Photoshop, it's possible to simulate the look of a hospital or security X-ray machine photo. Just layer up photographs that have been inverted (ie. turned into negatives) and make them semi-transparent so it's possible to see through one item onto the next. A dab of dark-blue tinting completes the illusion.

This tutorial will not only provide you with a cool-looking image, but will also teach you about how layers work in Photoshop. Editing pictures in separate layers is a key skill that will crop up time after time in digital imaging, so it pays to practice.

SCANNING

1

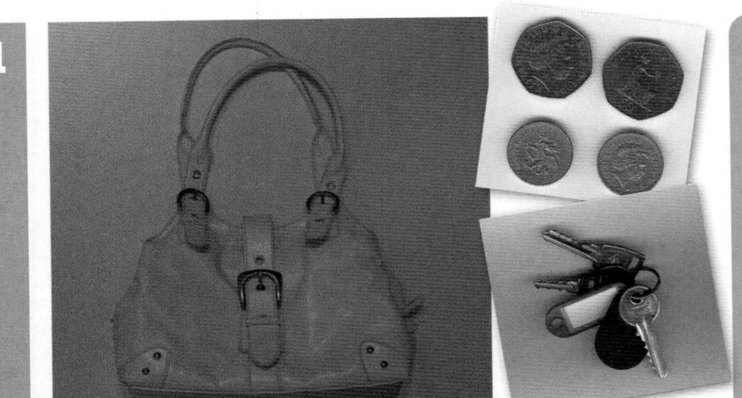

For this step, we use a flatbed scanner to create the images of the bag's 'contents'. Before that though, as the bag is too big for the scanner, we take a quick shot of it against a sheet of plain white board using ambient light. Then, using the scanner, we scan several ordinary objects that you might expect to see inside it.

2

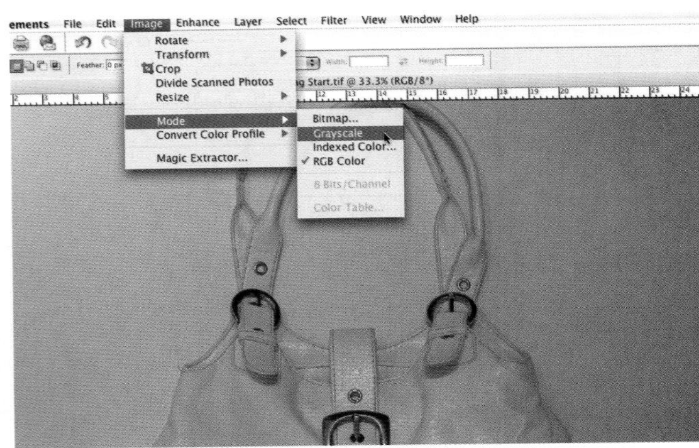

As you may be aware, an X-ray appears in monotone, which means that the colour spectrum of the image ranges from white to one other colour, usually a blue tone. To allow us to create this effect later on, we convert the image to Grayscale. To do this, go to ***Image>Mode>Grayscale*** clicking ***OK*** on the window that appears.

3

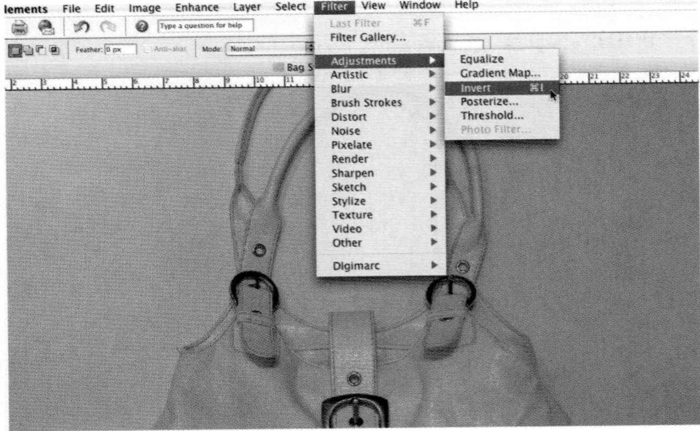

Another trait of X-rays is that they have the appearance of a film negative. Solid objects, such as anything metal, appear lighter whereas softer materials appear darker and more transparent. It is very easy to recreate this 'negative' effect; simply go to ***Filter>Adjustments>Invert***. The resulting effect isn't far off.

4

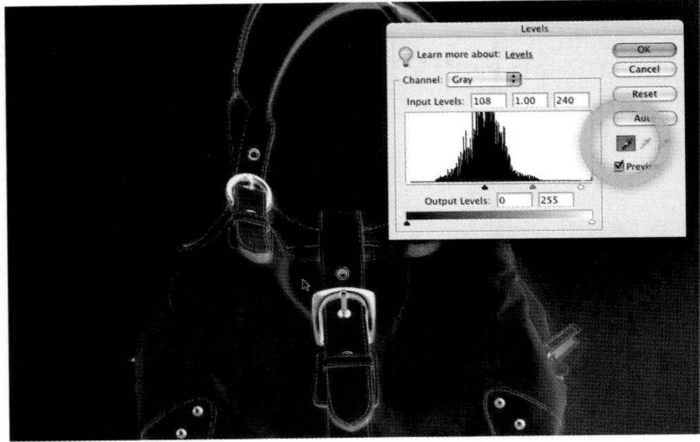

We now want boost the contrast without losing the detail of the bag's material. Using Levels is an effective way of achieving this. Go to ***Enhance>Adjust Lighting>Levels***, select the 'Set Black Point' dropper, the first of the three, then simply click on the image with the dropper icon in the area you want to appear blackest.

5

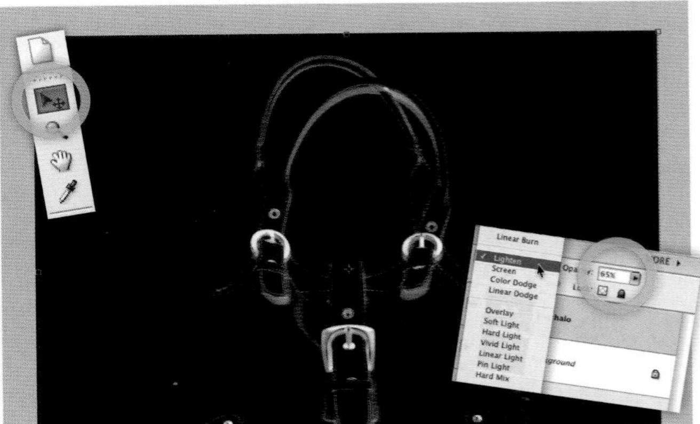

An X-ray looks fragmented, as items appear transparent. Photoshop doesn't allow for seeing through objects (yet!), but a similar effect is possible. Create a ***Layer>Duplicate Layer*** then set it to 65% Opacity with 'Lighten' as the blend mode; then, using the Move tool, nudge this layer sideways using the arrow keys.

6

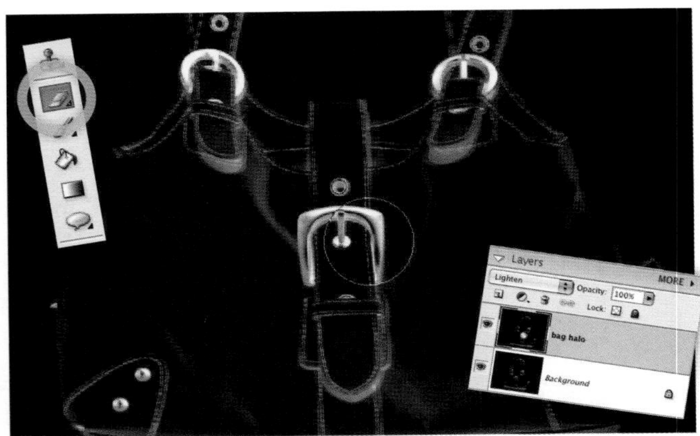

This new layer adds a fragmented effect, which is ideal, but for the lighter metal areas such as the buckles, we want to remove it so that they appear more defined. Using the Erase tool set to 50% Opacity, click over the metal areas of the image, removing sections of the layer, reducing the brush size for smaller areas like the studs.

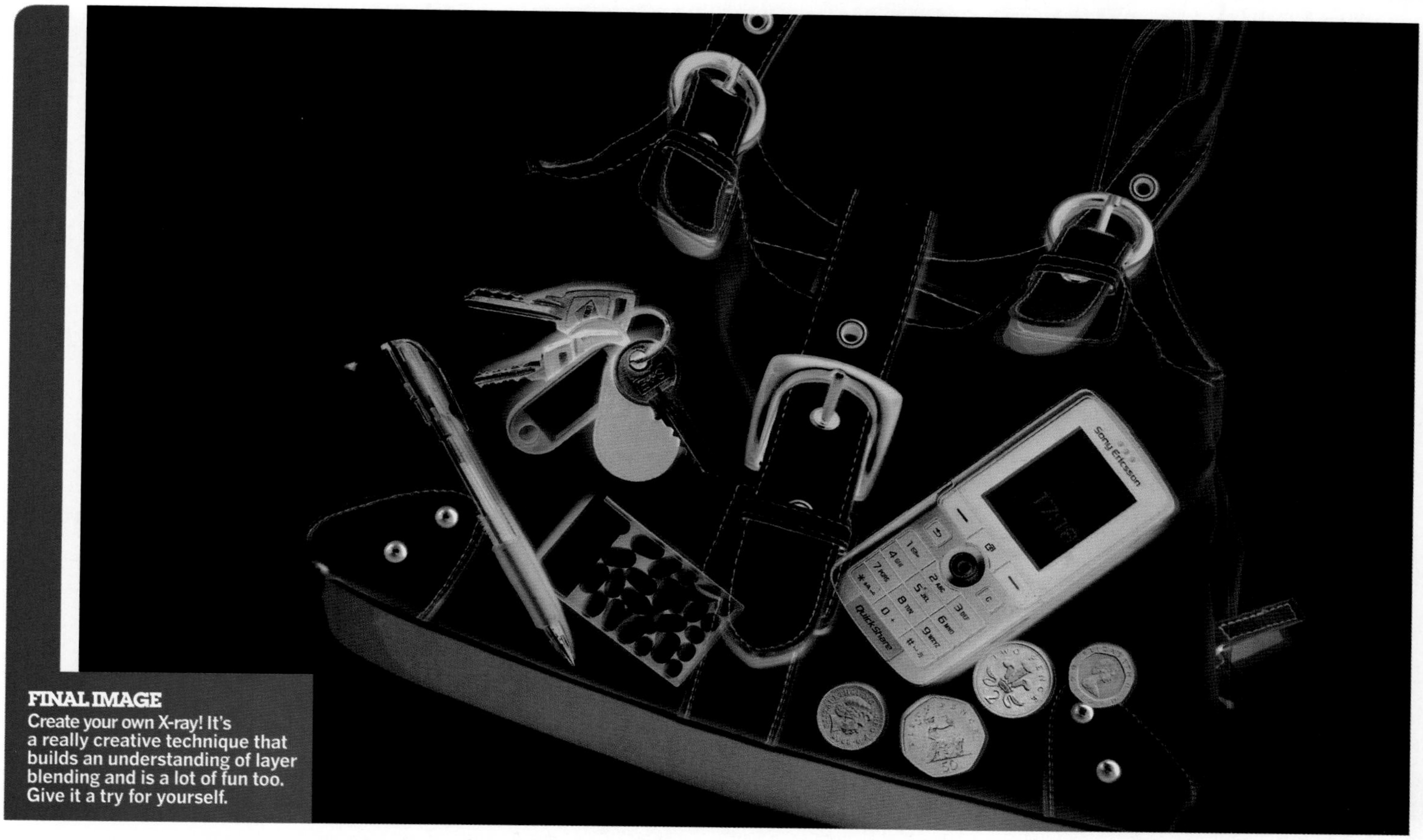

FINAL IMAGE
Create your own X-ray! It's a really creative technique that builds an understanding of layer blending and is a lot of fun too. Give it a try for yourself.

7

With the bag complete, it's time to drop in the contents. First, we open the phone scan and drag the image across to the bag canvas, automatically creating a new layer. Use ***Image>Transform>Free Transform***, adjusting the visible frame to resize the phone, and use the corner points to rotate then double-click.

8

Now to repeat steps four to six, we set the layer blend mode to Lighten at 60% Opacity, 'set the black point' in Levels and finally, create the Duplicate Layer at 30% Opacity, nudge it across and Erase some detail around the buttons. To complete the X-ray composition, we repeat this process for all the contents of the bag.

9

With all the contents in the bag, we do some small positional and rotational tweaks and then save the file as a Photoshop file (.psd) to preserve the layers we've created. Then use ***Layer>Flatten Image*** to flatten all layers to one image and then ***Image>Mode>RGB Color*** to allow us to put a colour tint into the image.

10

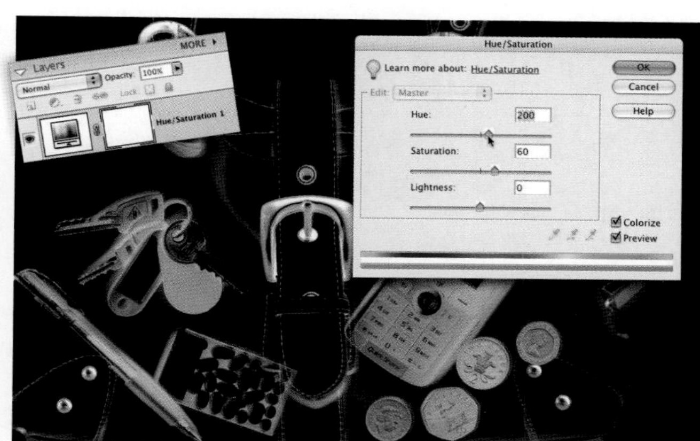

Next, tint the image to make it resemble an X-ray. Use ***Layer>New Adjustment Layer>Hue/Saturation***. In the window, click Colorize and move the Hue slider to around 200 for the blue range. Then use the Saturation slider to increase the colour intensity. To finish off, flatten the image and Save As a new file.

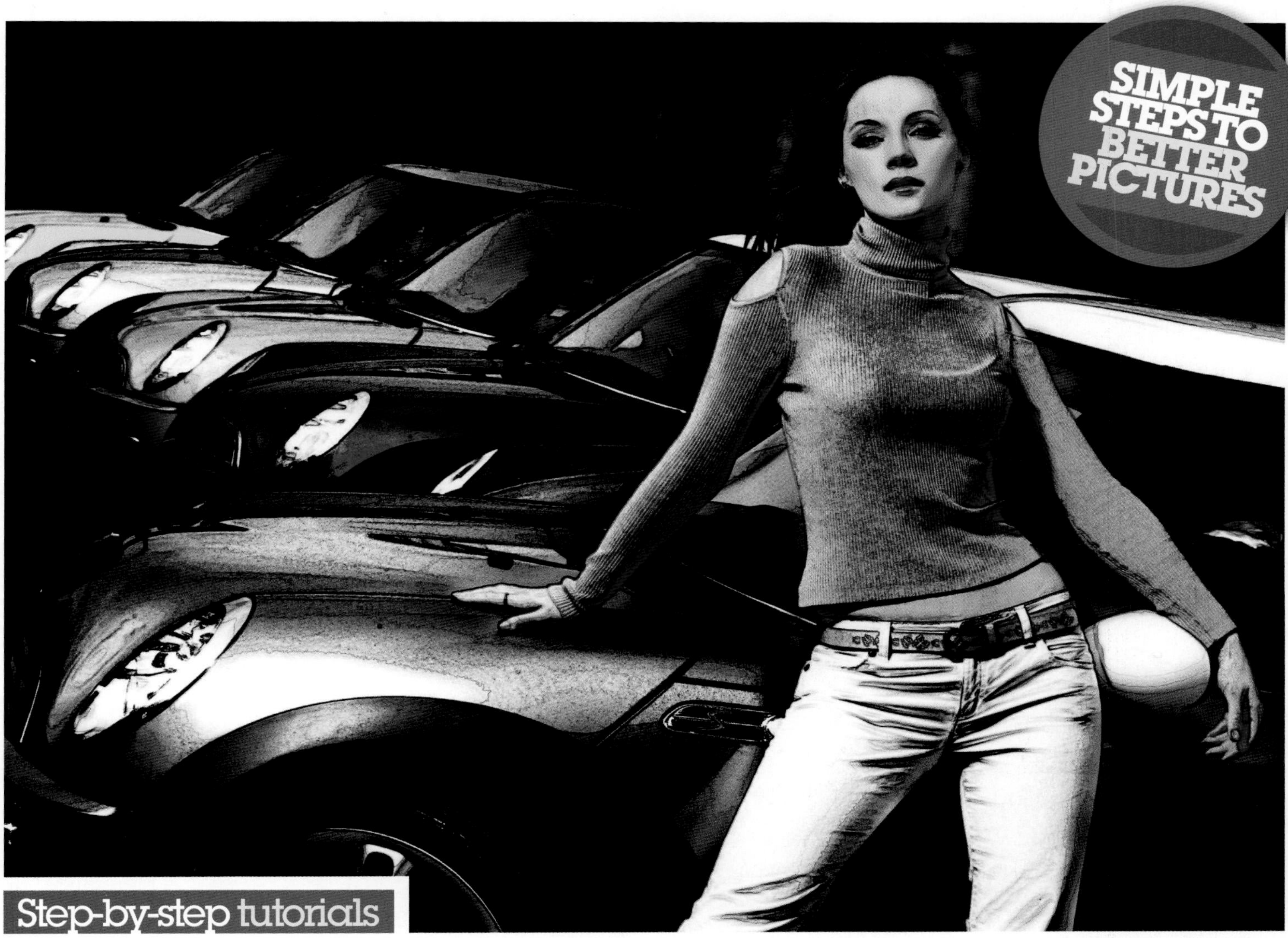

SIMPLE STEPS TO BETTER PICTURES

Step-by-step tutorials

ART TECHNIQUES

Our top choices for stylish effects that help add an extra dimension to photographs

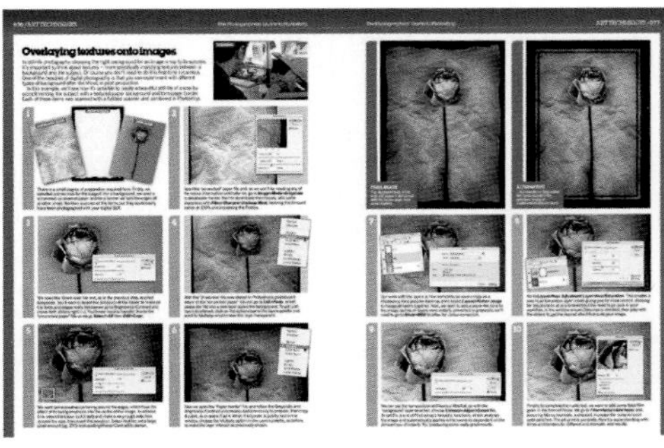
Overlaying textures onto images

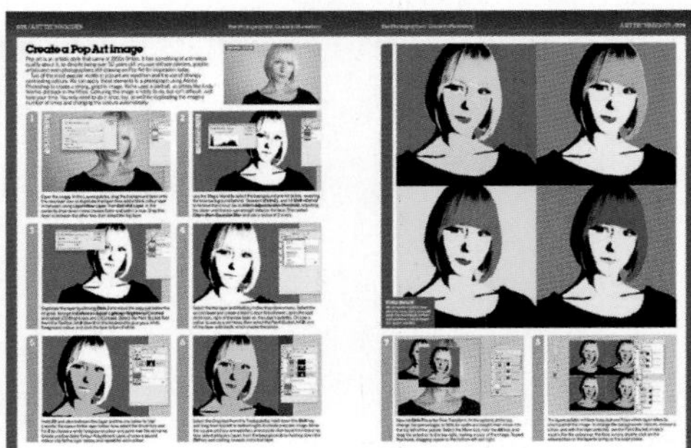
Create a Pop Art image

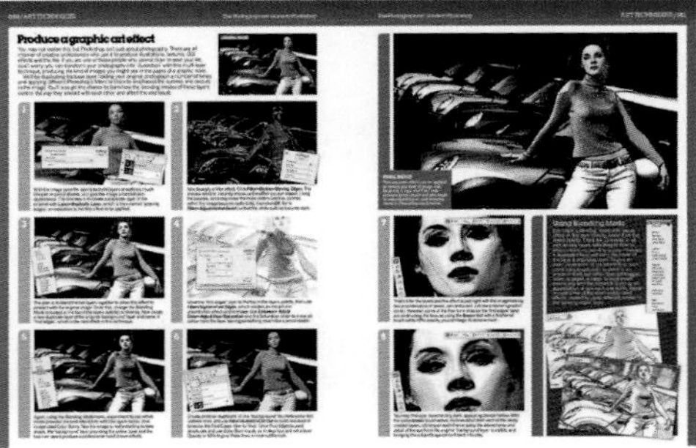
Produce a graphic art effect

Overlaying textures onto images

In still-life photography, choosing the right background for an image is key to its success. It's important to think about textures – more specifically matching textures between a background and the subject. Of course you don't need to do this first time in-camera. One of the beauties of digital photography is that you can experiment with different types of background after the shoot, in post production.

In this example, we'll see how it's possible to create a beautiful still-life of a rose by complimenting the subject with a textured paper background and torn-paper border. Each of these items was scanned with a flatbed scanner and combined in Photoshop.

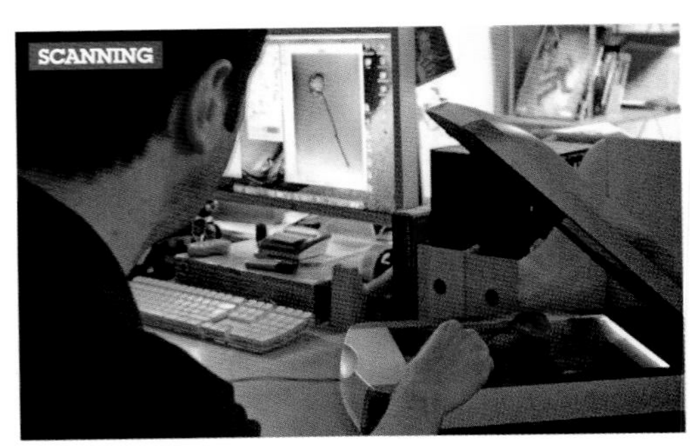

1

There is a small degree of preparation required here. Firstly, we selected a dried rose for the subject. For a background, we used a scrunched up sheet of paper and for a border, we tore the edges off another sheet. We then scanned all the items but they could easily have been photographed with your digital SLR.

2

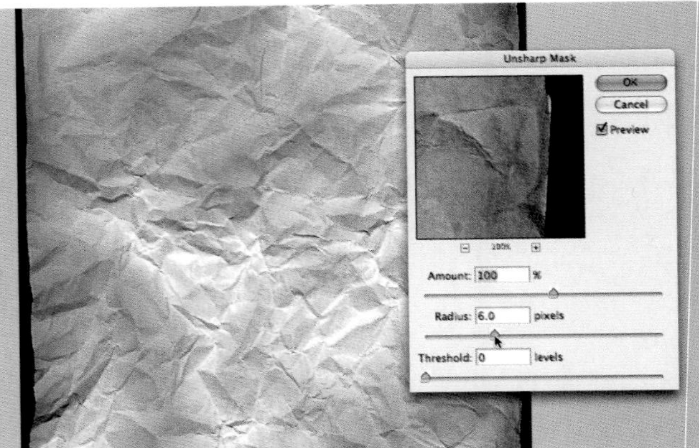

Open the 'scrunched' paper file and, as we won't be needing any of the colour information until later on, go to ***Image>Mode>Greyscale*** to desaturate the file, then to accentuate the creases, add some sharpness with ***Filter>Sharpen>Unsharp Mask***, keeping the Amount option at 100% and increasing the Radius.

3

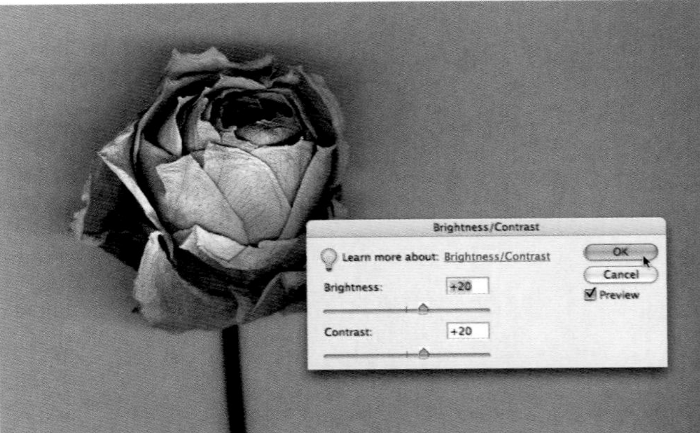

We open the 'Dried rose' file and, as in the previous step, applied Greyscale. You'll want to boost the definition of the flower to make all the folds and edges really bold so we go to Brightness/Contrast and move both sliders right (+). You'll now need to transfer this to the 'scrunched paper' file so we go ***Select>All*** then ***Edit>Copy***.

4

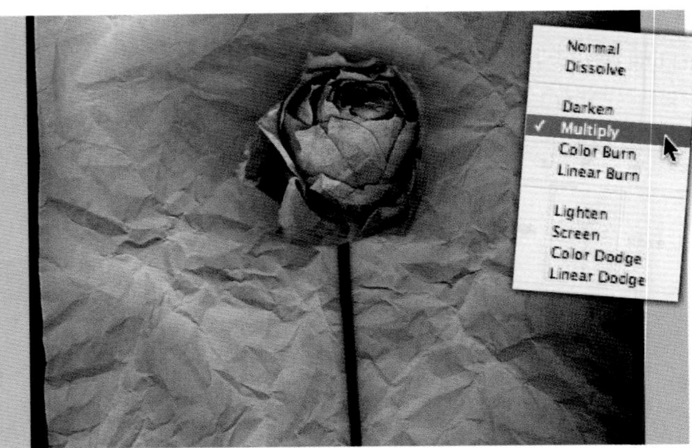

With the 'Dried rose' file now stored in Photoshop's pasteboard, return to the 'scrunched paper' file and go to ***Edit>Paste***, which pastes the file into a new layer above the background. To get both layers to interact, click on the options bar in the layers palette and scroll to Multiply, which make this layer transparent.

5

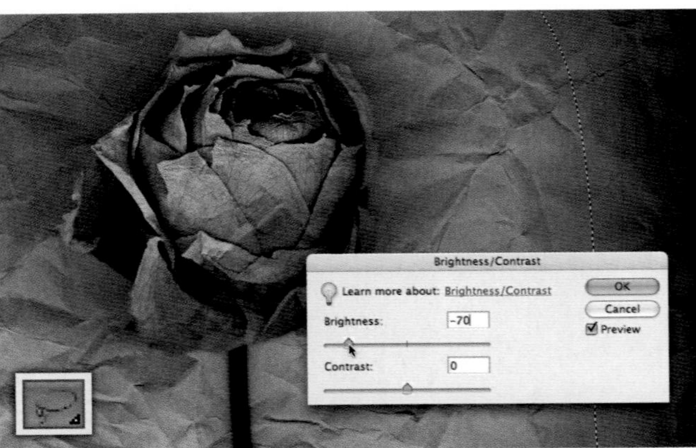

We want some creative darkening around the edges, which have the effect of throwing emphasis into the centre of the image. To achieve this, select the Lasso tool (inset) and make a very rough selection around the rose, than invert the selection. Select Feather, set a large pixel amount (eg. 100) and use Brightness/Contrast to darken.

6

Now we open the 'Paper border' file and follow the Greyscale and Brightness/Contrast processes used previously to prepare, then copy & paste, as in steps 3 ad 4. When the border is positioned in the window, choose the Multiply option in the Layers palette, as before, to make the layer interact as previously shown.

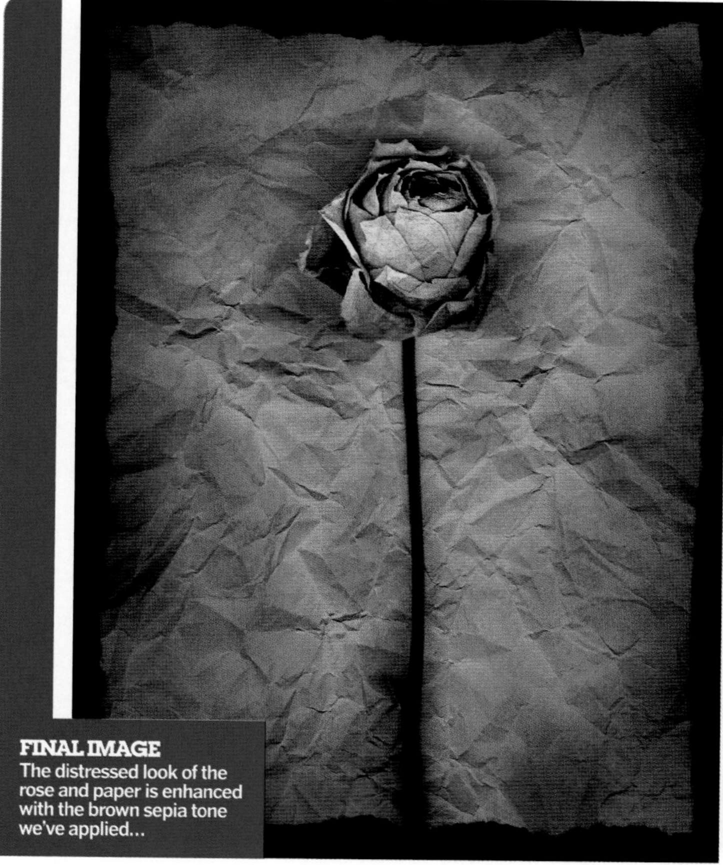

FINAL IMAGE
The distressed look of the rose and paper is enhanced with the brown sepia tone we've applied...

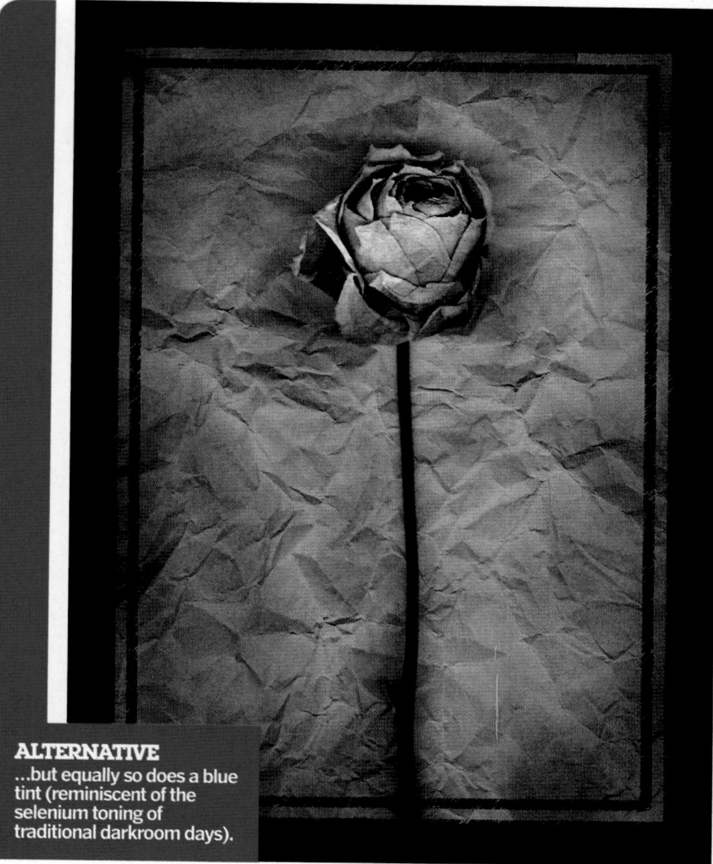

ALTERNATIVE
...but equally so does a blue tint (reminiscent of the selenium toning of traditional darkroom days).

7

Our work with the layers is now complete, so save a copy as a Photoshop file (.psd) for back-up, then select ***Layers>Flatten Image*** to merge all layers together. Next, we want to add a sepia-like tone to the image, but as all layers were initially converted to greyscale, we'll need to go to ***Mode>RGB*** to allow for colour correction.

8

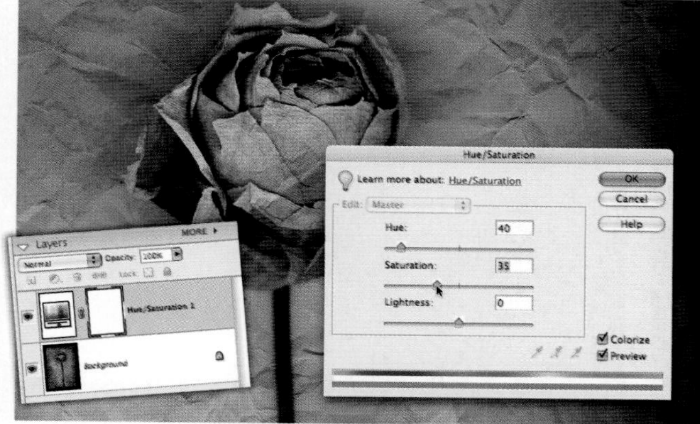

Go to ***Layers>New Adjustment Layer>Hue/Saturation***. This creates a new Hue/Saturation layer (inset) giving you far more control, allowing for adjustments at any time without the need to go back in your workflow. In the window ensure Colourize is checked, then play with the sliders to get the desired effect that suits your image.

9

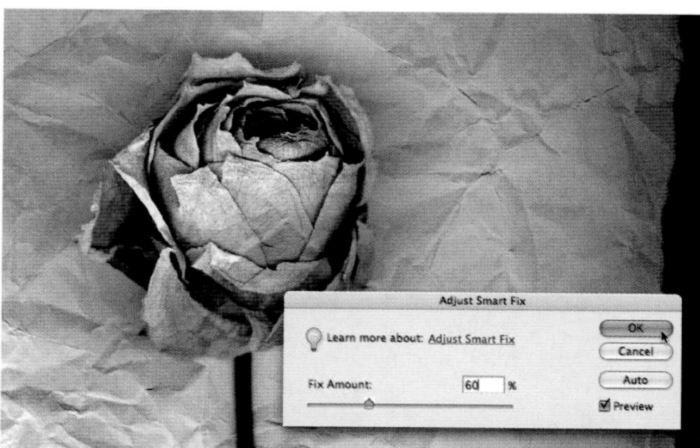

We can see the composition still looks a little flat, so with the 'background' layer selected, choose ***Enhance>Adjust>Smart Fix.*** Smart Fix is one of Photoshop's fantastic functions, which analyses the image and automatically applies enhancements dependent on the Amount you choose to 'fix,' producing some really great results.

10

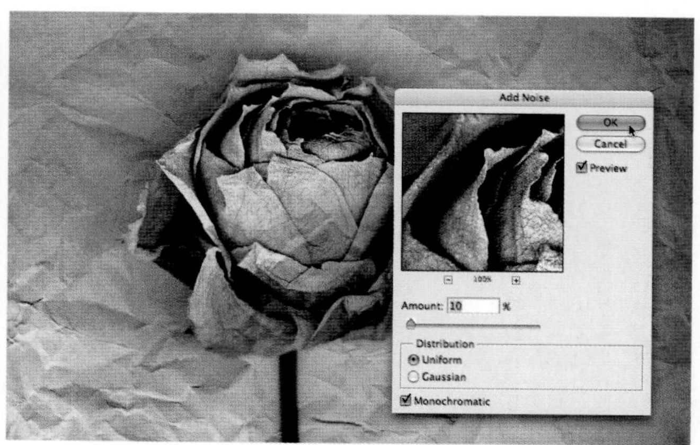

Finally, to complete the rustic feel, we want to add some false film grain in the form of Noise. We go to ***Filter>Noise>Add Noise*** and, ensuring Monochromatic is checked, increase the noise Amount until satisfied. The art print is complete. Now try experimenting with tones and borders for different and dramatic end results.

Create a Pop Art image

Pop art is an artistic style that came of 1950s Britain. It has something of a timeless quality about it, so despite being over 50 years-old, you can still see painters, graphic artists and even photographers still drawing on Pop Art for inspiration today.

Two of the most popular motifs in pop art are repetition and the use of strongly contrasting colours. We can apply these elements to a photograph using Adobe Photoshop to create a strong, graphic image. We've used a portrait, as artists like Andy Warhol did back in the fifties. Colouring the image is fiddly to do, but isn't difficult. Just take your time. You only need to do it once, too, as we'll be duplicating the image a number of times and changing the colours automatically.

1

Open the image. In the Layers palette, drag the background layer onto the new layer icon to duplicate the layer. Now add a blank colour layer in between using ***Layer>New Layer***, then ***Edit>Fill Layer***. In the contents drop-down menu choose Color and select a blue. Drag this layer in between the other two, then select the top layer.

2

Use the Magic Wand to select the background and hit delete, revealing the blue background behind. Deselect (***Ctrl+D***), and hit ***Shift+Ctrl+U*** to remove the colour. Go to ***Filter>Adjustments>Threshold,*** adjusting the slider until there's just enough detail in the face. Then select ***Filter>Blur>Gaussian Blur*** and use a radius of 2 pixels.

3

Duplicate the layer by clicking ***Ctrl+J*** and move the copy just below the original. Now go to ***Enhance>Adjust Lighting>Brightness/Contrast*** and select 100 Brightness and 0 Contrast. Select the Paint Bucket Tool from the Tool bar, hit ***D*** then ***X*** on the keyboard to give you a white foreground colour, and click the face to turn it white.

4

Select the top layer and Multiply in the drop-down menu. Select the second layer and create a Solid Colour Adjustment Layer (the split circle icon, right of the new layer on the Layers palette). Choose a colour to use as a skin tone, then select the Paint Bucket, hit ***D***, and fill the layer with black, which masks the colour.

5

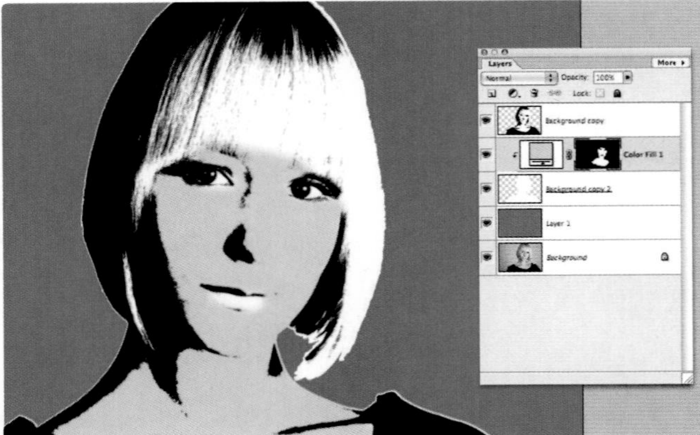

Hold ***Alt*** and click between this layer and the one below to 'clip' (isolate) the colour to the layer below. Now select the Brush tool and hit ***X*** to choose a white foreground colour and paint over the skin area. Create another Solid Colour Adjustment Layer, choose a second colour, clip to the layer below, and repeat for each colour.

6

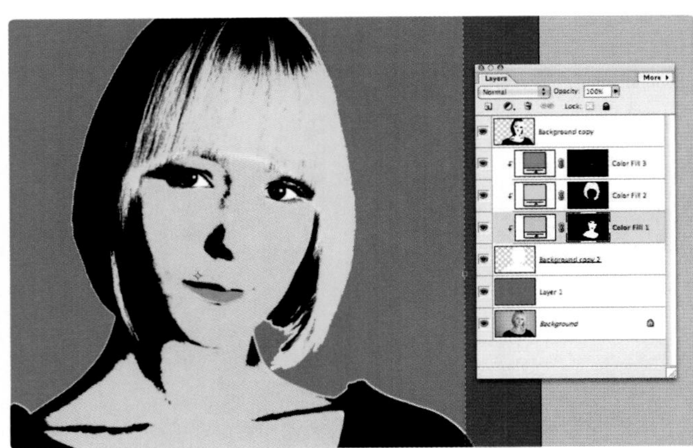

Select the Crop tool from the Tools palette. Hold down the ***Shift*** key and drag from top left to bottom right, to create a square image. Move the square until you are satisfied, and double click to perform the crop. Now select all layers (apart from the background) by holding down the ***Ctrl*** key and clicking on each individual layer.

FINAL IMAGE
We've made a grid of four pictures here, but you could push this technique further and produce a much larger 3x3 grid if you like.

7

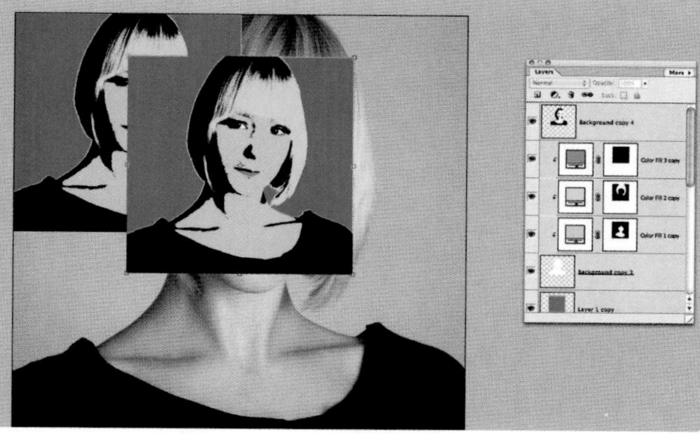

Now hit ***Ctrl+T*** to enter Free Transform. In the options at the top, change the percentages to 50% for width and height; then move it to the top left of the picture. Select the Move tool, hold the ***Alt*** key, and drag the selection to the top right, making a copy of the image. Repeat this twice, dragging copies to the bottom left and right.

8

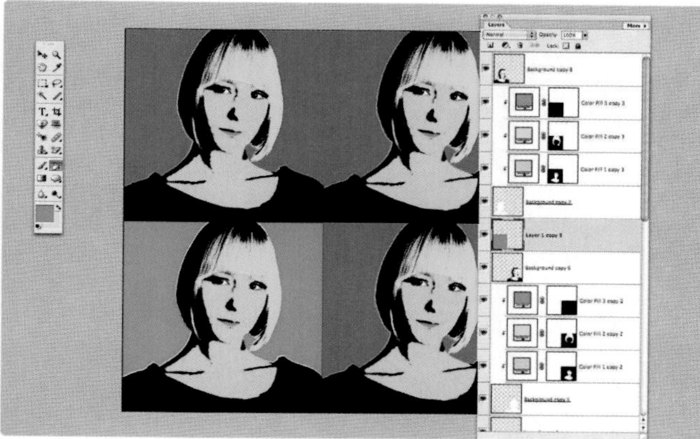

The layers palette will look busy, but you'll see which layer refers to which part of the image. To change the backgrounds' colours, choose a colour, and with the layer selected, use the Paint Bucket on each square. For the colours on the face, simply double-click on the coloured box on the layer to bring up the color picker.

Produce a graphic art effect

You may not realise this, but Photoshop isn't just about photography. There are all manner of creative professionals who use it to produce illustrations, textures, CGI effects and the like. If you are one of those people who cannot draw to save your life, don't worry: you can transform your photography into 'illustration' with this multi-layer technique, producing the kind of images you might see in the pages of a graphic novel.

We'll be duplicating the base layer holding your original photograph a number of times and applying different Photoshop's filters to them to emphasise the outlines and colours in the image. You'll also get the chance to learn how the blending modes of these layers control the way they interact with each other and affect the end result.

1

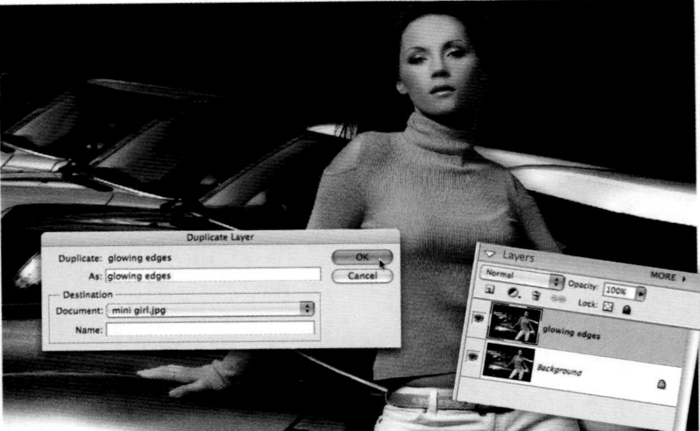

With the image open the plan is to build layers of outlines, much like pen or pencil strokes, and give the image a hand-drawn appearance. The first step is to create a duplicate layer of the original with ***Layer>Duplicate Layer***, which is then named 'glowing edges', an indication to the first effect to be applied.

2

Now to apply a filter effect. Click ***Filter>Stylize>Glowing Edges***. The preview window instantly shows us the effect you can expect. Using the preview, randomly move the three sliders until the outlines within the image become really bold, then click ***OK***. Go to ***Filter>Adjustments>Invert*** so that the white outlines become dark.

3

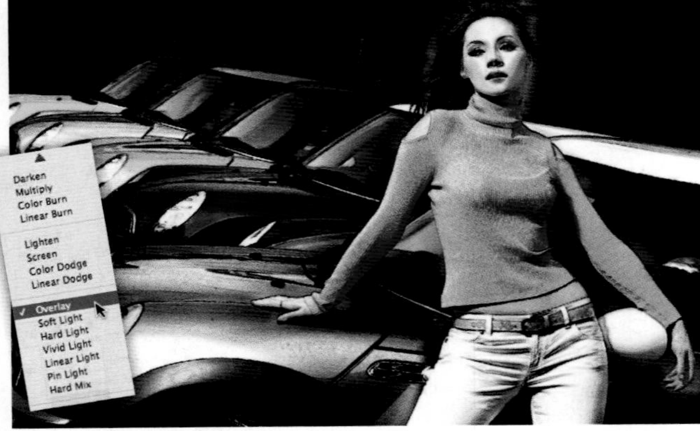

The plan is to blend the two layers together to allow this effect to interact with the original image. To do this, change the Blending Mode (situated at the top of the layers palette) to Overlay. Now create a new duplicate layer of the original 'background' layer and name it 'find edges', which is the next effect in this technique.

4

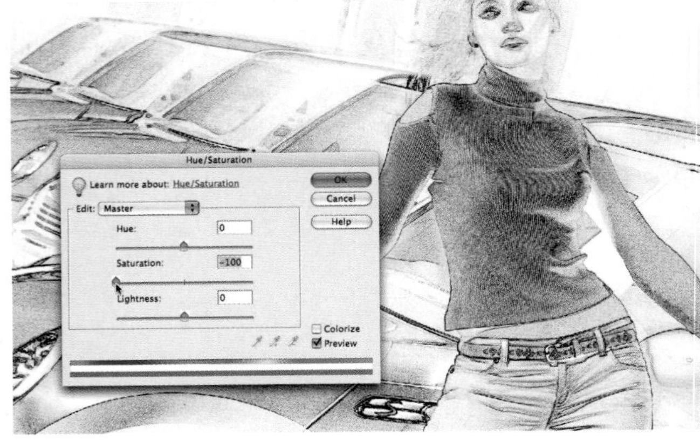

Move the 'find edges' layer to the top in the layers palette, then use ***Filter>Stylize>Find Edges***, which creates an instant and uncontrolled effect on the image. Use ***Enhance> Adjust Color>Adjust Hue/Saturation*** and the Saturation slider to erase all colour from the layer leaving something much like a pencil sketch.

5

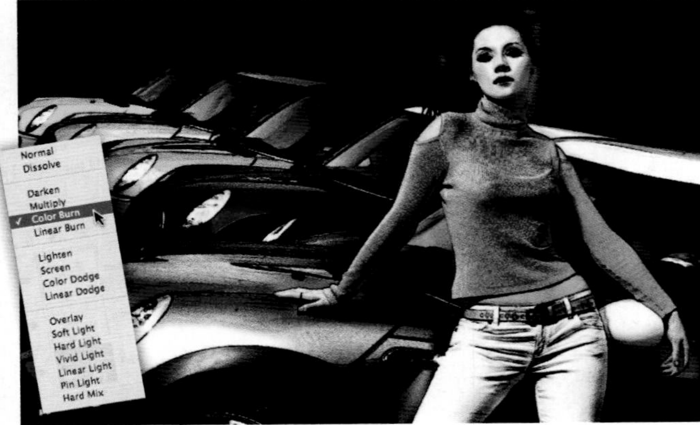

Again, using the Blending Mode menu, experiment to see which mode provides the best interaction with the layers below, (this image used Color Burn). Now the image is really starting to take shape, the 'background' layer providing the colour base and the two new layers produce a professional hand drawn effects.

6

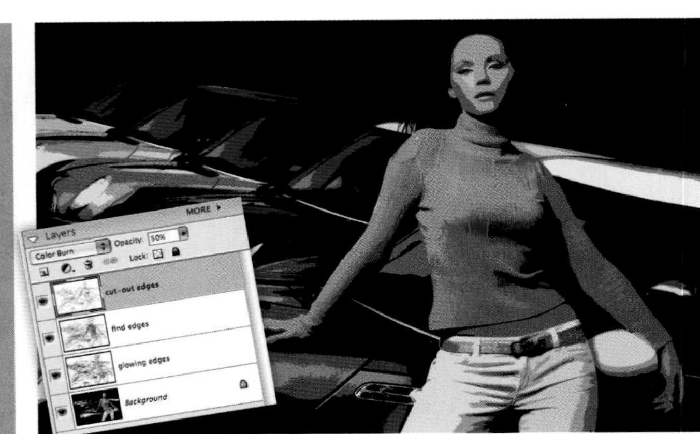

Create another duplicate of the 'background' to create some less uniform lines, and use ***Filter>Artistic>Cut Out*** to build new level of tones for the Find Edges filter to 'find'. Once Find Edges is used, desaturate and use Color Burn mode, as in step four, and set a layer Opacity of 50% to give these lines a more subtle look.

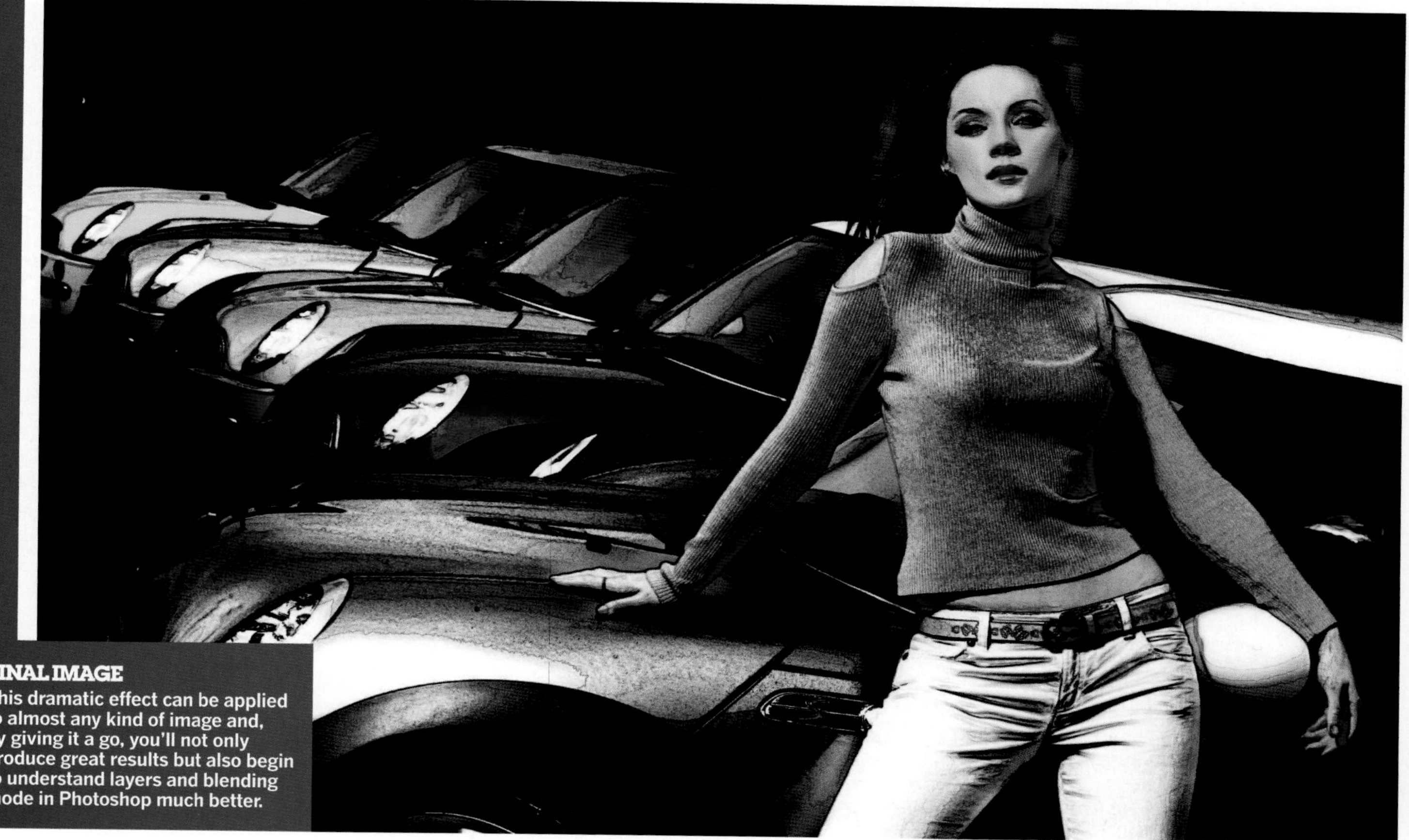

FINAL IMAGE
This dramatic effect can be applied to almost any kind of image and, by giving it a go, you'll not only produce great results but also begin to understand layers and blending mode in Photoshop much better.

7

That's it for the layers and the effect is just right with the image looking like a combination of pencil, pen and paint, just like a modern graphic comic. However, some of the free-form lines on the 'find edges' layer are obstructing the face, so using the **Eraser** tool with a feathered brush set to 45% opacity, you can begin to remove them.

8

You may find eyes become very dark, appearing almost hollow. With the same **Eraser** brush active, remove detail from each of the newly created layers, clicking on each then erasing the desired area until detail of the eye from the original 'background layer' is visible, and bringing the subject's eye contact back into play.

Using Blending Mode

Each layer's blending mode only has an effect on the layer directly below it on the layers palette. There are 23 modes in all with all new layers defaulting to Normal, which means no blending occurs. However, a duplicated layer will carry the mode of the layer it originated from. To give an exact explanation of the information each mode uses to calculate its blend is an article in itself, but rather than get bogged down by jargon, it helps to experiment extensively with the modes to build up an appreciation of how each one works. Below are just a few of the more widely used effects created by using different modes on the 'glowing edges' layer.

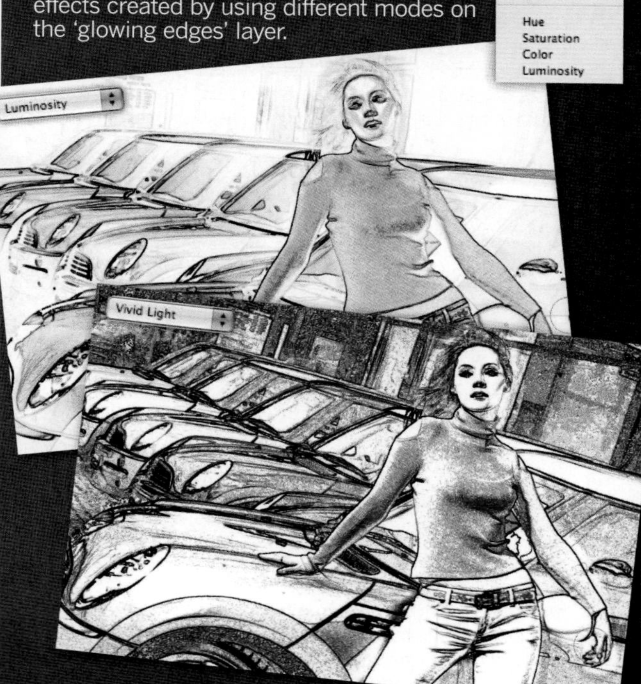

Use Gradient Map for colour impact

There is a temptation, sometimes, to be understated with your photography. Muted, subtle and discerning. Well that's all very good, but occasionally we'd encourage you to kick all of that into the long grass and go bold with your colours and contrast. This works best with simple, stark compositions, and there are a load of ways that you can boost and alter the colours in a photograph to add impact and punch.

Rather than simply playing with normal Saturation and Contrast controls, let's see how using the Gradient Map works. We'll apply this as an adjustment layer so we get more control over what is going on. With adjustment layers you can go back and change your settings at any point, depending on the look that you want.

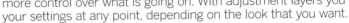

1

The first thing to do after opening the image is to create a duplicate of the original by using ***Layer>Duplicate Layer (or Ctrl + J)*** in the drop-down menu. This allows you to work on the image while preserving a copy which can be used later. This new layer is active by default and sits above the Background layer (inset).

2

Your next task is to create an adjustment layer that will allow you to place an effect over the new layer. For this, click on the black & white circular icon (circled) and select Gradient Map in the drop-down menu. The Gradient Map window appears with a default gradient set, which automatically previews on the image.

3

Clicking the gradient opens the Gradient Editor. There is a selection of preset gradients here, but you can create a custom gradient by clicking on the Color Stops pointers along the bottom of the long gradient (circled). These represent the colours used to create the gradient, seen here as a standard black to white gradient effect.

4

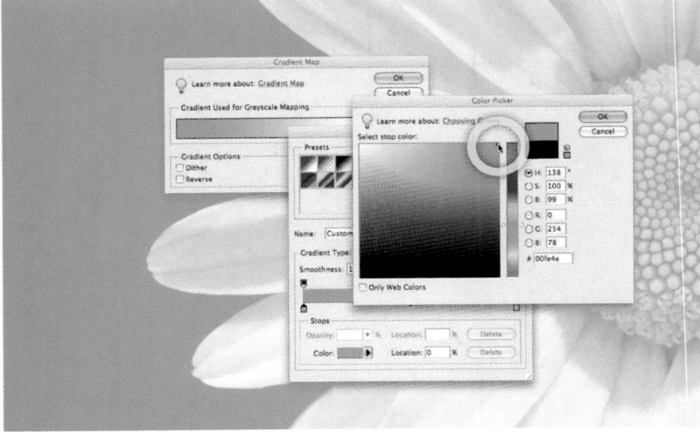

By double-clicking a Color Stop you can open the Color Picker, which works in the same way as any Photoshop swatch. First, select a hue using the vertical colour spectrum and then choose the colour temperature in the large colour field and click ***OK***. Don't be too concerned with accuracy here as the results are easily tweaked later.

5

Repeat this for the second Color Stop ensuring you use a colour that contrasts greatly with the first to give a really bold effect – use the preview to judge the results. To finish, add two additional color stop pointers by simply clicking under the gradient strip (circled), these are used as before and add a stronger tonal range to the effect.

6

Now click ***OK*** to leave the Gradient Editor and click it again to apply the final Gradient Map. The benefit of the gradient map is that you can now access the gradient to tweak if necessary. Once you're happy with the result, proceed by saving a copy, preserving the layers, then merging the gradient map with the duplicate layer using ***Layer>Merge Down***.

FINAL IMAGE
Using the Gradient Map is an excellent way to give your images a much needed colour-boost, not to mention creating infinitely unusual visual effects.

7

With the layers merged, any control of gradient map is gone – hence the need to save a copy. That said, you now have the opportunity to set **Linear Light** from the blend mode menu, situated at the top of the **Layer Palette** (inset). This allows the colour of the two remaining layers to interact, enhancing the effect further.

8

Finally, I can boost the overall effect by creating another layer – **Layer>Duplicate layer**. With this also set to **Linear Light,** all the contrast and colours are enhanced. The strength of this can now be controlled by reducing the layer **Opacity** as desired. All that remains now is to use **Layer>Flatten Image** and save the final version.

Experiment with *Layer Blend Mode*

Once a Gradient Map has been created, the Blend Mode of the layer is an excellent way to create an even more unusual and interesting effect. No two blend modes give the same results and the best way to find out which works best is to experiment with them – you'll soon discover which you prefer. If after trying all the modes you're still not satisfied, you can try using ***Filter>Adjustments>Invert***, inverting the layer, therefore changing the result of each blend mode.

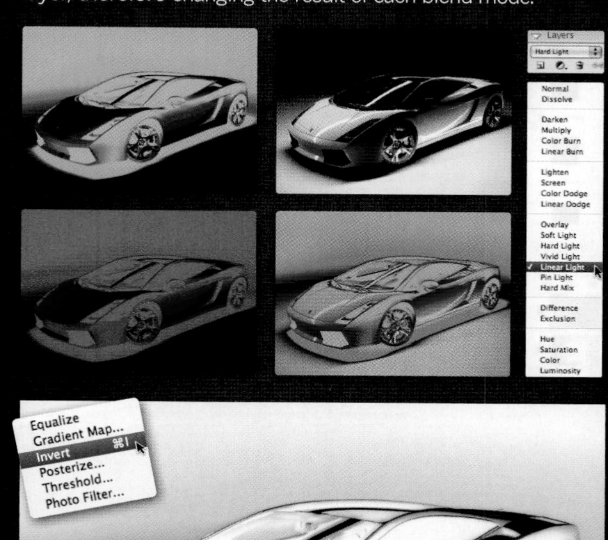

How to use muted colours to add mood

When it comes to colours, bolder is not always better. Most of us have had a go: a shot of a flower bursting with colour against an equally vibrant and suitably contrasting backdrop. Yet the result is often too overpowering to appreciate fully.

Subtle, muted colours can evoke a more sophisticated mood – just what you want when shooting fine-art to go on the wall. This Photoshop technique, which uses a combination of Filter effects, Layers and different blending modes, transforms that over-the-top image to one that is more muted. We've even limited the depth-of-field and sent some parts of the shot out of focus. The result is a more timeless image that you won't tire of as quickly as you would the bolder, more colourful version.

1

We need to combine mono and colour versions of the image, so, with the original open, click ***Layer>Duplicate Layer*** from the 'Background' and, as you will be working with the background layer, click the eye icon to the left of the newly created layer thumbnail (circled) and then click the background layer to activate it.

2

With the duplicate layer hidden and background layer active, use ***Enhance>Adjust Color>Adjust Hue/Saturation***, moving the Saturation slider left to about -80%, which reduces the overall colour in the image, but not completely. Now select the duplicated layer above to activate it, and click the 'eye' icon to reveal it.

3

Using the Magic Wand (inset), click to select the purple background and the flower's stem, holding the shift key to add to the selection. With the desired area selected, use ***Select>Feather*** at 1 pixel, to avoid any hard edges, then ***Edit>Delete*** to remove all detail from the selected area; in turn revealing the layer below.

4

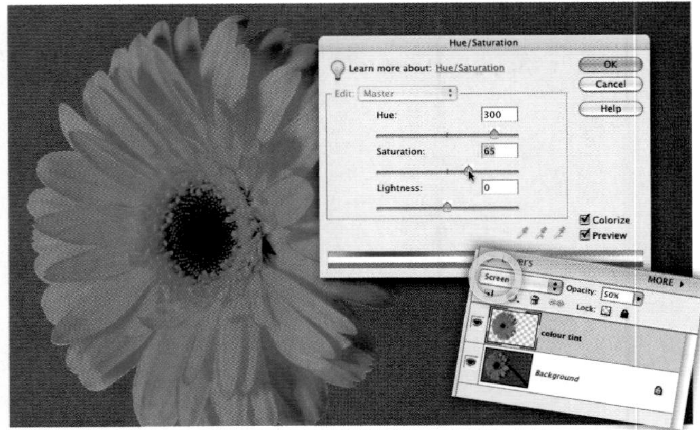

With this layer still active, revisit ***Adjust Hue/Saturation***, where, ensuring the ***Colorize*** box is ticked, you can boost the Hue and Saturation levels to give a deliberately vivid colour and click ***OK***. Now I can tone down the colour and create a really nice effect by changing the layer blend mode to Screen**,** with Opacity set to 50%.

5

The stem is proving to be a distraction, so we need to use a Gradient to minimise it. The selection made around the flower from step three will still be active and you need to utilise it again here. Go to ***Layer>New Layer***, name it 'Gradient' and drag the thumbnail in the Layers palette in between the two existing layers (inset right).

6

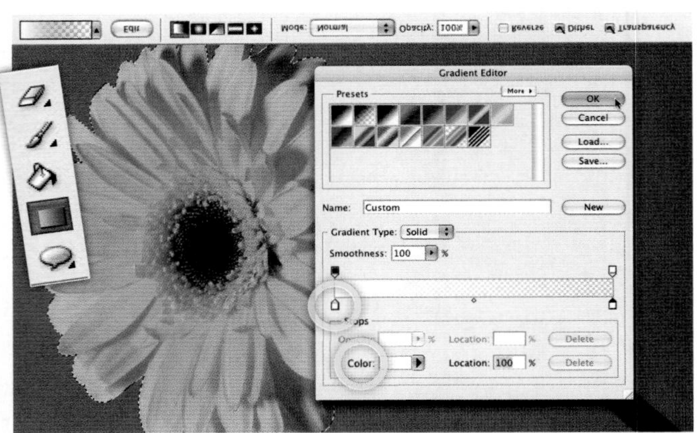

With the Gradient tool selected, click the ***Transparent*** box in the menu bar to the top right of the workspace, then the visual gradient, top left, to open the Gradient Editor. You want the gradient to run from white to transparent, so click the square 'color stop' sliders (circled), changing both to white in the Color field (circled).

FINAL IMAGE
A TINT OF COLOUR!
Bold and vivid colour in images is very striking, but a more subtle approach can often be just as effective!

7

Now click ***OK*** to exit the Gradient Editor then click and drag with the Gradient tool along the image, starting at the edge of the frame, releasing at the point you wish the gradient to end (in this case the centre of the flower). If the first gradient attempt isn't quite right you can click and drag again to re-draw until you're happy with the result.

8

To preserve all layers, use ***File>Save as,*** selecting a Photoshop (.psd) file then go ***Layer>Flatten Image***. Now we want to introduce a shallow depth-of-field. Use the Rectangular Marquee to create a selection either side of the flower's centre, Feather to the maximum 250 pixels, then use ***Filter>Blur>Gaussian blur*** to create the effect.

9

Create a new Rectangular Marquee half-way through the stem to the frame edge; Feather to 250 pixels and use the same Blur effect as before to increase the effect further. Switching to the Elliptical Marquee, make a selection within the flower's edge, then ***Select>Inverse*** before feathering to 150 pixels and Blur one last time.

10

With the Elliptical selection still active, click ***Enhance>Adjust Lighting>Brightness/Contrast*** and reduce the brightness substantially, further enhancing the focal area to the centre of the flower. Finish up by adding a little ***Filter>Noise>Add Noise***, but first ensuring that the Monochromatic box is ticked.

Turn your image into a sketch

There are plenty of photographers out there who, while being artistically talented with a camera, can't draw to save their life. Hence, Adobe Photoshop and Elements are popular applications with their range of filters and plug-ins that can create authentic-looking sketches and paintings in a wide variety of styles.

The thing about all of these filters, mind you, is that they are never going to give their best when used on their own as a 'one-click' solution. It's when they are combined with Element's other editing tools that the most effective results are produced. Let's see how an authentic pencil sketch effect can be applied using Elements Graphic Pen filter, combined with the Find Edges and Cutout commands.

1

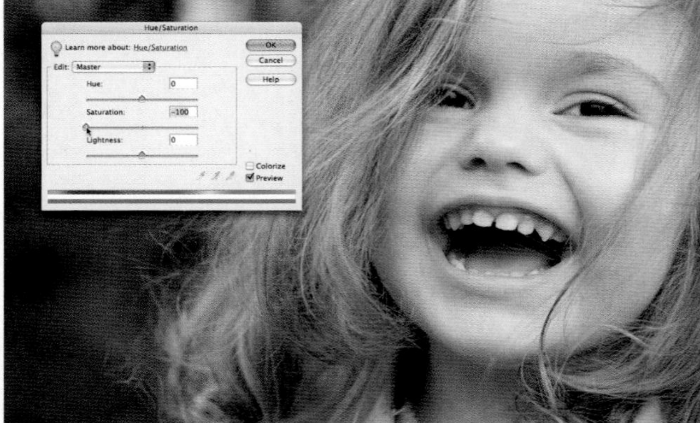

To achieve the sketch we'll need to create duplicate layers of the original, each containing a different filter effect that combine to give the end result. As the image will be presented in black & white, first desaturate using ***Enhance>Adjust Colour>Adjust Hue/Saturation***, taking the slider all the way left (–) to remove the colour.

2

As the filter effects work by manipulating the available detail, it doesn't hurt to give them a helping hand by boosting the contrast within your image, so use ***Enhance>Adjust Lighting>Brightness/Contrast*** and enhance the contrast by moving the slider to the right (+) until you are satisfied with the result.

3

Now it's time to create the new layers to combine the three effects you'll be creating. Go to ***Layer>Duplicate Layer*** and name the first layer 'tone', which will sit at the bottom. You can now hide the 'background' layer by clicking the eye icon next to it, then create two more duplicate layers named 'outline' and 'texture' respectively.

4

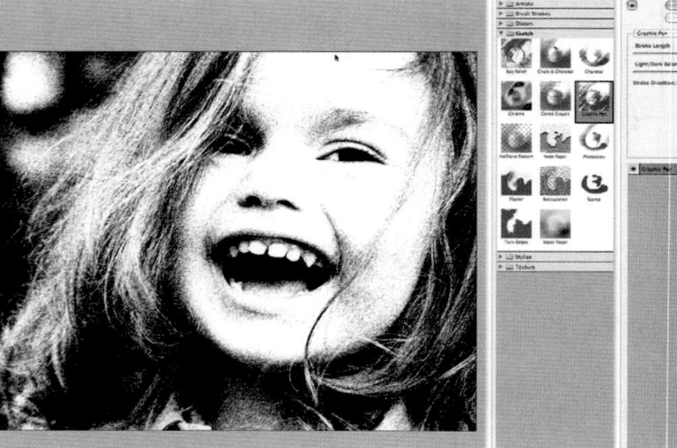

Now for the first effect. Make the 'texture' layer active by clicking it in the Layers palette, then go to ***Filter>Sketch> Graphic Pen***, and you'll get a simple preview window consisting of two sliders and a directional menu. Adjust these until happy then click ***OK***, then hide this layer by clicking the eye icon.

5

With the 'texture' layer hidden, click the 'outline' layer to make it active as we now want to create a pencil outline effect. To achieve this, use ***Filter>Stylize>Find Edges***, which pretty much does what it says on the tin. Boost the outline further with the Brightness/Contrast to complete the effect and once again hide the layer.

6

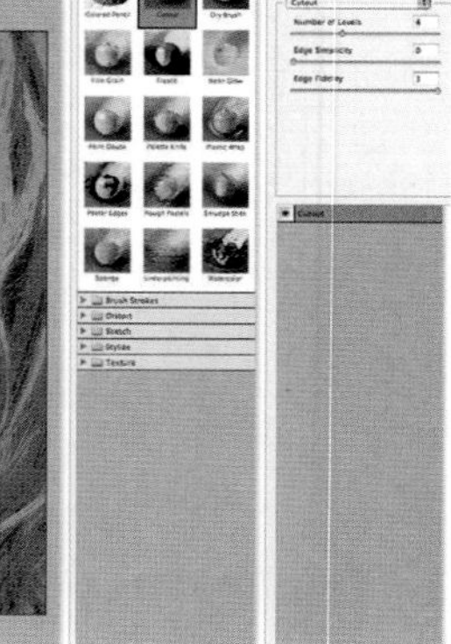

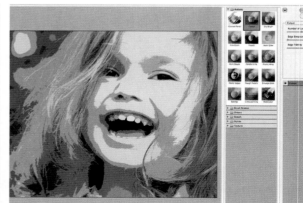

Now for the third and final effect, which will add a basic tonal shading to the image. Select ***Filter>Artistic>Cutout*** and you're presented with three sliders, although you should concentrate on 'number of levels', as this is the most important for deciding the amount of tonal separation, then click ***OK*** to apply the effect.

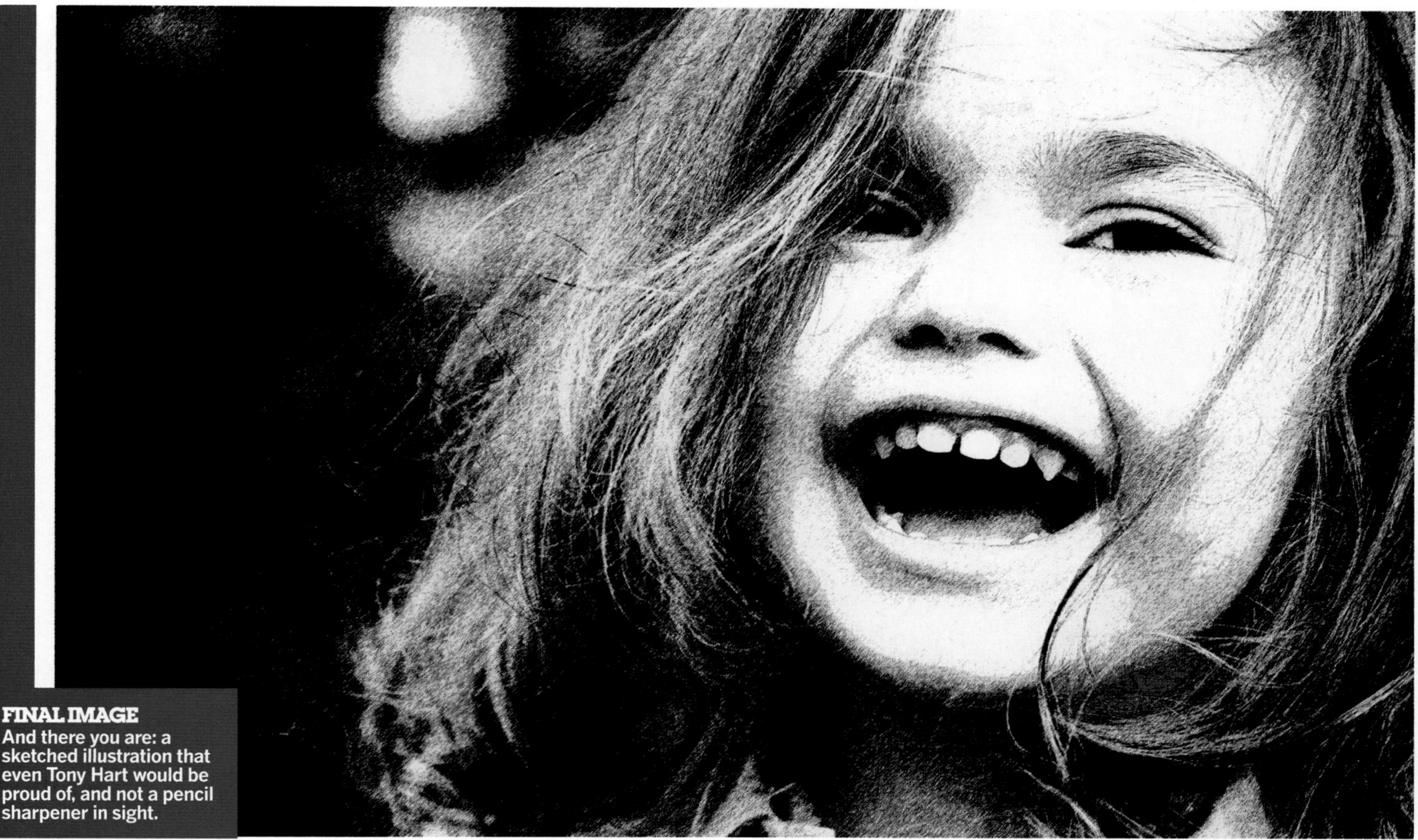

FINAL IMAGE
And there you are: a sketched illustration that even Tony Hart would be proud of, and not a pencil sharpener in sight.

7

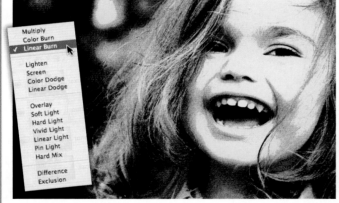

Now make all three layers visible by clicking on the empty eye icon box, however, only the top layer is viewable and the next stage is for the layers to interact. Set the 'texture' layer to 50% Opacity so the 'outline' layer becomes visible, which you set to ***Linear Burn*** in the drop-down menu, allowing it to blend with the 'tone' layer.

8

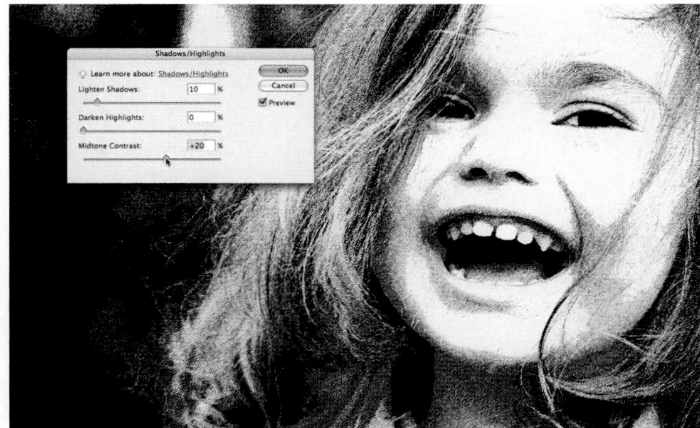

Save a copy as a Photoshop (.psd) file to preserve the layers. Then flatten the image so you can use it on the last process across the combined layers to lift out the textures, enhancing the 'sketched' appearance. For this, use ***Enhance>Adjust Lighting>Shadows/ Highlights*** and move the Midtone Contrast slider right (+).

Other subjects for the sketch effect

As you can see from these further examples, a sketch effect looks great with a variety of subjects and once you're confident using creative filters you should try to experiment as there are endless ways to reaching fantastic results. Why not try adding a hint of colour to the sketch or attempt to create the effect of pencil combined with watercolour.

PRESENTATION

Add the finishing touches to your favourite images with our top Photoshop presentations

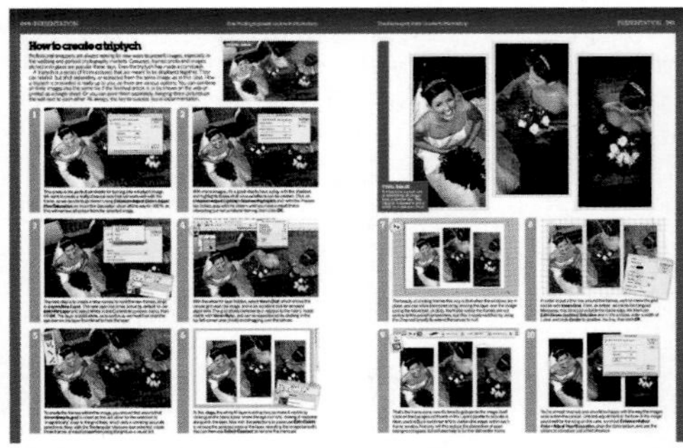

How to create a triptych

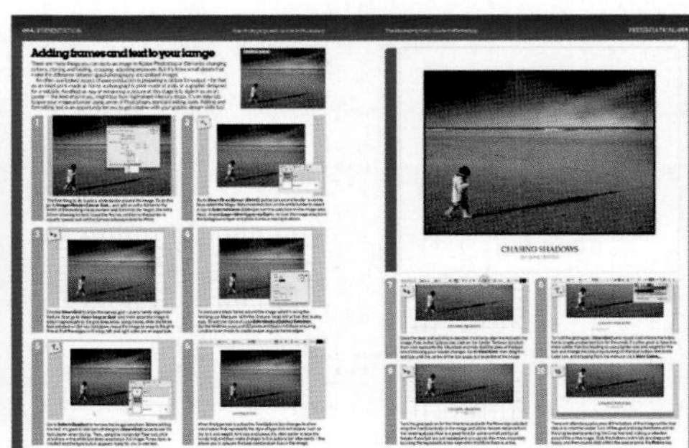

Adding frames and text to your image

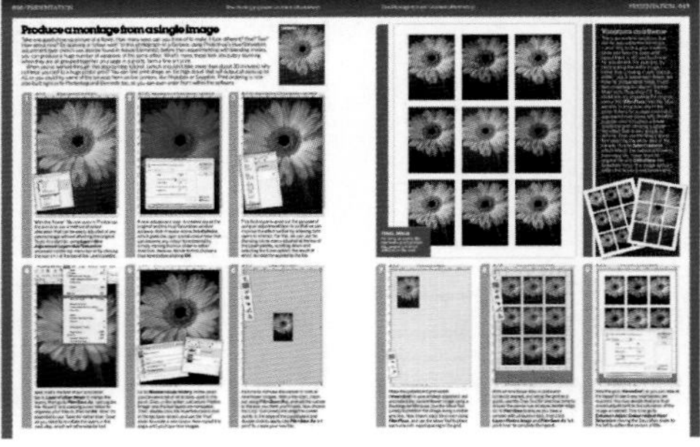

Produce a montage from a single image

How to create a triptych

Professional snappers are always looking for new ways to present images, especially in the wedding and portrait photography markets. Canvases, framed prints and images etched onto glass are popular these days. Even the triptych has made a comeback.

A triptych is a series of three pictures that are meant to be displayed together. They can related, but shot separately, or extracted from the same image, as in this case. How a triptych is presented is really up to you, as there are various options. You can combine all three images into the same file if the finished article is to be shown on the web or printed as a single sheet. Or you can print them separately, hanging three pictures on the wall next to each other. As always, the key to success lies in experimentation.

1

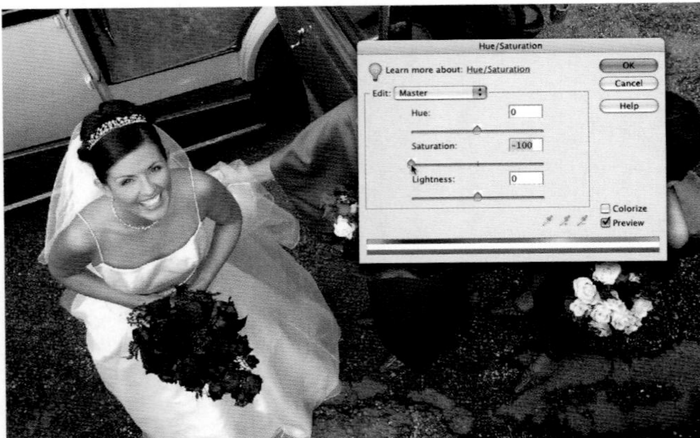

This photo is the perfect candidate for turning into a triptych image. We want to create a really classical look that will work well with the frame, so we decide to go mono! Using ***Enhance>Adjust Color>Adjust Hue/Saturation*** we move the Saturation slider all the way to -100%, as this will remove all colour from the selected image.

2

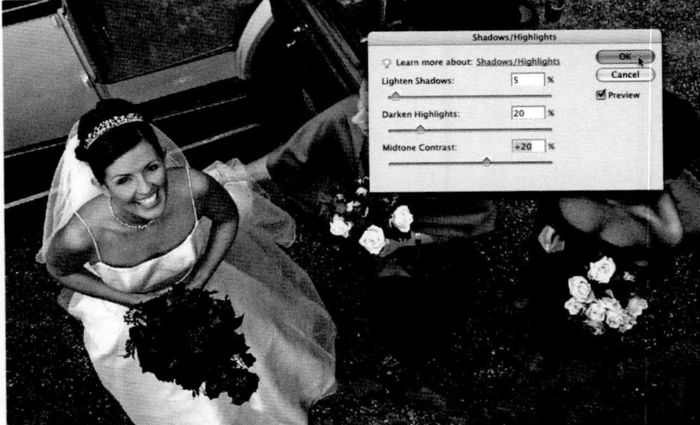

With mono images, it's a good idea to have a play with the shadows and highlights to see what unusual effects can be created. Click on ***Enhance>Adjust Lighting>Shadow/Highlights*** and, with the Preview box ticked, play with the sliders until you have a result that is interesting but not unnatural looking, then click ***OK***.

3

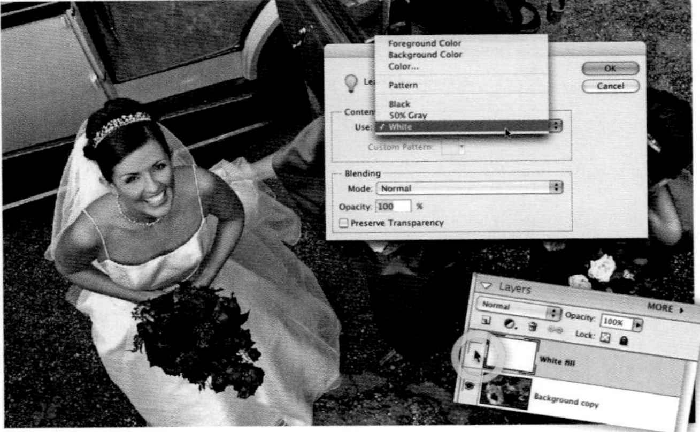

The next step is to create a false canvas to hold the new frames, so go to ***Layer>New Layer***. This new layer becomes active by default so use ***Edit>Fill Layer*** and select White in the Content drop-down menu, then hit ***OK***. The layer is solid white, so to continue, we must first click the eye icon on the layer thumbnail to hide the layer.

4

With the white fill layer hidden, select ***View>Grid***, which shows the canvas grid over the image, and is an excellent tool for accurate alignment. The grid shows increments in relation to the ruler), made visible with ***View>Ruler,*** and can be repositioned by clicking in the top left corner area (inset) and dragging over the canvas.

5

To create the frames within the image, you should first ensure that ***View>Snap to grid*** is ticked as this will allow for the selection to 'magnetically' snap to the grid lines, which aids in creating accurate selections. Now, with the Rectangular Marquee tool selected, create three frames of equal proportion using the grid as a visual aid.

6

At this stage, the white fill layer is still active, so make it visible by clicking on the blank space where the eye icon sits, making it reappear along with the layer. Now with the selections in place use ***Edit>Delete*** to remove the selected areas of the layer, revealing the image beneath. You can then use ***Select>Deselect*** to remove the marquee.

FINAL IMAGE
A triptych is a great way of presenting an image from a special day. This triptych is bound to put a smile on someone's face!

7

The beauty of creating frames this way is that when the windows are in place, you can refine their position by moving the layer over the image (using the Move tool, circled). You'll also notice the frames are not central to the overall composition, but this is easily rectified by using the Crop tool (inset), to extend the canvas to suit.

8

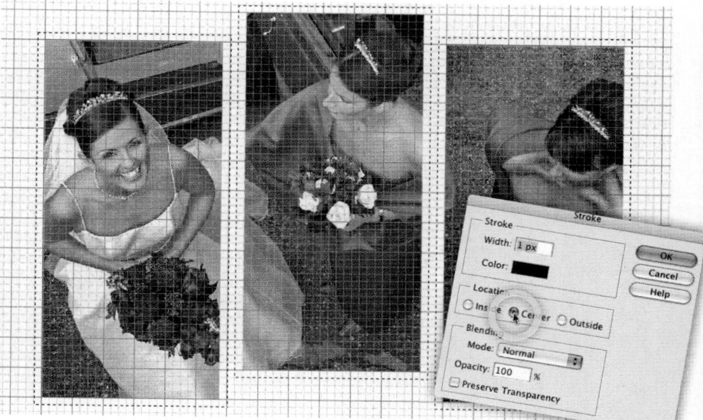

In order to put a thin line around the frames, we first make the grid visible with ***View>Grid.*** Then, as before, we create Rectangular Marquees; this time just outside the frame edge. We then use ***Edit>Stroke (outline) Selection*** and in the window, enter a width of 1 pixel and click ***Center*** to position the line, then click ***OK***.

9

That's the frame done, now it's time to go back to the image itself. Click on the background thumb in the Layers palette to activate it. Next, use the Burn tool (inset left) to darken the edges within each frame window. Not only will this reduce the distraction of open background space, but will also help to further define the frame.

10

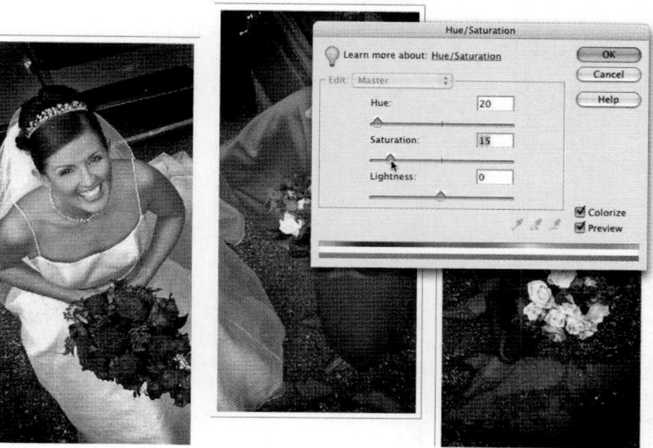

You're almost finished, and should be happy with the way the images work within the canvas. One last adjustment to the tone of the image could well be the icing on the cake, so revisit ***Enhance>Adjust Color>Adjust Hue/Saturation***, click the Colorize box, and use the sliders to introduce just a hint of colour.

Producing a photographic calendar

We're all taking more pictures than ever before, yet we are printing them less and less. In fact, the general trend amongst digital photographers is that they just don't do enough with their pictures. This is odd as there's never been more ways to output your images: prints, canvases, mugs, t-shirts, greetings cards. The list is virtually endless.

A great way of showing-off your pictures is to select 12 of them and assemble a calendar for the coming year. You don't even have to wait until January; your creation could run from October to September. This is your creation, after all. Many commercial services will make a calendar from your pictures for a few pounds, although we've provided some templates so you can do it for free. Download them from our website.

1

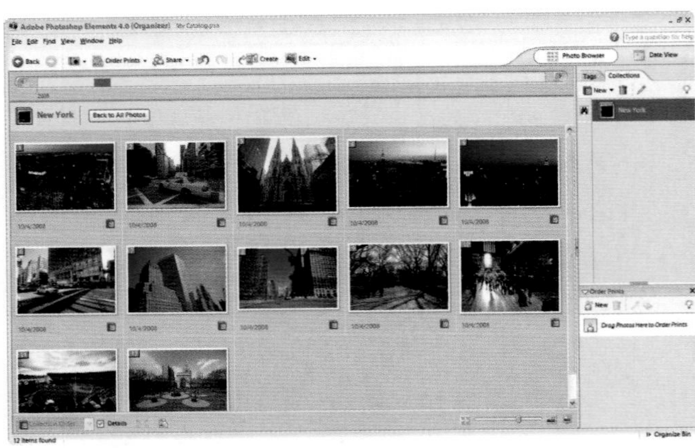

A successful calendar needs a well-selected image set. Choose a theme or style that helps the images work together, such as matching images to the seasons. Also ensure that the shots are in the same format – either landscape or portrait. You'll need to choose 12 images, plus one for the cover, although this can be one of the 12.

2

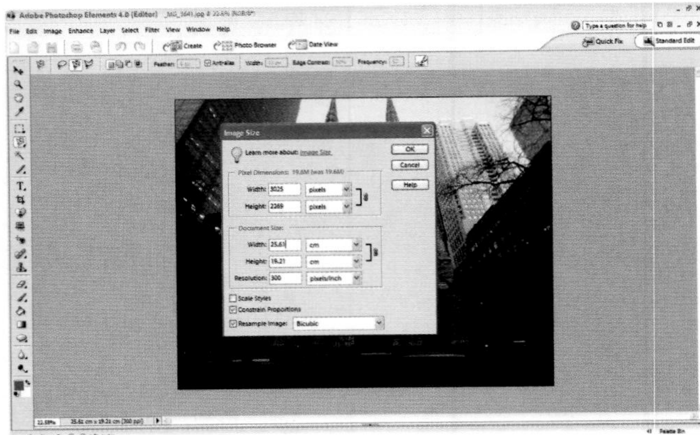

Make sure that your shots are all around the same size – in this instance, just smaller than A4. Open each image and go to ***Image>Resize>Image size***. First, ensure that the Resample Image box is not ticked, and change the drop-down boxes to show the Width and Height in cm, and the Resolution in pixels/inch.

3

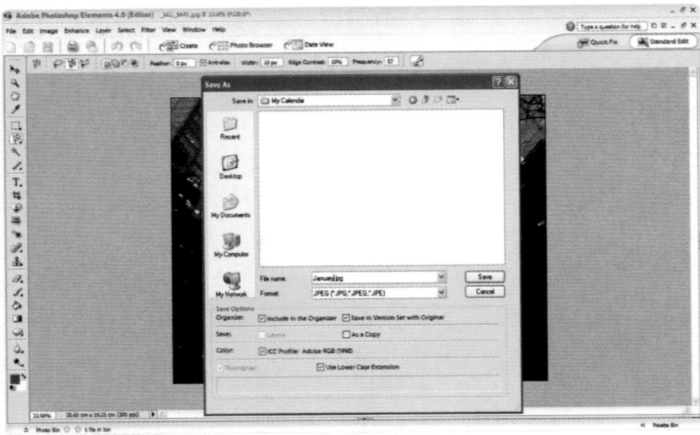

Set a Resolution of 300ppi and check the new size. If your longest value is above 30cm, you'll need to reduce the size. Click on the Resample image box and enter a new value for the Width or Height. Images less than 20cm may be too low res so, if possible, use another image. Save the image into a new folder as a JPEG (level 12).

4

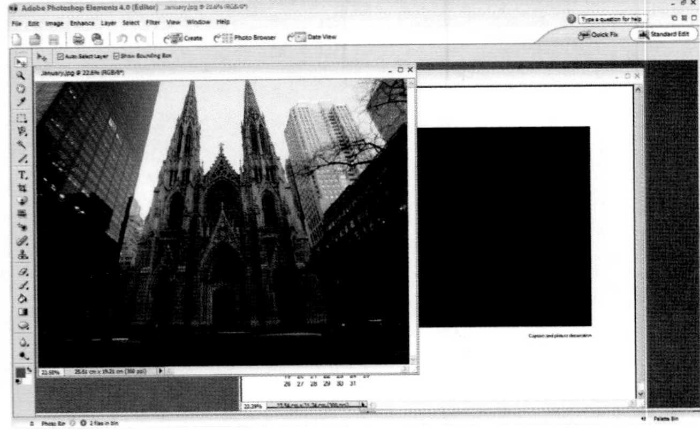

Open your first image and first template. You can find the templates in the download section on *www.digitalslrphoto.com*. With both documents in view, select the Move tool from the tool bar, click on your image and drag your mouse over to the template and release. The image should now appear as a new layer on the template.

5

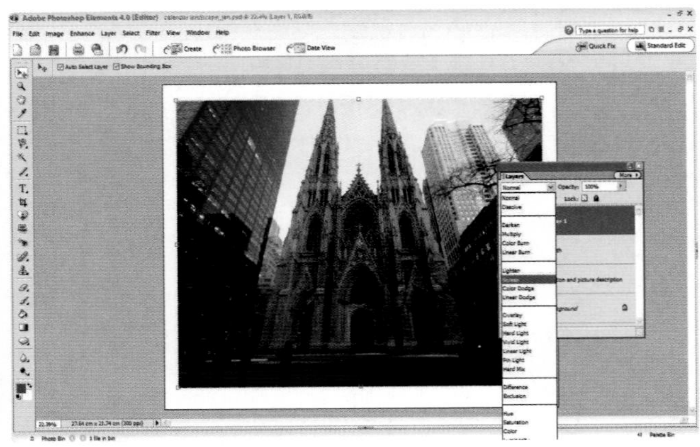

Close your original image, and use the Move tool again to shift your shot over the black square in the template – it doesn't matter if it's slightly too big or small at this stage. Next, bring up the Layers palette (***F7***). With your new layer selected, change the Mode in the drop-down menu from Normal to Screen.

6

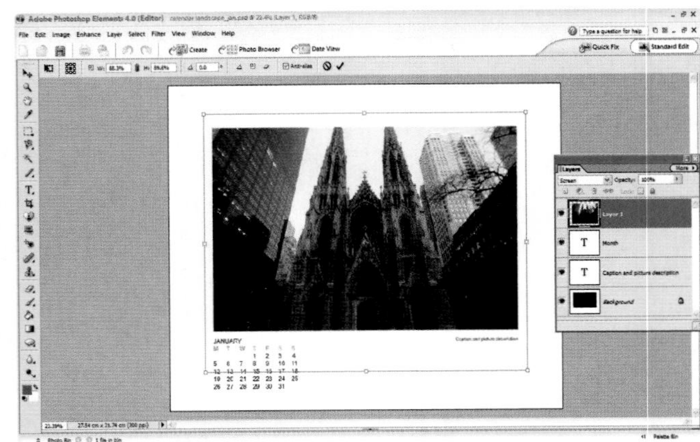

Your image should now only be visible in the previously black box. Now, with the ***Shift*** key held down (to maintain the perspective), click and drag on one of the corner boxes. (In the full version of Photoshop, hit ***Ctrl+L*** to enter Free Transform first.) Once you're happy, hit ***Enter*** on the keyboard or ***double-click*** on the image.

JANUARY

M	T	W	T	F	S	S
			1	2	3	4
5	6	7	8	9	10	11
12	13	14	15	16	17	18
19	20	21	22	23	24	25
26	27	28	29	30	31	

St Patrick's Cathedral

FINAL CALENDAR
A calendar is a great way to show off your talent to friends and family, and makes a good Christmas present, too.

7

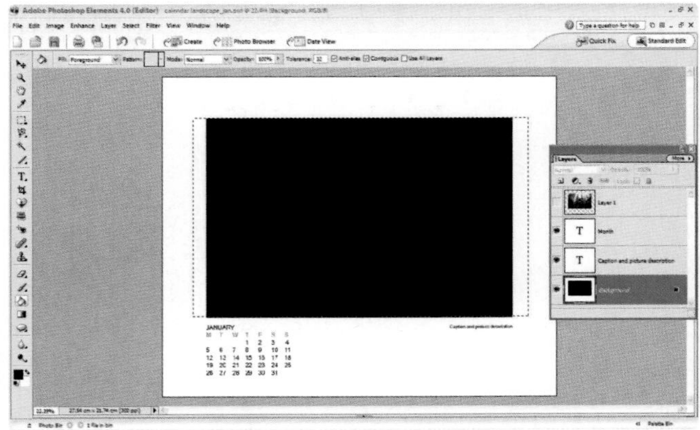

If you're feeling creative, you can change the size of the image on the page by adding to or deleting some of the black square. To do this, select the background layer, then choose the Rectangular Marquee tool from the tool palette. Click and drag your area, and hit the backspace to delete or use the Paint Bucket tool to fill it with black.

8

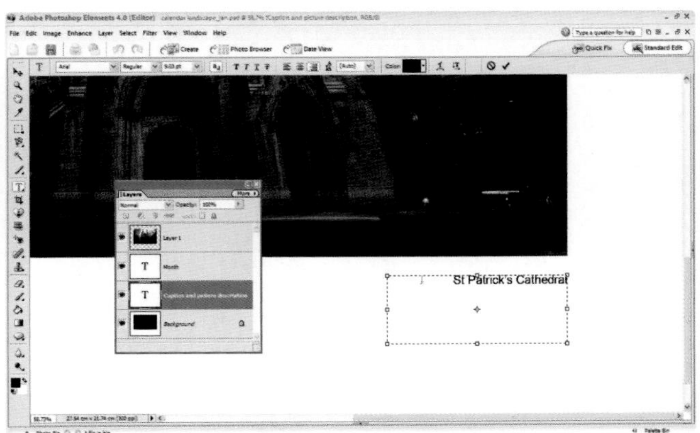

Finally, select the Type tool from the tool Palette and click on the 'my caption here' text under the image. You can then type in your own name or picture description. Once you're happy with your text, go ***Layer>Flatten image*** and save under a new name (such as January.jpg). Do this for each month and don't forget the cover!

Putting the calendar together

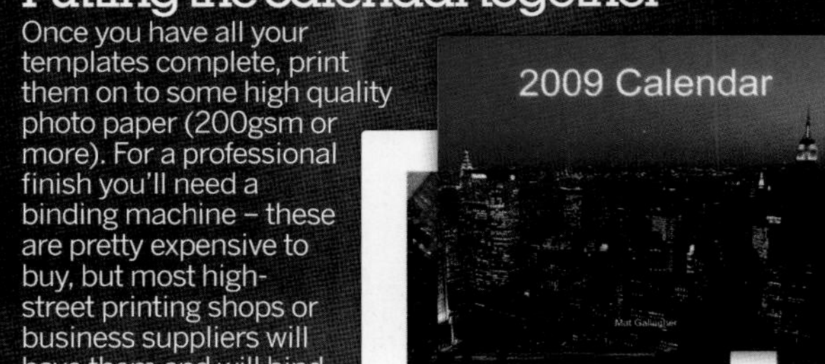

Once you have all your templates complete, print them on to some high quality photo paper (200gsm or more). For a professional finish you'll need a binding machine – these are pretty expensive to buy, but most high-street printing shops or business suppliers will have them and will bind your creation for you for just a few pounds.

Looking for an easier option?

If you want to produce a calendar quickly, most online printing companies can now produce one for you. All you need to do is supply the photos. JPics, the new online photo site from Jessops can produce wall calendars from just £5 with a range of templates to choose from. ***Visit www.jpics.co.uk***

Creating a calendar in Elements

Users of Elements from version 4.0 upwards can already create calendars using the software's Create function. This works like an auto assistant, taking you through the process and giving you the opportunity to print it yourself (Elements 4 only), create a PDF, share it by email or print it via the online Kodak Easyshare Gallery, which will return it to you as a finished calendar. ***Visit www.adobe.com/uk for more details.***

Adding frames and text to your iamge

There are many things you can do to an image in Adobe Photoshop or Elements: changing colours, cloning and healing, cropping, adjusting exposure. But it's those small details that make the difference between good photography and brilliant images.

An often overlooked aspect of post-production is preparing a picture for output – be that as an inkjet print made at home, a photographic print made at a lab, or a graphic designed for a website. An effective way of enhancing a picture at this stage is to style it as an art poster – the kind of print you might buy from high-street interiors shops. It's an easy job to give your image a border using some of Photoshop's standard editing tools. Adding and formatting text is an opportunity for you to get creative with your graphic design skills too!

1

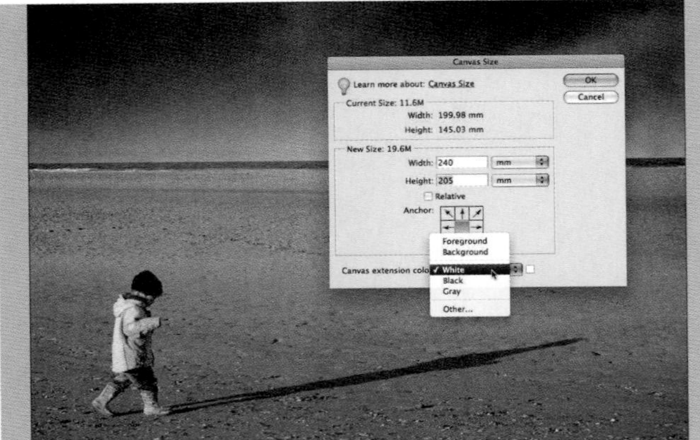

The first thing to do is add a white border around the image. To do this go to ***Image>Resize>Canvas Size...*** and add an extra 40mm to the width of the existing measurement and 50mm to the height, the extra 10mm allowing for text. Leave the Anchor centred so the border is equally spaced and set the Canvas extension color to White.

2

Go to ***View>Fit on Screen*** (***Ctrl+0***) so the canvas and border is visible. Now select the Magic Wand tool and click on the white border to select it. Go to ***Select>Inverse*** (***Ctrl+I***) to turn the selection on the image area. Next, choose ***Layer>New>Layer via Cut*** to remove the image area from the background layer and place it onto a new layer above.

3

Choose ***View>Grid*** to show the canvas grid – a very handy alignment feature. Now go to ***View>Snap to Grid***, which will allow the image to snap magnetically to the grid lines when being moved. With the Move tool selected or Ctrl key held down, move the image to snap to the grid line so that the edges on the top, left and right sides are an equal size.

4

To produce a black frame around the image select it using the Rectangular Marquee. With the Grid and Snap still active, this is very easy. To add the frame choose ***Edit>Stroke (Outline) Selection***. Set the Width to a value of 20 pixels and black in Colour, ensuring Location is on Inside to create proper angular frame edges.

5

Go to ***Select>Deselect*** to remove the image selection. Before adding the text, it's good to first turn off the grid (***View>Grid***) so as to see the text clearer when typing. Then, using the Horizontal Type tool, click anywhere in the white bordered area below the image. A new layer is created and the type cursor appears ready for you to add text.

6

When the type tool is active the Tool Options bar changes to show information that represents the style of type that will appear, such as the font and weight, font size and colour. It's often easier to type the words first and then make changes to the options bar afterwards – this allows you to preview the best combination live on the image.

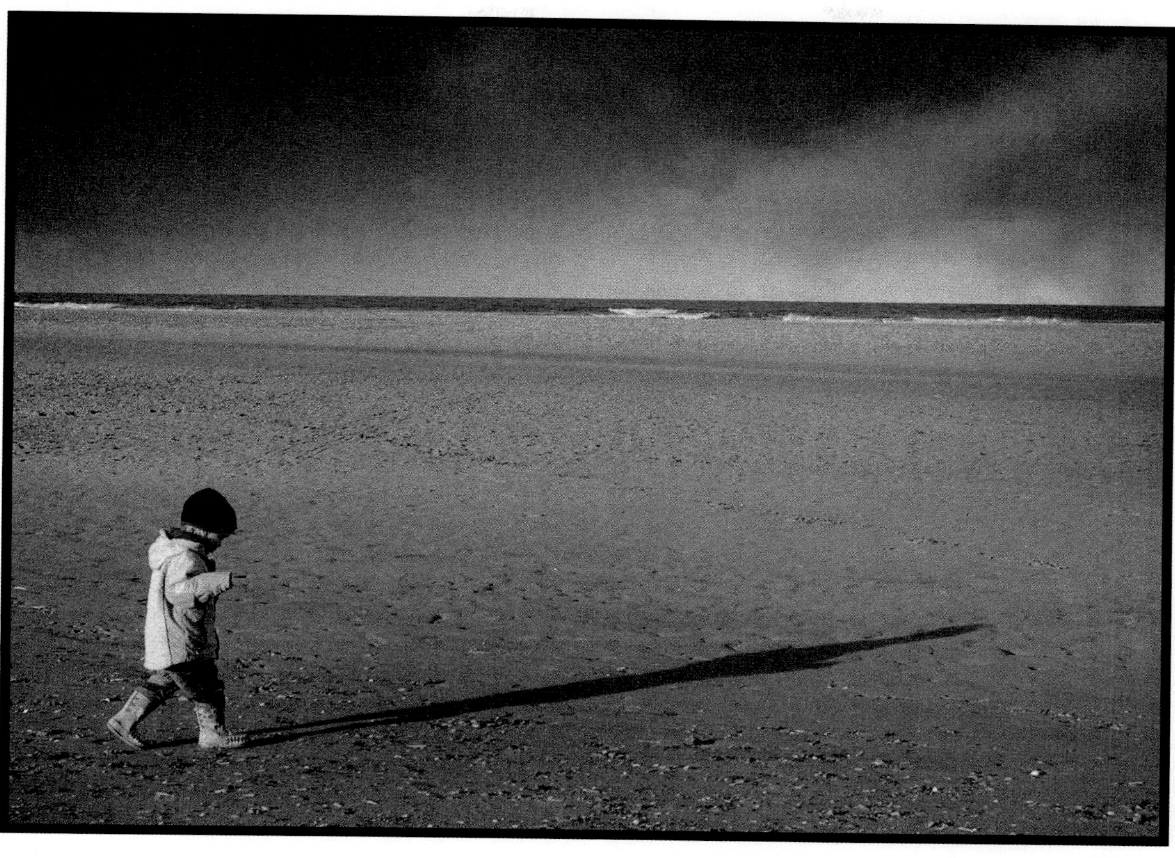

7

Once the style and wording is decided it's time to align the text with the image. First, In the Options bar, click on the Center Text icon (circled) then click back onto the Move tool and note that the state of the type box containing your header changes. Go to ***View>Grid***, then drag the text box until the centre of the box snaps to the centre of the image.

8

Turn off the grid again (***View>Grid***) and repeat instructions from step five to create another text box for the credit. It's often good to have this more subtle than the heading so use a lighter size and weight for the font and change the colour by clicking on the blue button next to the Color box and choosing from the menu or click ***More Colors...***

9

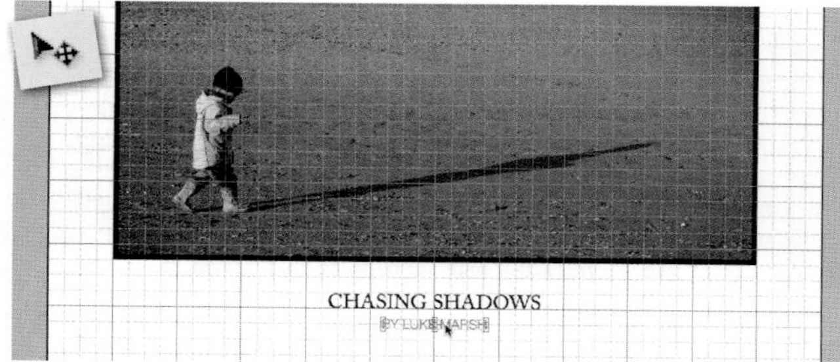

Turn the grid back on for the final time and with the Move tool selected snap the credit centrally to the image and at the desired distance from the heading above. Now is a good time for some overall positional tweaks if you feel any are needed and you can do this more accurately by using the keyboards arrow keys while the Move tools is active.

10

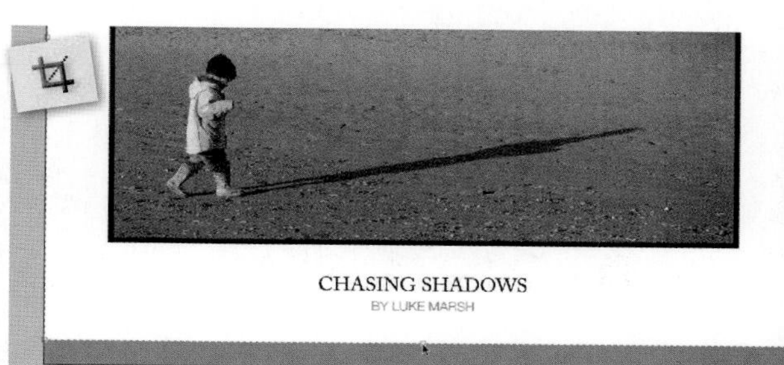

There will often be surplus area at the bottom of the image so the final step is to crop the border. Turn off the grid and snap functions and do the crop by eye by selecting the Crop tool and making a selection around the entire image. Grab the bottom centre tab and drag until happy and then double click within the area or press the ***Return*** key.

Produce a montage from a single image

Take one good close-up picture of a flower. How many ways can you think of to make it look different? One? Two? How about nine? By applying a 'colour wash' to this photograph of a Gerbera using Photoshop's Hue/Saturation adjustment layer (which can also be found in Adobe Elements), before then experimenting with blending modes, you can produce a huge number of variations of the same effect. What's more, these look absolutely stunning when they are all grouped together on a page in a grid to form a fine-art print.

When you've worked through this step-by-step tutorial, (which shouldn't take more than about 30 minutes) why not treat yourself to a huge poster print? You can find print shops on the high street that will output at sizes up to A1, or you could try some of the services from on-line printers, like Photobox or Snapfish. Print ordering is now also built right in to Photoshop and Elements too, so you can even order from within the software.

1

With the 'flower' file now open in Photoshop, the aim is to use a method of colour alteration that can be easily adjusted at any desired stage without affecting the original. To do this start by using ***Layer>New Adjustment Layer>Hue/Saturation*** accessed via the top menu bar or by clicking the icon ( ) at the top of the Layers palette.

2

A new adjustment layer is created above the original and the Hue/Saturation window appears. With Preview active, tick ***Colorize***, which gives the layer a solid colour tone that can become any colour tone desired by simply moving the Hue slider in either direction. Here we decide to first choose a blue tone before clicking ***OK***.

3

This technique is good but the purpose of using an adjustment layer is so that we can improve the effect further by allowing both layers to interact. For this, we can use the Blending Mode menu situated at the top of the Layer palette, scrolling down and selecting the Color option, the result of which is instantly applied to the file.

4

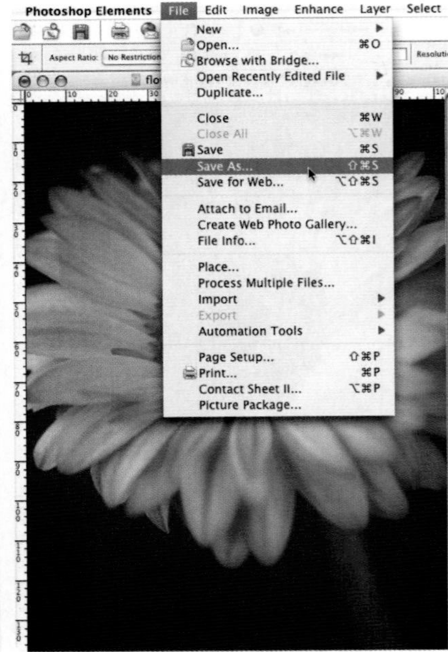

Well, that's the first of our nine done! Go to ***Layer>Flatten Image*** to merge the layers, then go to ***File>Save As***, naming the file 'flower1' and creating a new folder to organise your files in, then hit ***OK***. Note: it's essential to use 'Save As' rather than 'Save' as you need to reinstate the layers in the next step, which will otherwise be lost.

5

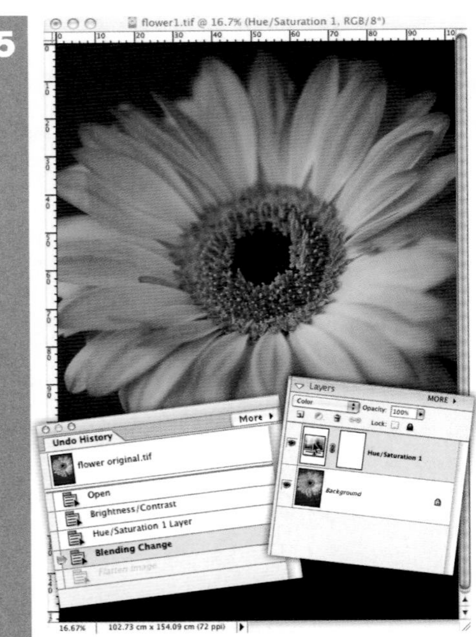

Go to ***Window>Undo History***. In the panel you can see a list of all actions used to this point. Click on the action just before 'Flatten Image' and the lost layers are reinstated. Then, double-click the Hue/Saturation icon in the top layer (inset) and use the 'Hue' slider to create a new colour. Now repeat the steps until you have nine images.

6

It's time to increase the canvas to hold all nine flower images. With a file open, zoom out using ***File>Zoom Out***, and set the canvas to the size you think you'll need. Now choose the Crop Tool (inset) and drag the corner points to the edge of the pasteboard and double-click to apply. Use ***File>Save As*** 'art print' to create your new file.

FINAL IMAGE
An array of motifs like this looks good printed big, properly framed and put on the wall.

Variations on a theme

There are endless variations that can be applied to this technique – your only limit is your creativity. Once you have the basic grid layout there is still plenty of room for adjustment. For example, try desaturating the entire image, rather than creating a pure black & white – you'll notice each flower will have its unique tonal range, much like converting to b&w in Channel Mixer with Photoshop CS. You could also try importing the original colour file (***File>Place***) into the b&w version, placing it on any of the other flowers for a more minimalist approach (inset below left). Another popular idea is to place a flower inside the grid, creating a jigsaw-like effect that is very simple to achieve. First use the Magic Wand tool selecting the white area of the canvas, choose ***Select>Inverse***, which selects the individual flowers, then copy any flower from its original file and ***Edit>Paste*** into Selection. Voila! The image appears within the boxes (inset below right).

7

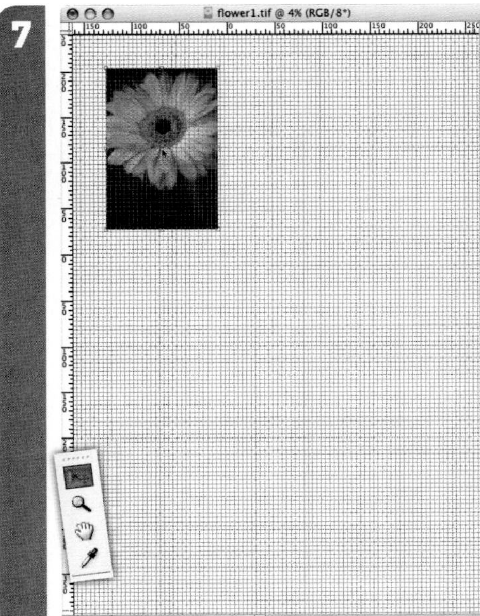

Make the pasteboard grid visible (***View>Grid***) to give an ideal alignment aid and select the current flower image using a Rectangular Marquee. Use the Move Tool (inset) to position the image along a visible grid line. Now import each file in turn using ***File>Place***, and use the Move Tool to place each one with equal spacing in the grid.

8

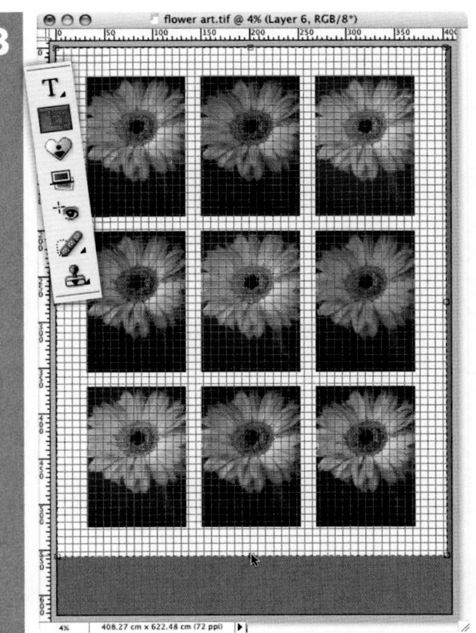

With all nine flower files in place and correctly aligned, and using the grid as a guide, use the Crop Tool for one final time to ensure the canvas has an equal border edge. Go to ***File>Save*** to ensure you have a version with all layers intact, then click ***Layer>Flatten Image*** and ***File>Save As*** 'art print final' to complete the layout.

9

Hide the grid (***View>Grid***) so you can look at the layout to see if any final tweaks are required. You may decide that one final overall adjustment to the saturation of the image is needed. This time go to ***Enhance>Adjust Colour>Adjust Hue/ Saturation*** moving the Saturation slider to the left to soften the colours a little.

Step-by-step tutorials

SIMPLE STEPS TO BETTER PICTURES

BLACK & WHITE

Master monochrome as we provide several techniques for converting colour to b&w

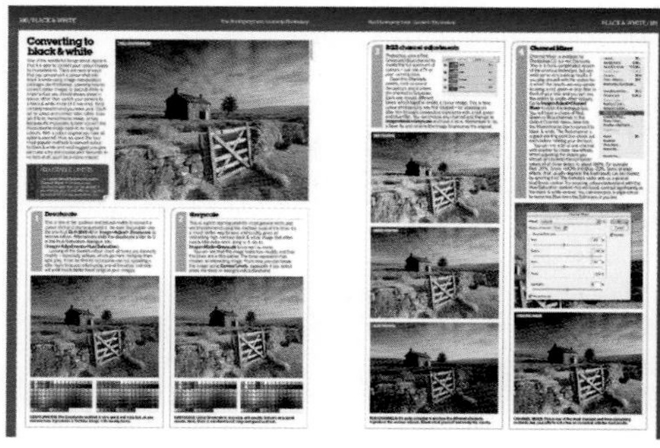

Converting to black & white

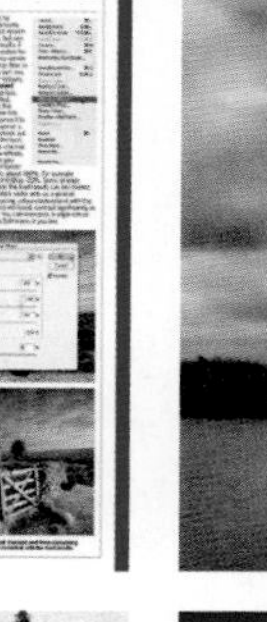

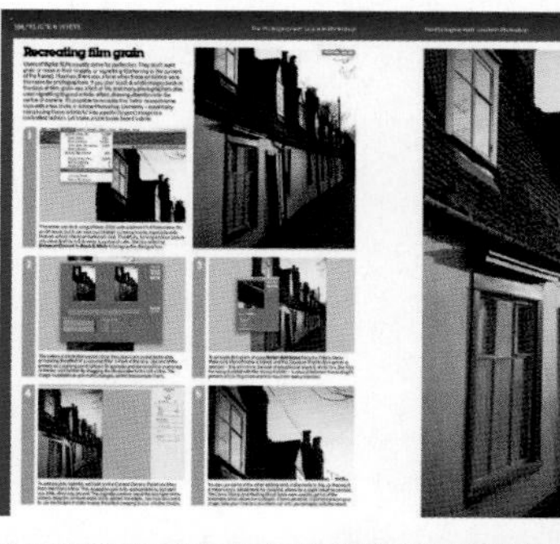

Recreating film grain

Create a toned black & white image

Converting to black & white

One of the wonderful things about digital is that it is easy to convert your colour images to monochrome. There are several ways that you can convert a colour shot into black & white using image manipulation packages like Photoshop. Learning how to convert colour images to black & white is important as you should always shoot in colour, rather than switch your camera to a black & white mode (if it has one). We'd certainly recommend you leave your DSLR set to colour and convert later, rather than set it to its monochrome mode, simply because it's impossible to later convert the monochrome image back to its original colours. With a colour original you have all options covered. Here we cover the four most popular methods to convert colour to black & white and we'd suggest you give each one a try and choose your favourite. In no time at all, you'll be a mono master!

PRO TIPS

ADJUSTABLE LAYERS

Use ***Layer>NewAdjustment Layer>Channel Mixer***. It creates a new adjustable layer that can be altered if you change your mind later on. Use this technique for Curves and Levels, too

ROSS HODDINOTT

1 Desaturate

This is one of the quickest and easiest routes to convert a colour shot and you've guessed it, the least favourable! Use the shortcut ***Ctrl+Shift+U*** or ***Image>Adjust> Desaturate*** to remove colour. Alternatively slide the desaturate slider to 0 in the Hue/Saturation dialogue box: (***Image>Adjustments>Hue/Saturation***).

Looking at the Swatch colour chart, all tones are distinctly muddy – especially yellows, which go more mid-grey than light grey. It can be fine for occasional use but spending a little more time and effort using one of the other methods will yield much better tonal range in your images.

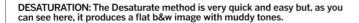

DESATURATION: The Desaturate method is very quick and easy but, as you can see here, it produces a flat b&w image with muddy tones.

2 Greyscale

This is a good starting point for most general shots and we'd recommend using this method most of the time. It's a much better way forward and quickly gives an interesting high contrast black & white image that often needs little extra work doing to it. Go to: ***Image>Mode>Greyscale*** to convert to mono.

You can see that the image looks less muddy and that the blues are a little darker. The tonal separation has created an interesting image. From here you can tweak the image using ***Curves/Levels***, especially if you select areas like skies or backgrounds beforehand.

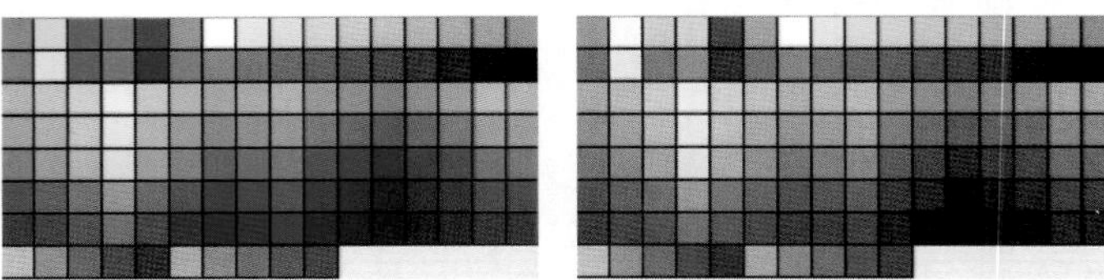

GREYSCALE: Using Greyscale is very easy and usually delivers very good results. Here, there is excellent tonal range and good contrast.

3 RGB channel adjustments

Photoshop uses a Red, Green and Blue channel to create the full spectrum of colours – just like a TV or your camera does.

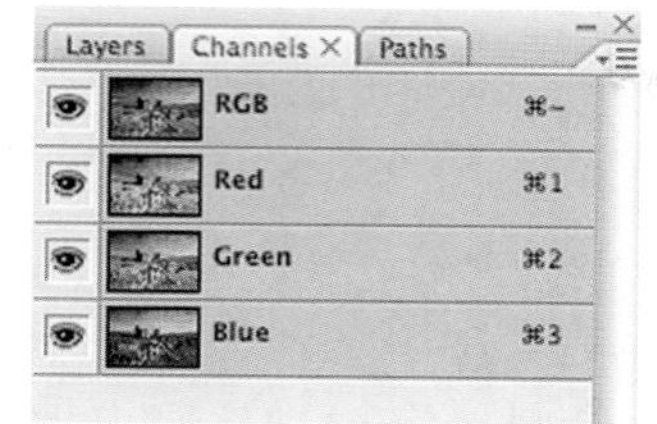

Open the Channels palette, click on one of the colours and it shows the channel in Greyscale. Each one reveals different tones, which together create a colour image. This is how colour photography was first created – by shooting on b&w film through consecutive exposures with a red, green and blue filter. You can choose any channel and then go to ***Image>Mode>Greyscale*** and save it as is. Remember to do a Save As and rename the image to preserve the original.

RGB CHANNELS: It's quite amazing to see how the different channels reproduce the various colours. Shoot a test yourself and study the results.

4 Channel Mixer

Channel Mixer is available for Photoshop CS but not Elements. This is a more complicated version of the previous technique, but can yield some very exciting results if you play around with the sliders for a while! The results are very similar to using a red, green or blue filter in front of your lens and you can mix the sliders to create other colours. Go to ***Image>Adjust>Channel Mixer*** to open the dialogue box. You will have a choice of Red, Green or Blue channels in the Output Channel menu. Now tick the Monochrome box to convert to black & white. The Red channel is a good starting point but check out each before making your decision.

You can mix a bit of one channel with another to create new effects. When adjusting the sliders you should aim to keep the combined values of all three sliders to about 100%. For example Red -20%, Green +140% and Blue -20%. Some strange effects (that usually degrade the final result) can be created by ignoring this! The Constant slider acts as a general brightness control. Try boosting colours beforehand with the Hue/Saturation control, this will boost contrast significantly in the black & white version. You can even pick a single colour to boost like Blue from the Edit menu if you like.

Levels... ⌘L
Auto Levels ⇧⌘L
Auto Contrast ⌥⇧⌘L
Auto Color ⇧⌘B
Curves... ⌘M
Color Balance... ⌘B
Brightness/Contrast...
Hue/Saturation... ⌘U
Desaturate ⇧⌘U
Match Color...
Replace Color...
Selective Color...
Channel Mixer...
Gradient Map...
Photo Filter...
Shadow/Highlight...
Exposure...
Invert ⌘I
Equalize
Threshold...
Posterize...
Variations...

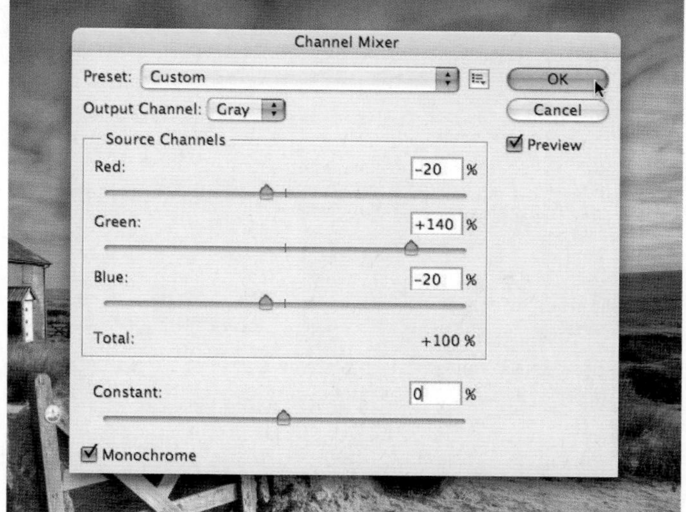

CHANNEL MIXER: This is one of the most involved and time-consuming methods, but your efforts will often be rewarded with the best results.

Hand-printed monochrome images

In days gone by, film photographers shooting black & white would use a traditional darkroom full of noxious chemicals to make prints. In fact some photographers still do this today. While it's an expensive, time-consuming and smelly process, it produces good results because of the control it gives over the final print. Black & white darkroom workers have great control over contrast and can 'dodge' and 'burn' light into various parts of the scene to selectively lighten and darken areas.

Fast forward to 2009, and this is now possible with Adobe Photoshop and Elements. Let's have a look at a simple method to transform a scene into monochrome, fine-tune its contrast and selectively change brightness using the Dodge and Burn tools.

1

Not every image is suitable for the mono treatment, so selecting your subject is important; but many photos (such as this one) can benefit from it. The conversion will add a bit of punch, hopefully transforming the shot from lack-lustre snapshot to dynamic masterpiece.

2

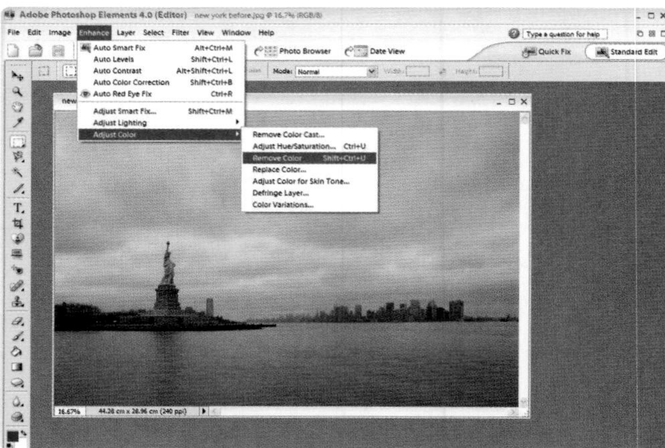

Removing the colour is just the first step (or the second in this tutorial), but can be done quickly and easily by going to ***Enhance>Adjust Color>Remove Color***. The result will be a rather grey looking image, but one that has undoubtedly changed to mono.

3

To revitalise your shot, go to ***Enhance>Adjust Lighting>Levels (Ctrl+L)***. Under the histogram you'll notice three small triangles. Drag the left and right ones inwards and the centre triangle slightly to the right until you are happy with the result, then click ***OK***.

4

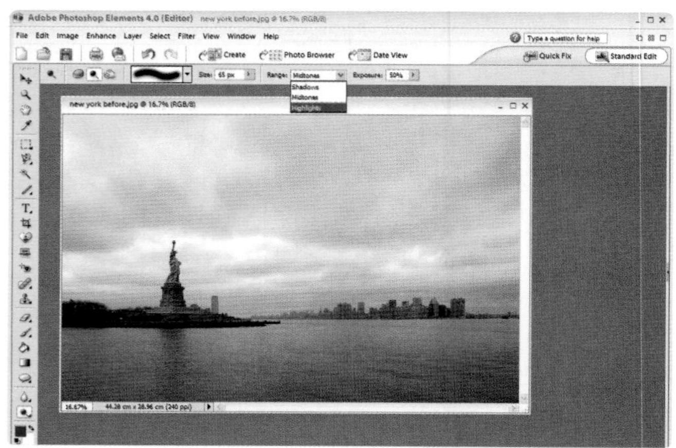

Select the Dodge tool (the bottom icon) from the tool palette. If you see a Sponge or Burn icon, click and hold the mouse over it and change it to Dodge (the lollipop-shaped icon). Set the Range to Highlights and the Exposure to around 4%. You're now ready to apply changes.

5

Use a large size brush to paint over the lighter areas to make them brighter. Then click and hold the Dodge icon, to change it to Burn (the hand icon). This time set the Range to Shadows with a 4% exposure and paint over the areas you want to make darker.

6

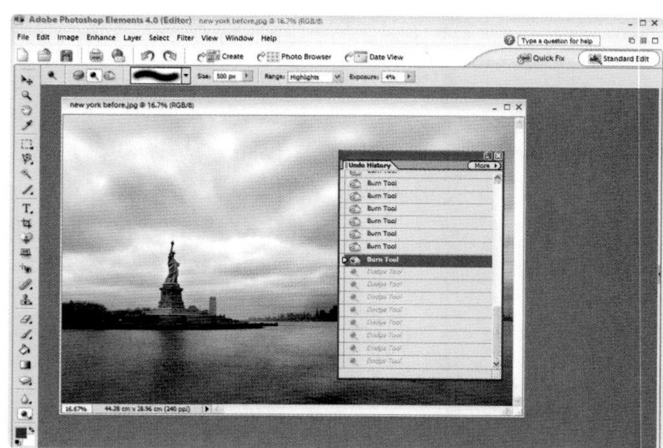

Swap between the Dodge and Burn tools to bring out the highlights and shadows. If you go too far, go to ***Window>Undo History***, which brings up the history palette and allow you to step back over the last few operations, or just hit ***Alt+Ctrl+Z*** to undo.

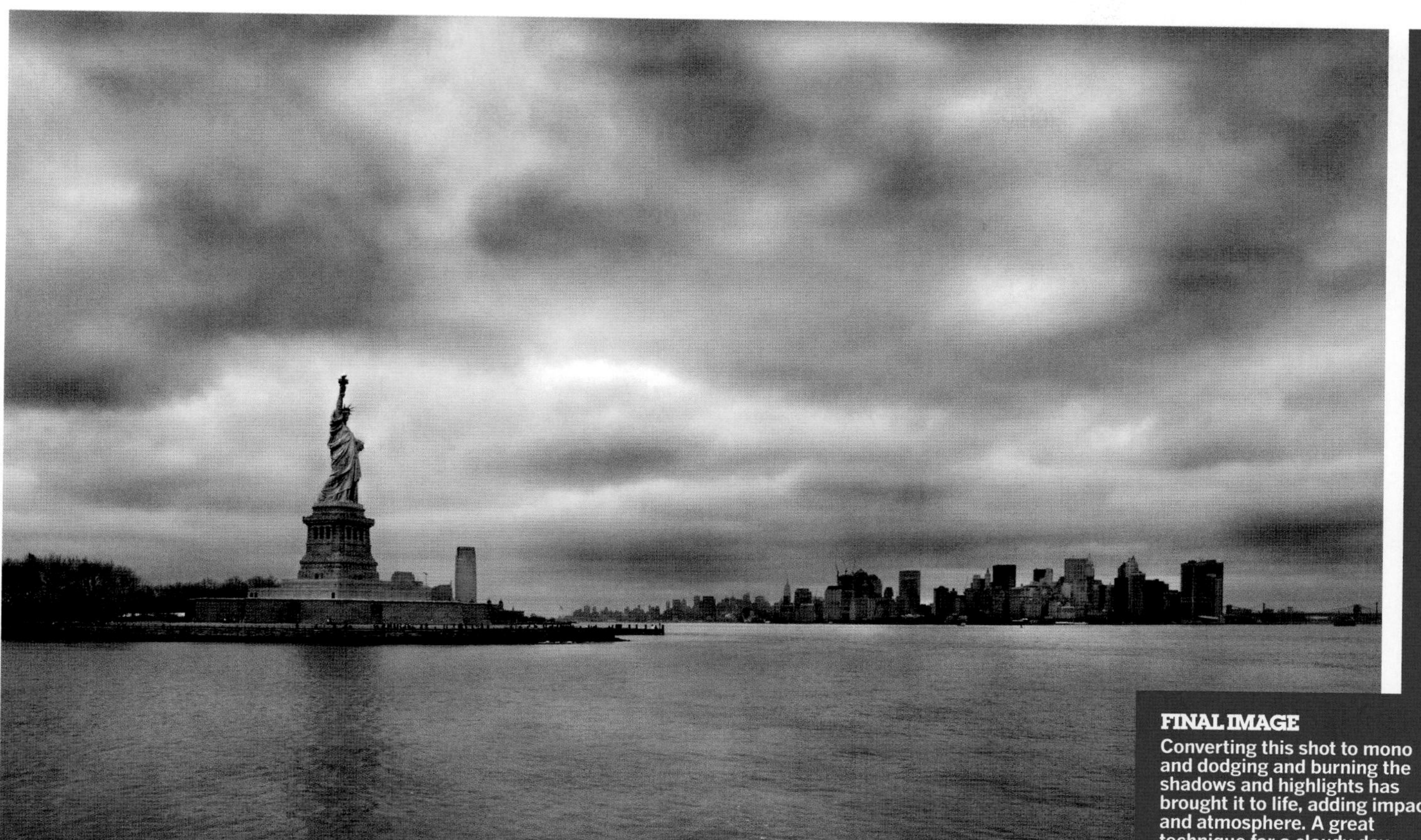

FINAL IMAGE
Converting this shot to mono and dodging and burning the shadows and highlights has brought it to life, adding impact and atmosphere. A great technique for a cloudy day.

Advanced adjustments using channels and filters

If you are using the full version of Photoshop or a newer version of Photoshop Elements (version 6 or higher), you can take more control over the colour removal process. Older versions of Photoshop dealt with this by using the Channel Mixer adjustment, but both Photoshop CS3 and Elements 6 have specific black & white conversion options, with a range of presets, that can be used in place of step 2.

Elements 6

From the menu bar, go to ***Enhance>Convert to Black & White***. This brings up a dedicated palette showing before and after images, a range of presets and manual adjustment of the Red, Green and Blue colour channels, as well as Contrast.

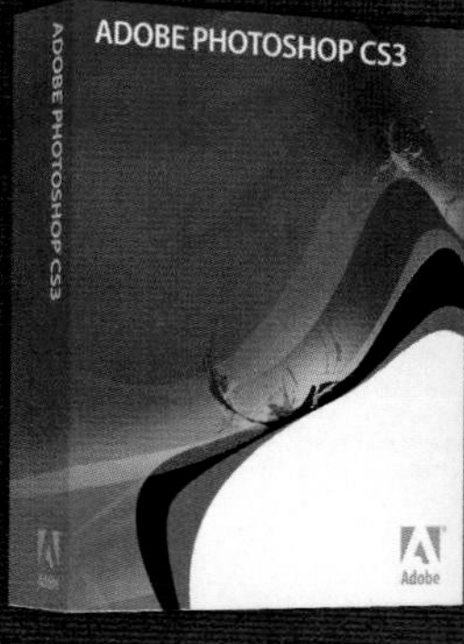

Photoshop CS3

From the menu bar, go to ***Image>Adjustments>Black & White***. This more advanced looking palette provides an extensive list of presets, a six-channel mixer for manual adjustment, plus colour tinting options to produce toned images.

Create a toned black & white image

There is so much you can do with a black & white photograph. You can play with its tones and contrast, make local 'dodging' and 'burning' adjustments to parts of the scene and even apply coloured tones or tints to give a certain look and feel.

This last part is easy to do badly, but looks great when it's done well. A slightly warm, brown cast (known as 'sepia') is reminiscent of those old photographs of yesteryear and gives the picture a classic look. Alternatively a cooler blue tone gives pictures a more modern, contemporary look. The secret is to experiment and not go over the top.

Toning a black & white picture well needs a good monochrome conversion to start with though. Here's how to really take control of your image and make the best job of it.

1

Open up your image and add a Black & White adjustment layer by clicking the half-black, half-white circle at the bottom of the layers palette. In earlier versions of the software, you can use a Channel Mixer adjustment layer instead.

2

Adjust the colour sliders until your image contains a pleasing array of tones, or choose a preset from the drop-down menu. In the Channel Mixer, check Monochrome and alter the sliders, ensuring they still add up to 100.

3

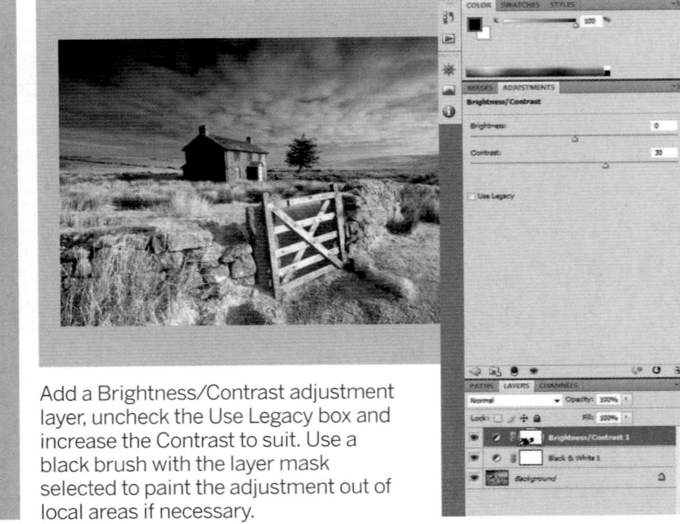

Add a Brightness/Contrast adjustment layer, uncheck the Use Legacy box and increase the Contrast to suit. Use a black brush with the layer mask selected to paint the adjustment out of local areas if necessary.

4

Now we need to think about dodging and burning. Add a Curves adjustment layer and push the curve hard upwards with a single point. Select the layer mask (the blank rectangle) and invert by pressing ***Ctrl + I***.

5

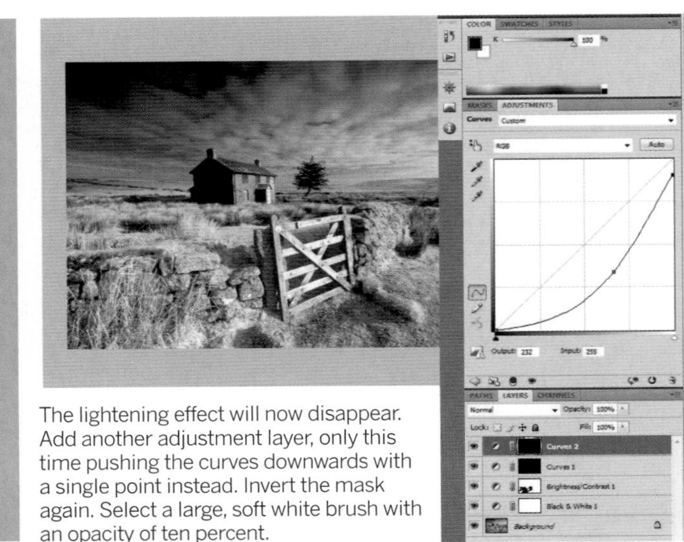

The lightening effect will now disappear. Add another adjustment layer, only this time pushing the curves downwards with a single point instead. Invert the mask again. Select a large, soft white brush with an opacity of ten percent.

6

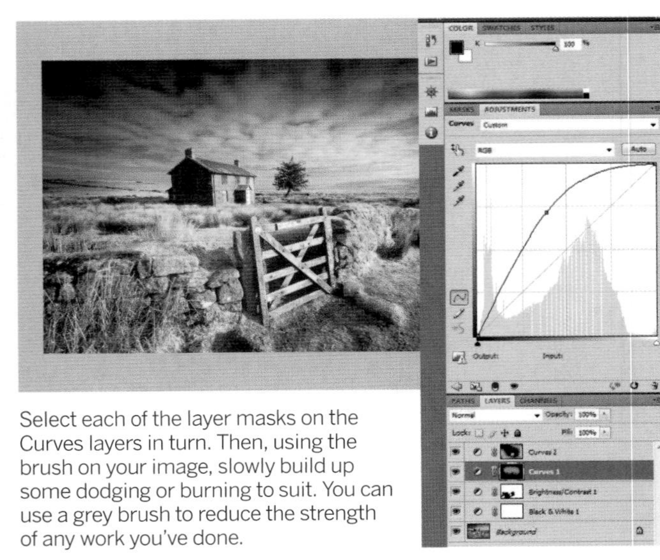

Select each of the layer masks on the Curves layers in turn. Then, using the brush on your image, slowly build up some dodging or burning to suit. You can use a grey brush to reduce the strength of any work you've done.

FINAL IMAGE
The final step is to merge all the layers together and add the final colours, again using a Colour Balance adjustment, to give an 'old' look to the photograph.

7

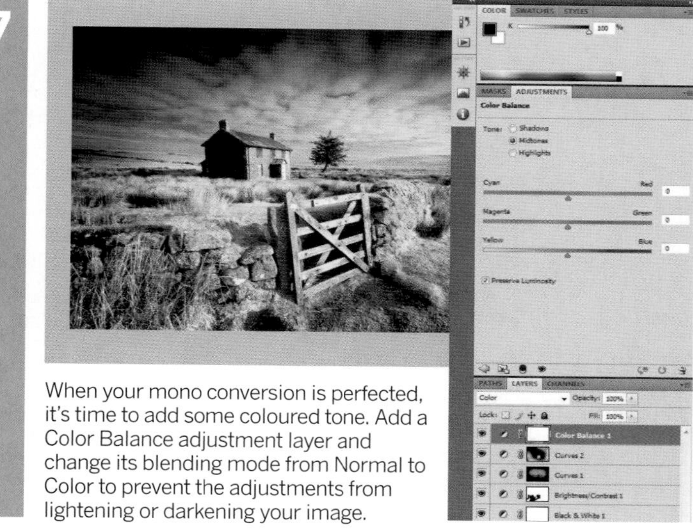

When your mono conversion is perfected, it's time to add some coloured tone. Add a Color Balance adjustment layer and change its blending mode from Normal to Color to prevent the adjustments from lightening or darkening your image.

8

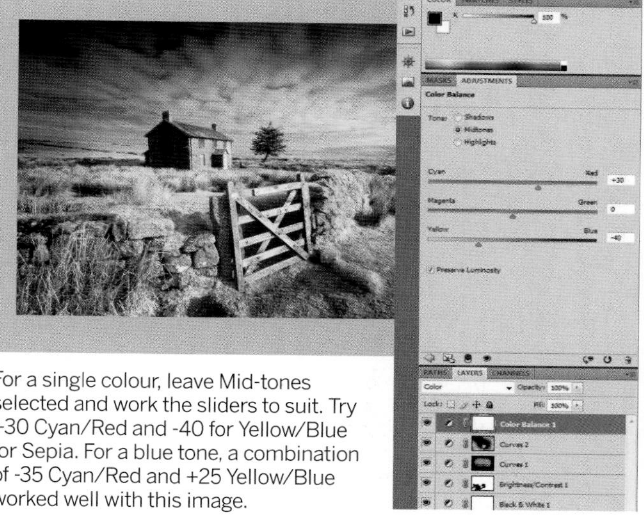

For a single colour, leave Mid-tones selected and work the sliders to suit. Try +30 Cyan/Red and -40 for Yellow/Blue for Sepia. For a blue tone, a combination of -35 Cyan/Red and +25 Yellow/Blue worked well with this image.

9

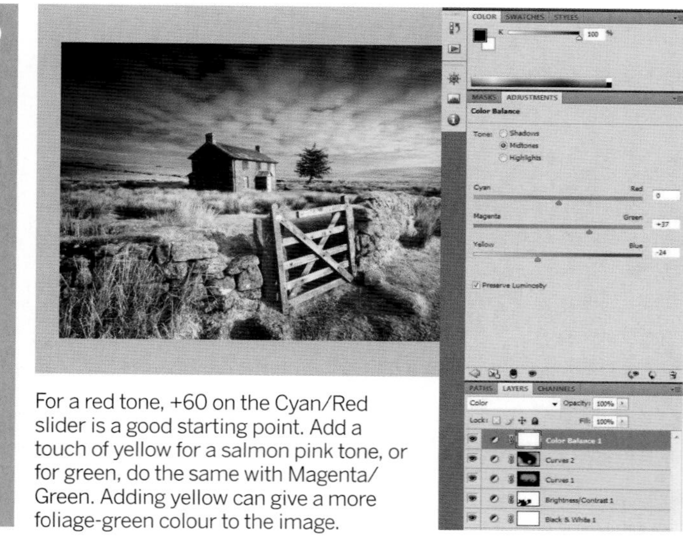

For a red tone, +60 on the Cyan/Red slider is a good starting point. Add a touch of yellow for a salmon pink tone, or for green, do the same with Magenta/Green. Adding yellow can give a more foliage-green colour to the image.

10

For split-toning, leave the mid-tones at zero and make changes to Shadows and then Highlights instead. As you increase the strength for each, the colours will seem to meet in the mid-tones, as with traditional toning.

Non-destructive Dodging and Burning

The Dodge and Burn tools in Adobe's Photoshop and Elements software are often used to selectively lighten or darken areas of a photograph. Black & white photographers are especially fond of this technique, which is perhaps not surprising, as it was invented in the monochrome darkroom. Traditional printers selectively shield ('dodge') and focus ('burn') light onto areas of light-sensitive photographic paper. In the digital darkroom, however, the process is much easier, as the Dodge and Burn tools can be used to paint-in these effects.

The problem with the Dodge and Burn tools in Photoshop and Elements, though, is that they are destructive. This means that they permanently alter the pixels in an image, and the only way of undoing their effects is to go back through the History, meaning all actions performed following dodging or burning will be lost too. It would be much better to be able to apply these edits as an adjustment layer that could be edited independently of the image.

You can do this by creating a new layer and painting it with black, white and grey colours before changing the blending mode to either Soft Light or Overlay. You can then edit this layer using the Brush tool, meaning it's possible to fine-tune the effects until they are to your exact taste.

ORIGINAL IMAGE

Technique watch

CHOOSING A BLENDING MODE

The Soft Light blending mode can produce subtle effects. If you want a more punchy result, use Overlay instead. Both these modes work by comparing corresponding pixels in the base layer and upper layer – darkening the base-layer pixel if the upper-layer pixel is darker, and brightening it if it's lighter. Soft Light does this to a lesser extent than Overlay.

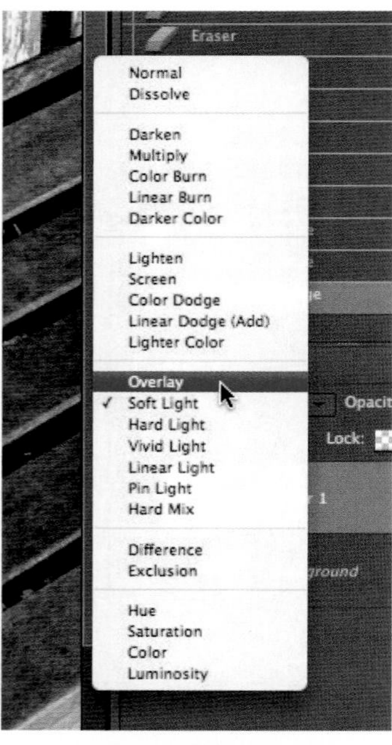

1

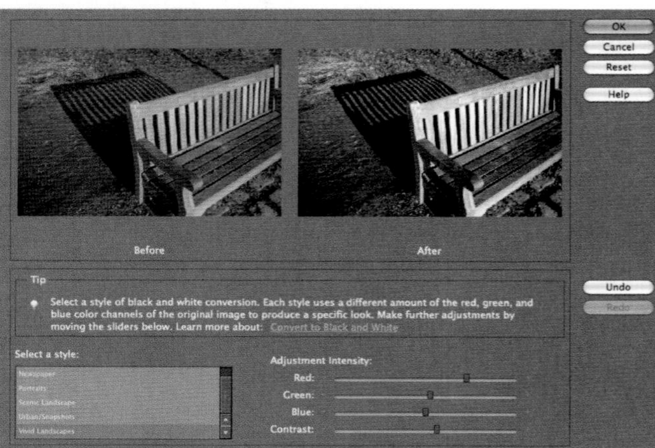

The original picture is transformed to black & white with the ***Enhance to Black and White*** command, which is found in the Enhance menu. Use the Vivid landscape preset and increased the contrast a bit for some added punch. Experiment with these settings to find the best for your picture.

2

The conversion isn't bad to be honest, but the wood of the bench is slightly bright and the shadow areas are a bit dark. To improve the image, correct this by burning and dodging these areas in a separate layer.

3

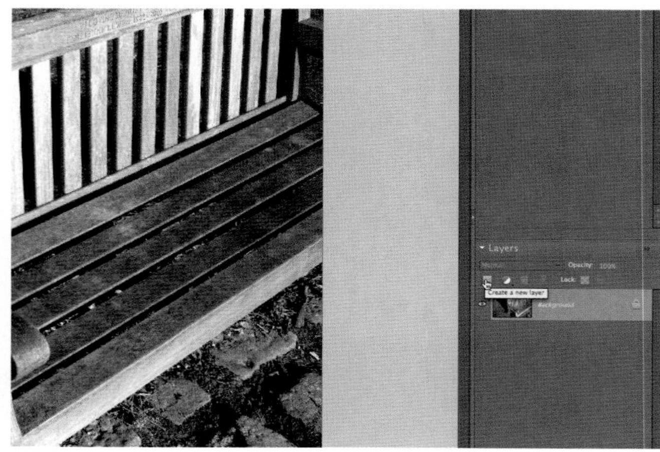

Create the new layer that will hold the dodging and burning effects by clicking the New Layer button. You can rename it by double-clicking the layer and typing in a new name. Change the blending mode to Soft Light.

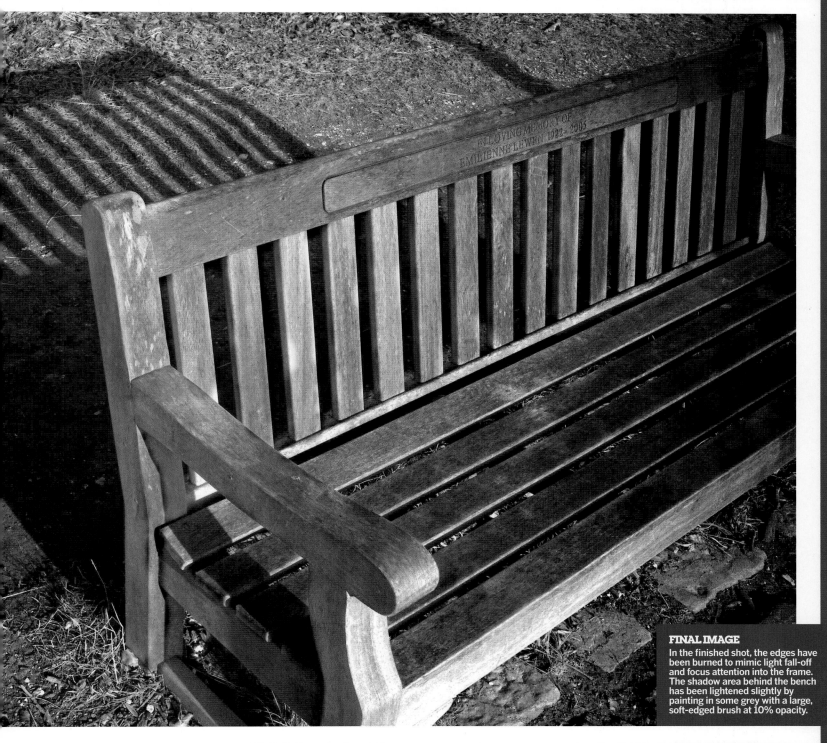

FINAL IMAGE
In the finished shot, the edges have been burned to mimic light fall-off and focus attention into the frame. The shadow area behind the bench has been lightened slightly by painting in some grey with a large, soft-edged brush at 10% opacity.

4

Using the Brush tool, paint black onto the areas you want to burn (darken) and white on the areas you want to dodge (lighten). You can use grey shades too if pure black or pure white would be too extreme.

5

Use all of the available brush options for the best results, playing with size and hardness, depending on the area you are dodging or burning. You may want to use a graphics tablet for added precision.

Recreating film grain

Users of digital SLRs usually strive for perfection. They don't want grain or noise in their images, or vignetting (darkening in the corners of the frame). However, there was a time when these problems were the norm for photographers. If you shot black & white images back in the days of film, grain was a fact of life, and many photographers also used vignetting to good artistic effect, drawing attention into the centre of a scene. It's possible to recreate this 'retro' monochrome look with a few tricks in Adobe Photoshop Elements – essentially introducing these 'artefacts' into a perfectly good image in a controlled fashion. Let's take a look to see how it's done.

1

This scene was shot using a Nikon D700 with a 50mm f/1.4 Nikkor lens. It's an OK result, but it can look much better in monochrome, especially with that old-school chemical-darkroom look. Thankfully, turning a colour picture into black & white in Elements is a piece of cake. Start by selecting ***Enhance>Convert to Black & White*** to bring up the dialogue box.

2

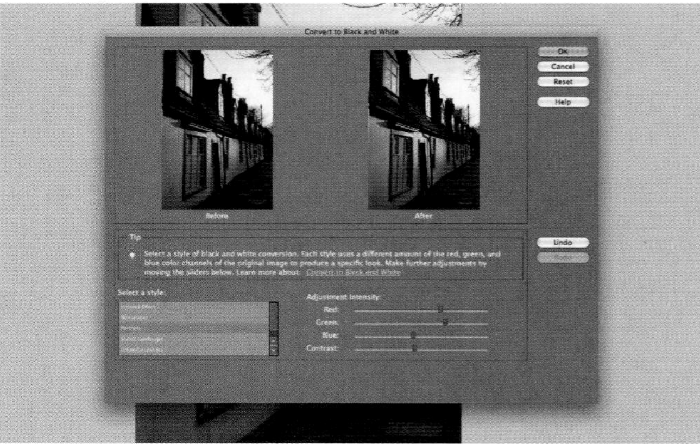

The sliders at the bottom control how the colours are converted to grey, simulating the effect of a coloured filter in front of the lens. Use one of the presets as a starting point (Urban/Snapshots) and darkened the blue tones in the sky a bit further by dragging the Blues slider to the left a little. The image is updated as you make changes, so feel free to experiment.

3

To simulate film grain, choose ***Noise>Add Noise*** from the Filters menu. Make sure Monochrome is ticked, and the Gaussian Distribution option is selected – this will mimic the look of a traditional black & white film. Don't be too heavy-handed with the Amount slider – a value of between five and eight percent is fine. Any more and the result will look unrealistic.

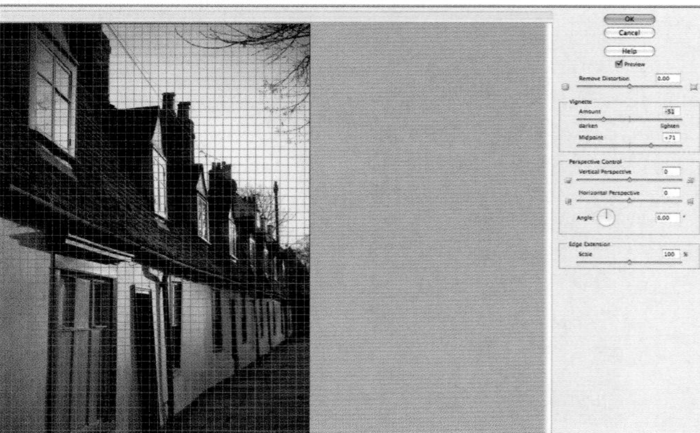

To add a subtle vignette, we'll call on the Correct Camera Distortion filter, from the Filters menu. This is usually used to fix such problems, but we'll use it the other way around. The Vignette controls are at the top-right of the screen. Drag the Amount slider left to darken the edges. You may also want to use the Midpoint slider to stop the effect creeping too far into the middle.

5

You can use some of the other editing tools in Elements to tidy up the result. A minor Levels adjustment, for instance, allows for a slight tweak to contrast. The Clone Stamp and Healing Brush tools were used to get rid of the telephone wires above the cottages. If there are other imperfections on your image, take your time to clone them out until you're happy with the result.

FINAL IMAGE
You could be forgiven for thinking that this final image was an old print from the mid-20th Century, all thanks to a few simple tweaks in Photoshop Elements.

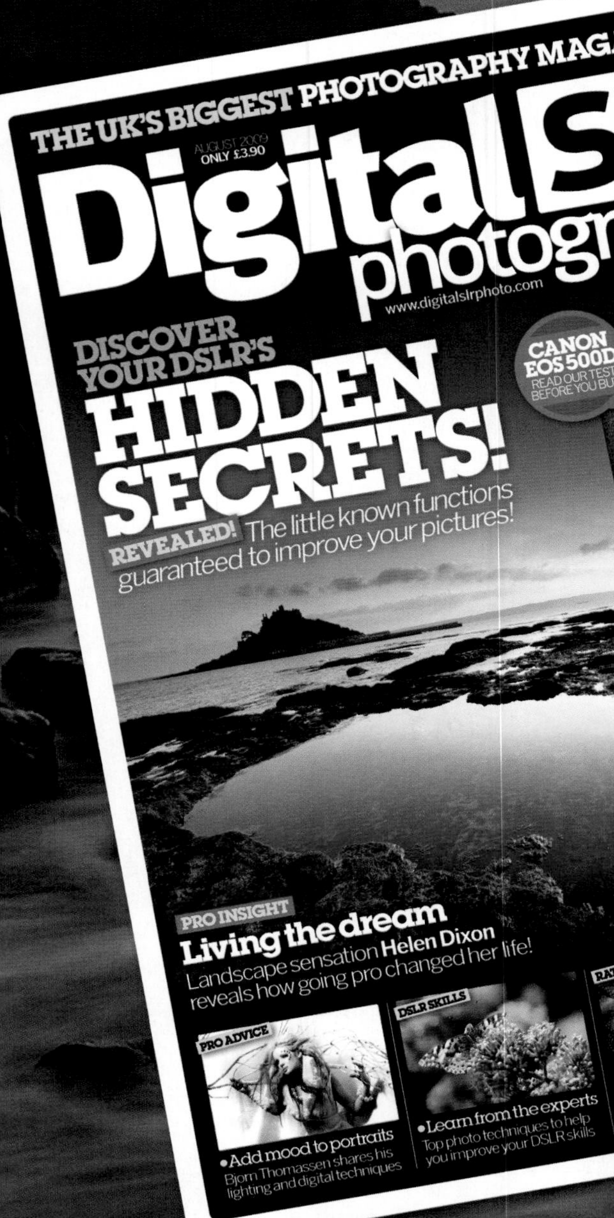

THE UK'S BIGGEST PHOTOGRAPHY MAGA
AUGUST 2009 ONLY £3.90
Digital S
photogr
www.digitalslrphoto.com
DISCOVER YOUR DSLR'S
HIDDEN SECRETS!
REVEALED! The little known functions guaranteed to improve your pictures!
CANON EOS 500D
READ OUR TEST BEFORE YOU BUY
PRO INSIGHT
Living the dream
Landscape sensation Helen Dixon reveals how going pro changed her life!
PRO ADVICE
Add mood to portraits
Bjorn Thomassen shares his lighting and digital techniques
DSLR SKILLS
Learn from the experts
Top photo techniques to help you improve your DSLR skills

3 issues for £1
when you subscribe today

Subscribe to *Digital SLR Photography* today and get your first 3 issues for just £1

If you decide that *Digital SLR Photography* is the magazine for you, then your subscription will **save you 18%** on the shop price – that's just **£3.16 an issue**, instead of £3.90 in the shops! Whether you're a beginner, enthusiast or a professional, *Digital SLR Photography* is packed with all the essential advice, reviews and tips you need to take your best-ever images!

Including: ✔ Expert tips and tricks ✔ Easy to follow step-by-step guides ✔ Essential equipment advice ✔ Inspirational articles

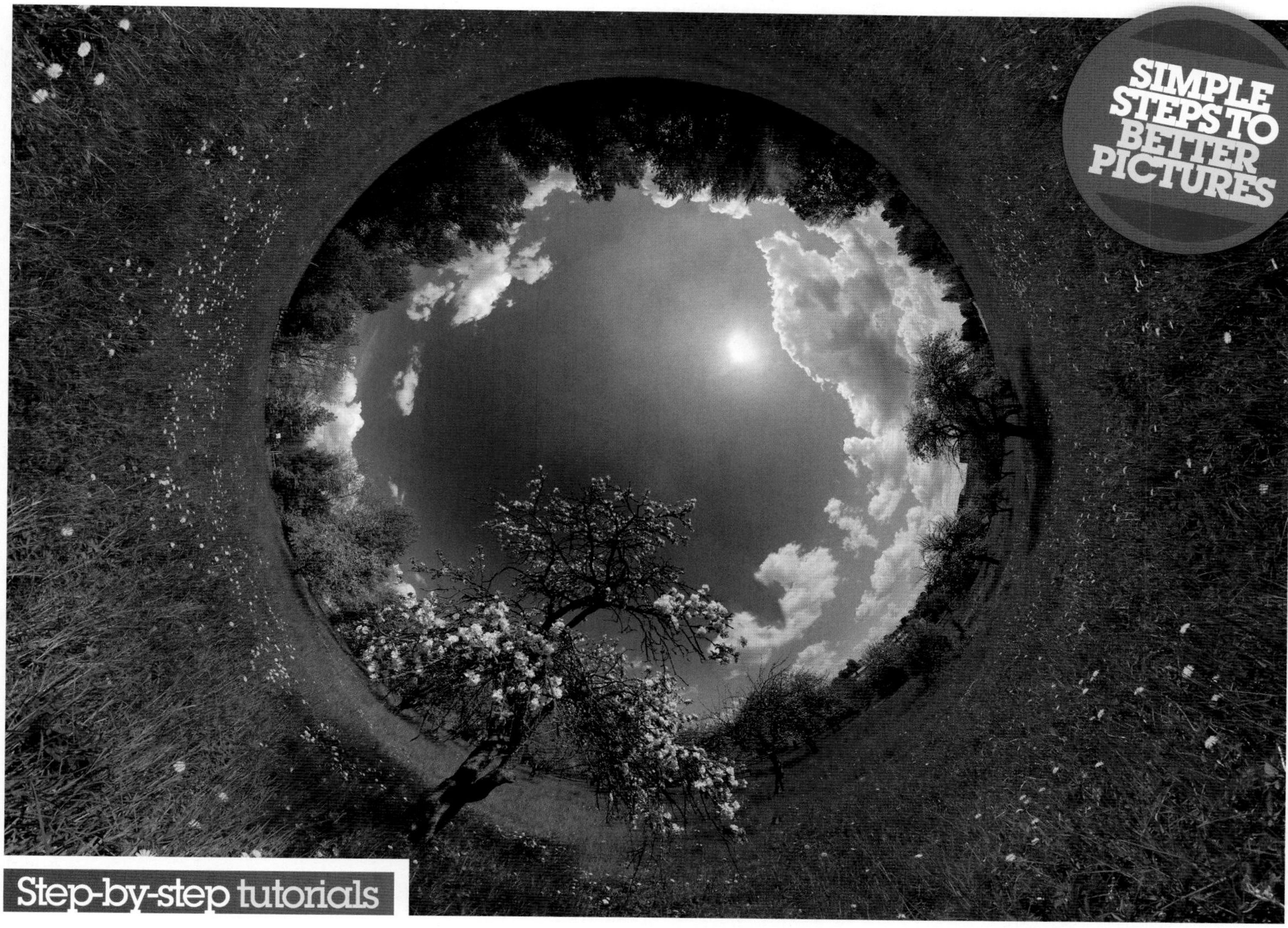

SIMPLE STEPS TO BETTER PICTURES

Step-by-step tutorials

PRO TECHNIQUE

Our team of leading experts provide advice for mastering advanced Photoshop skills

Using textured layers in Photoshop

How to create a digital panoramic

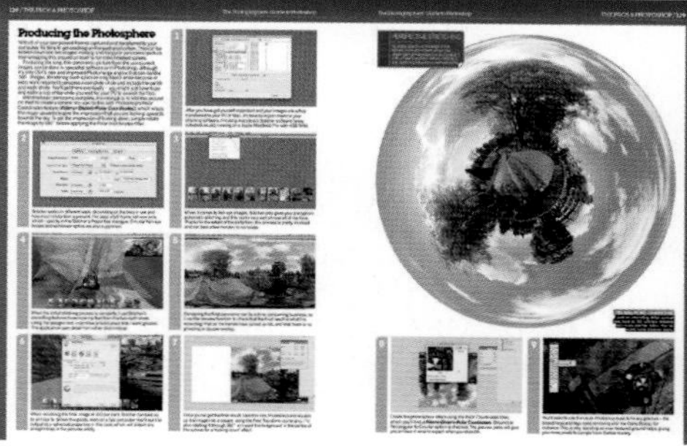
Producing the Photosphere

Pro advice: Adding textures

Lara Jade

Lara's sensational photographs made her one of the darlings of the website Flickr, but more recently her romantic mixture of self-portraiture and fashion work has attracted the attention of some big name professional clients too.

ADDING LAYERS of texture is a technique that is becoming increasingly popular among contemporary photographers. Essentially, it involves placing one image on top of the other, and once you've got the hang of it, it's really quite simple. The 'textures' could be anything, from an image of a tree bark or a leaf, to a scanned three-dimensional objects. Here, we'll show you how you can use them to enhance your shots and give them a unique look.

I first discovered textures when I was at college. I was learning on film cameras, so I began to study the work of a lot of the great film photographers. I noticed that quite a lot of their shots had an unusual look to them, so I started to search for a way of incorporating that effect into my own digital photography. I began looking on the internet for different textures, and I came across lots of grungy wood images. I started experimenting by laying them over my pictures to get that particular effect. There were several ways in which film photographers would achieve this look, whether it be using multiple layers, different chemicals, or even scratching the negatives or wet prints with metal implements like scissors. At the time, I spent many hours browsing the DeviantArt website, and I found a lot of this sort of texturing effect in the work I saw there. These days you can find it anywhere and, at the moment, I find Flickr is a really good place to look for inspiration.

To try and get that 'film look' in my own work, I initially tried adding the textures manually in Photoshop. I soon began downloading stock textures, which I could place on top of my images and eventually started to go out and shoot my own. I would bring them back and start mixing them with my images, just experimenting with different ways of adding and adjusting them in Photoshop.

Textured layers are actually very versatile, and without them, that look is very hard to achieve in Photoshop. With them, you can add different types of vignetting by darkening the corners of the texture, or you could overlay two different textures to create an image that's unique and different. When you add textures to a portrait, it helps to focus the viewer's attention on the subject by acting as a frame, helping to guide their eye towards it. They can be used in many ways, to convey different meanings.

I've found that textures work very well with my conceptual images in which the subject is quite far away and there's a bit of a story involved. With close-up portraits, where the subject fills the frame, they can be a bit overpowering, distracting the viewer's attention from the subject. For this type of work smoother textures tend to work best, especially those that are slightly blurry, with no distinct edges. Good examples of this are close-ups of leaves or a canvas. Anything that's not too busy, essentially. However, the best way to find this out is by experimenting. There's no set rule for each different picture, but with experience, you'll get to know what is more likely to work for a particular image.

When adding a texture to an image, it's a good idea to keep in mind that textures are meant to enhance a picture, not to make it. If your original is not very good, adding textures will not remedy this. However, if it's a great shot then textures can be used to compliment the result.

Often, less is more: too many textures in an image will overcomplicate it, making it too busy, and therefore distracting. Additionally, the result will be too focused on the digital side of things, rather than the photography.

To get you started, DeviantArt and StockExchange offer some really useful free textures that, despite not being very large, helped me to get started, and to learn what sort of textures worked with different images. On StockExchange, you just type in what sort of texture you want, and then download the files.

These days, though, I try and shoot my own textures when I'm out and about. I often have good luck finding what I want in abandoned locations – rusty walls, crumbling rock and so on. All fantastically grungy. I also use smoother textures, for example an out-of-focus shot of some fairy lights on a tree, which gives a lovely effect of colourful, blurred circles. Anything works really. You can even find things in your own house, such as the surface of a table, or a sponge in the bathroom!

I'd say that my favourite textures are those that occur in the natural world though. I was recently visiting the Lake District on a shoot, and I was photographing everything from the grass to the trees, including the mud on the ground and some old, crumbling leaves.

Girl leaning back
I wanted to achieve the old film look, so I found various textures relating to film, and overlaid them. I also added a light texture of fingerprints and made the whole image slightly sepia.

"There are other programs that can be used to add or enhance textures, but Photoshop is, in my experience, by far the best option, as it allows you the most control over each texture"

Male with grass
This was made by experimenting with various textures – paint strokes, green canvas and inversion. I also erased areas to keep the focus on the model.

Because of the time involved, I don't go out specifically to shoot textures anymore, but I do tend to take a few every time I'm out on a location shoot. Because of that, I just use whichever kit I have with me at the time. I usually shoot them handheld, in the middle of the afternoon, but, depending on the lighting conditions, a tripod and a flash can come in handy too. I also find that the Canon 24-70mm zoom lens I'm using at the moment is ideal, as the range allows me to stand a bit further back and take a variety of different shots of a single subject without having to move around too much, which saves time.

I give each texture in my library a specific name, such as 'colourful' or 'red'; and each goes into a folder, based on these names. It's really important to do this, as when you're looking through your textures folders, it will make it much easier to find exactly what you're looking for – libraries tend to build up quickly, so it's best to start as you mean to go on!

I do adjust my textures in the library too. In some of them, just the contrast will be enhanced, or a vignette added, but with others, I may have created them in Photoshop, by mixing them, blurring a layer, inverting them and adding them again; so some of them look very digital, whereas others look quite natural.

There are other programs that can be used to add or enhance textures, but Photoshop is, in my experience, by far the best option, as it allows you the most control over each texture, and how you can apply it to your image. There is a number of ways in which a texture can be added to an image. First of all, I copy them over the top of the original image, in a new layer. Then, using the layer blending modes in the Layers panel, I will most frequently experiment with the Soft Light, Multiply and Hard Light modes, (clicking 'Undo' if it doesn't look right!) Sometimes, I'll invert the texture and repeat the process, adding the inverted texture on top of the original texture layer, and desaturating it if necessary. You'll soon see what looks best with your picture. Reducing the opacity can help a texture to blend better with a certain image, as can erasing the middle of a texture, to help a portrait to stand out, leaving the texture as a vignette around the edge. For more conceptual images, I might reduce the opacity, and just delete creatively! Layer masks can also be used, but I've never found them necessary with the texture work I do. ■

Essential information

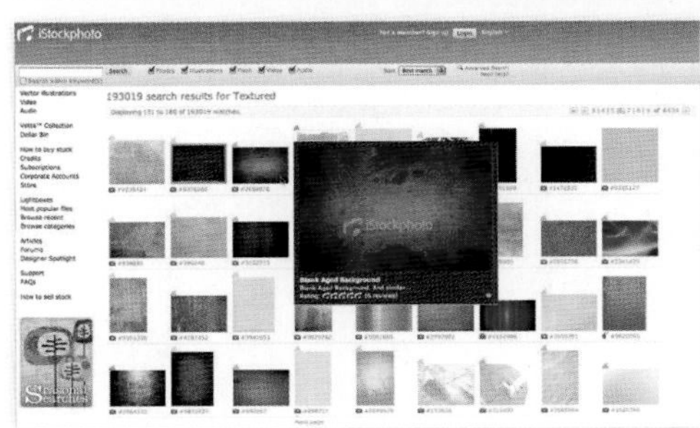

DOWNLOADING TEXTURES

Lara has two great textures packs for sale. Usually £50 per pack, readers of this MagBook can order them for £39 each. For details, please email larajadephotography@gmail.com. Here are some more great textures resources...

Stock Exchange - www.sxc.hu
CG Textures - www.cgtextures.com
Stock Vault - www.stockvault.net
Image After - www.imageafter.com
istockphoto - www.istockphoto.com

Using textured layers in Photoshop

Once you've shot your textures and decided which image you want to apply it to, it's time to fire up Photoshop and get cracking. The principle involves stacking a texture (or textures) on top of the original picture as a new layer, before changing the blending mode and reducing the opacity. There are parts of the picture that don't respond well to this treatment so it's important to be discerning and use the eraser or layer mask tools to select where you want the texture to appear.

PRO TIPS

RESOLUTION

When looking for textures, make sure you download high-quality files with enough resolution to work with. It's no good shooting Raw at the best quality and adding a low quality texture

1

Open the image and texture files in Photoshop and place them next to each other on the workspace rather than on top of each other. Usually we use Raw files, but for this step-by-step, we can work with a JPEG conversion, focusing on how you can add layers of texture to an existing image.

2

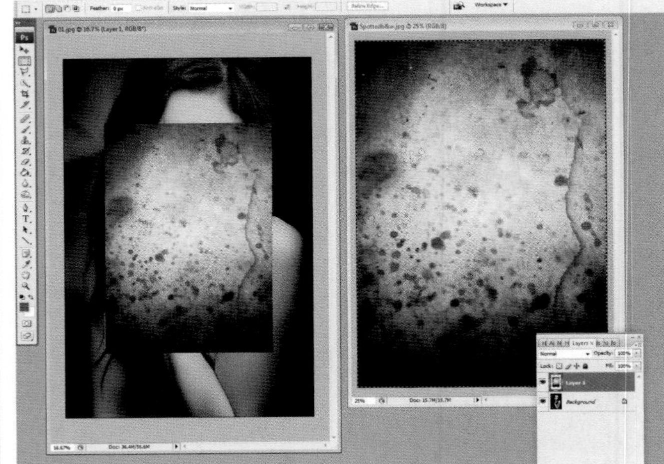

Now we need to take the texture and place it onto a new layer of my image file. To do this, select the texture (***Ctrl+A***) then copy it (***Ctrl+C***) and paste it onto the original image (***Ctrl+V***). By default, the texture will appear in a new layer on top of the background image.

3

On the layers palette, turn down the opacity of your texture to suit your photo (here, we chose an Opacity of 90%). We then changed the layer blend mode to Soft Light. Next, go to Free Transform (***Ctrl+T***) and drag the texture edges to fit the image. Remember to save as you go.

4

On portrait shots, textures can be quite unflattering in key areas, so it's always best to remove them from skin, facial features and any parts of the photograph that stand out. Using a large, soft-edged brush, we can erase texture from such areas of the image.

5

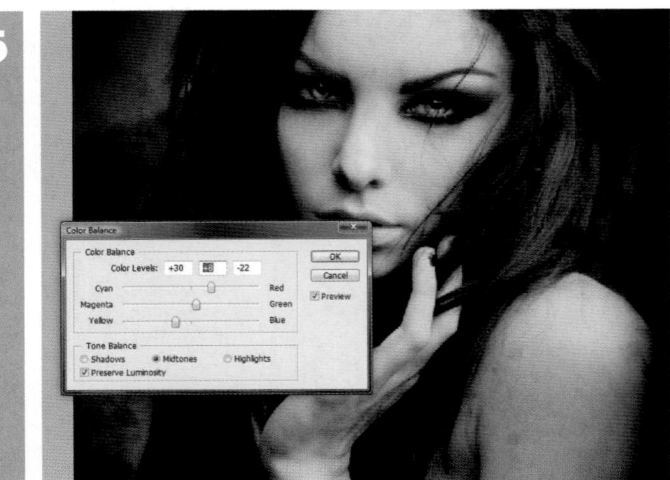

With a basic texture in place, we can decide to add some colour (ensuring the image mode is set to either RGB or CMYK). There are various ways to do this, but we'll use ***Image>Adjustments>Color Balance*** and play around with sliders to create a sepia-like effect over the photo.

6

Multiple texturing can often be a benefit to your technique, so, following the process seen in steps 1-4, we add one final texture; though here we invert the texture using ***Image>Adjustments>Invert*** and change the layer blend mode to Screen, turning the Opacity down to 45%.

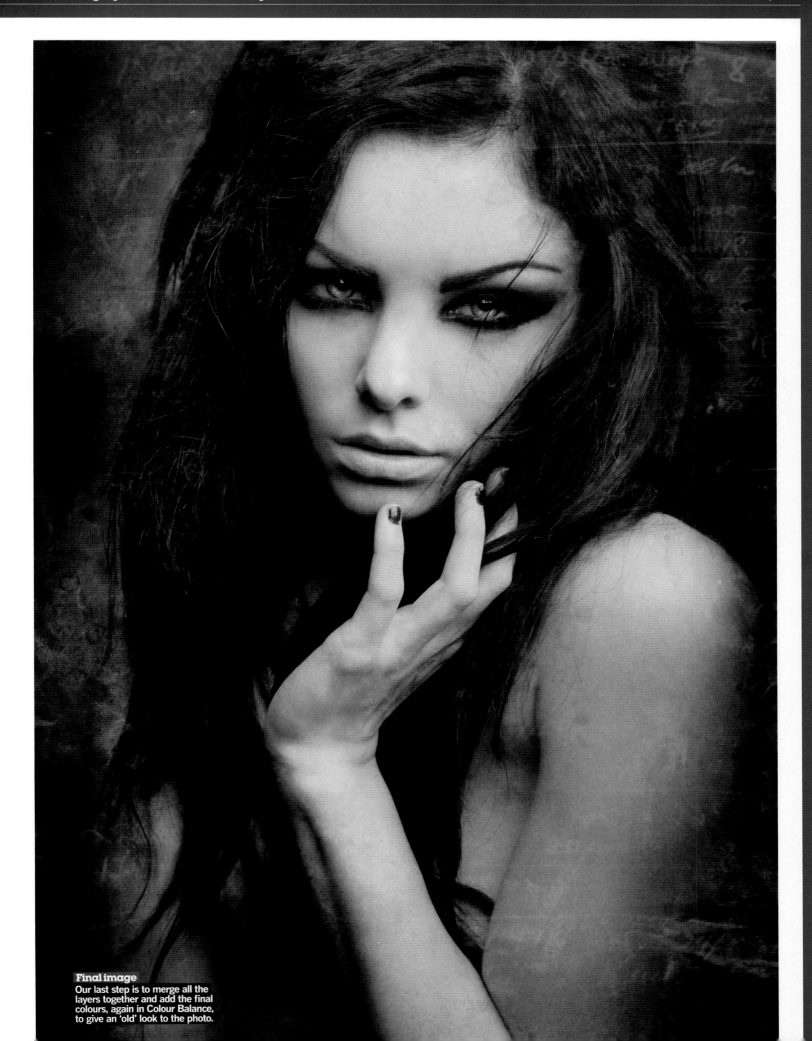

Final image
Our last step is to merge all the layers together and add the final colours, again in Colour Balance, to give an 'old' look to the photo.

Pro advice: Panoramics

Lee Frost

Lee's the author of several best-selling books on photography and brings with him years of expertise and unrivalled photo technique advice. You can read Lee's thoughts on photography each month in *Digital SLR Photography* magazine.

PANORAMIC PHOTOGRAPHY has played a central role in my career for many years now. I was first inspired to try it after buying a copy of Colin Prior's *Highland Wilderness* back in the early '90s. It's a book of his shots of the wild landscape of northern Scotland, taken with a 6x17cm panoramic rollfilm camera. It was as if I had found the missing piece to my own creative jigsaw, and after months of saving, I managed to scrape enough money together to buy a second-hand Fuji G617.

It was the start of a love affair that endures to this day and has seen me work with a range of different cameras, from Hasselblad XPans, Horseman 612s and Art 617s, to a Fotoman, a Fuji GX-617 which I still own and use, and even a natty handmade 360° camera called a Lookaround. Oh, and along the way I wrote a best-selling book on the art of panoramic photography, funnily-enough titled *Lee Frost's Panoramic Photography*. You should buy a copy – it really is very good!

However, since I stepped over the to dark side, with the purchase of my first digital SLR, I've discovered a whole other side to panoramic photography in the form of image stitching, and I have to say that I'm impressed.

Initially, I refused to believe that any digital technique could match the quality I was achieving with my Fuji GX-617 and Fuji Velvia slide film. When the resulting 6x17cm trannies are scanned on a high-end Imacon scanner (admittedly at £9 a pop), I'm able to output enormous prints where every detail is as clear as a bell – some of my panoramas have been printed as big as 3x1m and they still look good. What's more, those images are created with one shot, so there's no faffing around at a computer.

Oh, I knew what I was talking about. I'd been at this game for years and I had honed my craft. No digital upstart was going to convince me to part with my beloved Fuji. Then out of curiosity, I secretly shot a sequence of images with my Canon EOS-1Ds MkIII, stitched them together, sat back and thought, 'WOW!'

So simple, so quick, and so good. Yet again, I realised that being a stubborn old git, when it came to embracing digital technology, was doing me more harm than good. It's great to have principles, but the reality is that I'd sell my granny for the sake of a great shot, so I realised it was time to stop being silly and just face facts – creating digital panoramas is not only easy, but it's versatile and offers the photographer endless creative potential.

With a panoramic film camera, you're limited to the field-of-view offered by the lens or lenses available for that particular model, and the widest focal length rarely captures any more than you could in a single shot with a 17mm lens on a DSLR. But if you shoot a series of digital images and stitch them, not only can you use any of the lenses in your kit, from super-wide to telephoto, you can also take as many individual frames as you like and cover any angle up to 360°. If you're really serious you can shoot more than one row of images and stitch them all together to create gigantic image files. At the heart of this technique is the software you use to stitch the images together, and the good news is that it's now better than ever, making the task of creating perfect results with the minimum of fuss, both quick and easy.

A friend of mine started making digital panoramas in the days when each frame had to be picked up and dropped onto an enlarged canvas in Photoshop and manually blended, using layer masks and the brush tool, to merge them together without showing the joins. The

Essential information

KEEP KIT LEVEL!

It is crucial to make sure your camera is level. There's no point setting up your tripod, sticking a spirit level on the camera's hotshoe and levelling the camera, because as soon as you pan left or right to take the next shot, it will go off-level. Instead, ensure the base on which the tripod head sits is level in all directions – either by adjusting the tripod legs or by purchasing a levelling base that sits between the tripod legs and head. I use a Gitzo Levelling base, giving me 15° of adjustment with its cup and half-ball design and a bullseye bubble to check for level. The latest model (GS5120LVL) costs aroubd £100. Manfrotto produces a simpler model known as the MN338 Levelling Base (£70), which uses three thumbwheels to create a level platform. Once the platform is level, adjust the head itself to make sure it's level too – then, it should be possible to pan through 360° without a hitch.

ST MARY'S LIGHTHOUSE,
Even when shooting in low-light with long exposures, the latest stitching software can produce seamless images. I shot ten individual frames for this dusk scene.

NEWCASTLE QUAYSIDE
This panorama was created from a sequence of eight frames, all shot handheld with an infrared-modified DSLR then stiched using Photomerge in Photoshop CS3.

results looked fantastic, but it took hours for him to construct a single panorama, and he was already a Photoshop wizard. Looking back, it was probably watching him that put me off digital imaging – it seemed far more complicated than just pressing the shutter release of a panoramic camera and capturing a scene on film.

But like most things digital, advances and improvements have been made and literally all you need to do now is put the individual images that will make up the final panorama into a folder on your computer, open your stitching software, browse your folders to find the right one, click OK, and sit back while the software does all the hard work. Minutes later, a perfect panoramic image appears on your screen

I use Photomerge in Adobe Photoshop CS3 to do all my stitching at the moment, and I have to say that it's absolutely fantastic; but the Photomerge tool in Photoshop CS2 was pretty terrible in comparison. So if you've tried stitching images with software that's more than a couple of years old, only to be disappointed with the results, it's probably time to upgrade to a later version, or maybe you should try a different package altogether. That's exactly how I ended up using Photoshop CS3. I was more than happy with CS2, until I sat down one day with the intention of stitching some images and Photomerge in CS2, struggled, to the point that I gave up, phoned a mate and asked for help. His response was: "Download the free trial for CS3 and try that". I did, and it worked brilliantly. Needless to say, as soon my free trial ended I purchased an upgrade and have been using it ever since – and I'm told that Photomerge in CS 4 is even better, so I look forward to giving that a try some time soon!

If you don't have a recent version of Photoshop that you can upgrade, or if you don't use it at all, you'll need to buy some proprietary ▸

VAL D'ORCIA, TUSCANY
At dawn, the Val d'Orcia in Tuscany has to be one of the most beautiful views in the world, but I never tire of shooting it, or rising at 4.30am to get there in time. It was made for the panoramic format.

Essential information

GADGETS & GIZMOS

Once you start looking, you'll find all kinds of gadgets, designed to help create perfect stitched panoramas – levelling bases/heads, panoramic plates, nodal slides and brackets, etc. Some cost hundreds of pounds and look so complicated that you'd need a degree in engineering to set them up. To be honest, most of these gizmos are unnecessary, simply because modern stitching software is so good, it automatically corrects distortion and parallax. I use a Gitzo levelling base which allows me to level the tripod head even if the tripod isn't level. Once the camera platform on the tripod head is level, I can rotate the camera, which will remain level. I've also shot sequences handheld where the camera wasn't level, and the results still looked great.

If you want a pukka panoramic system, Really Right Stuff offers the most comprehensive range of accessories. The snag is that no UK distributor imports it, so you need to buy it from the States. Pro snapper Jon Hicks swears by his RRS kit – a ball head and panning clamp, an 'L' plate that lets him turn the camera on its side without adjusting the tripod head, and a flat rail that rotates the camera on the lenses optical centre. The gear isn't cheap, thanks to the exchange rate (around £600 for that set-up), but it will last a lifetime. An alternative is to buy a multi-purpose rail for your tripod head, so you can adjust the camera position to avoid parallax. Macro focusing rails are ideal, such as the Manfrotto 454 Micro Positioning Plate that costs just £56 or the Novoflex Castel-L at £140. These gadgets may seem expensive, but levelling your camera is the most important factor when capturing panoramics.

stitching software. There are various options (see panel), but I know several other photographers who use the application PTGui (www.ptgui.com) and say it's fantastic. Costing only £75 for the latest personal version, it also represents excellent value for money.

So, as long as your software will handle the stitching, all you need to do then is make sure you produce a set of photographs that the application can work with to construct a seamless panorama.

The key here is control and planning – you need to decide what you're going to do before you do it, ie. getting yourself organised and establishing a work routine that you can repeat time after time so it becomes almost second nature when you are working in the field.

You can shoot panoramic sequences handheld and successfully stitch them afterwards (in fact I have, on many occasions) but there's a greater chance that the camera will drift out of level as you move it between shots. This means that the software has to work harder and you might end up with a jagged edge to the stitched panorama that must be cropped off – which could mean losing vital subject matter, like the top of a building. To avoid this, set your zoom to a wider focal length, so you've got more room for error if you do have to crop later on. A far better option, though, is to mount your camera on a tripod, so you can level it properly, keep it level from frame to frame, and not have to worry about camera shake.

Though it isn't essential to do so, it also makes sense to turn your camera on its side so that the pixel depth of the panorama will be maximised. With my Canon EOS-1Ds MkIII on its side, the output depth at 300dpi is almost 19in, whereas if I were shooting in landscape format it would be less than 13in.

TARANSAY, OUTER HEBRIDES
Coastal landscape photography is my main passion – there's something hypnotic about the sea. This panorama shows the view from Taransay towards the south of Harris in the Outer Hebrides.

With the camera on a tripod, you need to decide where the panorama will begin and end. In the countryside, I rarely cover more than 90° and more often than not, much less. However, in urban locations or when shooting interiors, markets and so on, you could go for a full 360° pan – the results look amazing.

In terms of lens choice, that's really down to individual situations and needs. I tend to use my Canon 24-70mm f/2.8L zoom more than any other, and occasionally a 70-200mm. If you go too wide there will be a lot of distortion in each image and even if the software manages to cope with it, the results can look odd. Saying that, you don't always have to create panoramas that look natural, so be prepared to experiment and throw caution to the wind – you could be pleasantly surprised by the outcome.

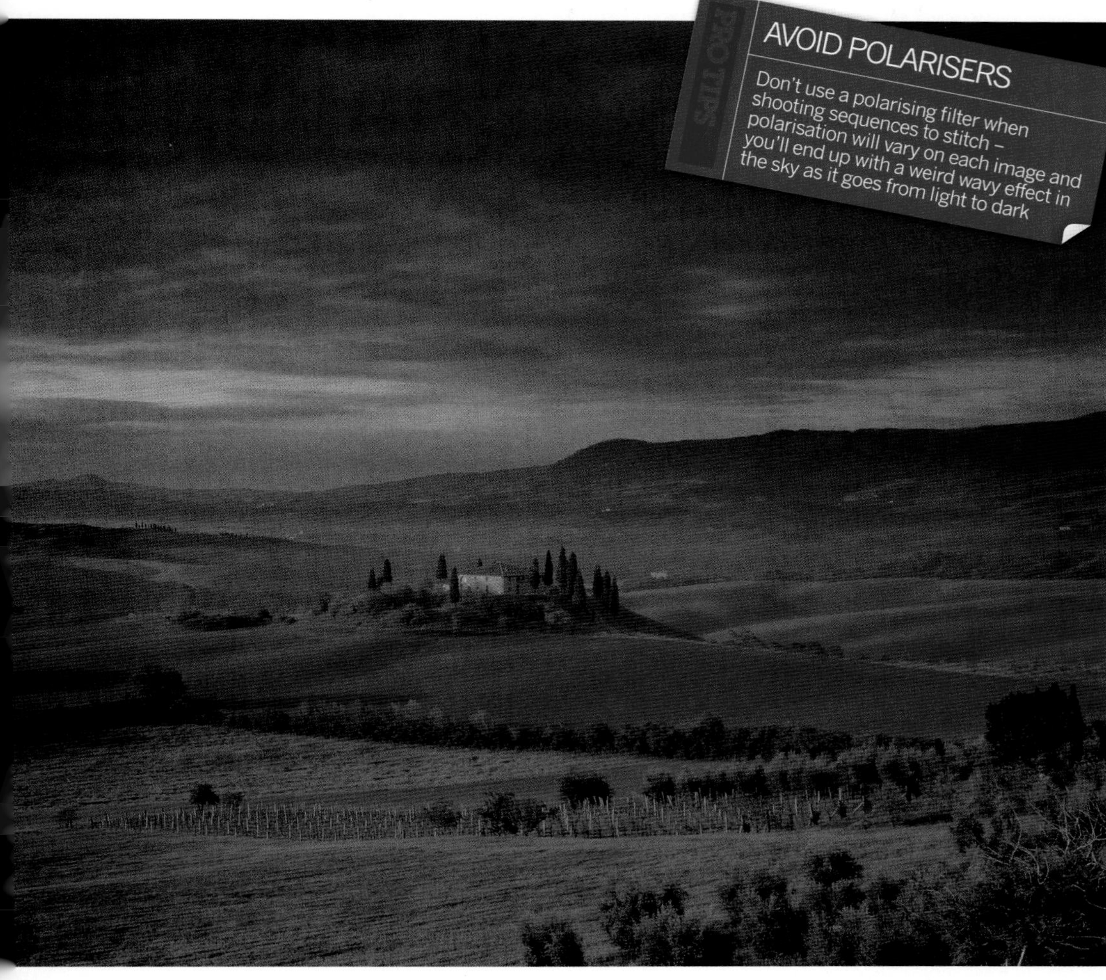

PRO TIPS

AVOID POLARISERS

Don't use a polarising filter when shooting sequences to stitch – polarisation will vary on each image and you'll end up with a weird wavy effect in the sky as it goes from light to dark

Essential information

PARALLAX ERROR & THE NODAL POINT

The main technical issue you have to face when shooting panoramas is parallax error, which is caused when you rotate the camera between frames and the alignment of elements in the scene changes slightly; so the frames don't line up perfectly when stitched. The wider the focal length you use for the individual frames, the more obvious this will be.

A couple of years ago, this was the main factor that caused stitching software to struggle, but if you make sure that the frames in your sequence overlap the one before by at least 30%, the latest software manages to overcome parallax error with ease, because you're giving it the space to find a suitable blending path through each pair of images, therefore areas where parallax error is a problem can be avoided. To actually find the optical centre of a lens, or a focal length setting on a zoom, set up two objects roughly one metre apart – poles in the ground work well, or coloured pencils taped to a tabletop (as shown below). Position your camera so that the two objects are perfectly aligned and the camera is levelled as though you were about to shoot a sequence of images to be stitched together to make a panorama.

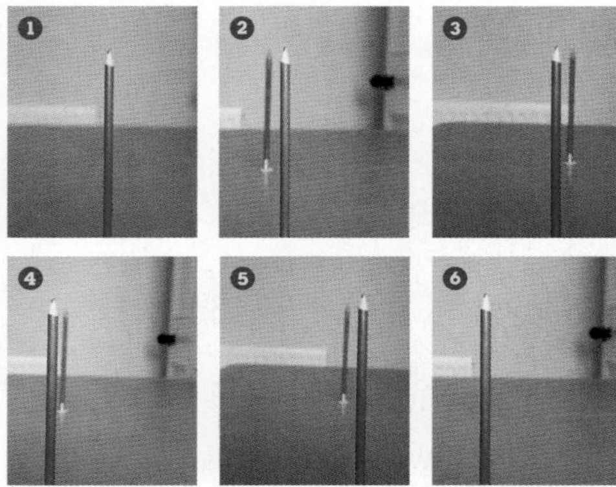

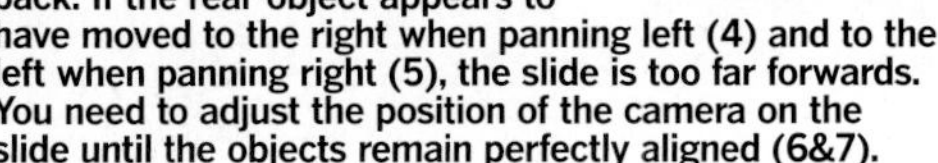

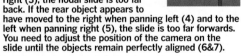

(1) First take a shot with the two objects aligned in the centre of the frame, then pan the camera to the left, take a second shot, then pan right and take a third. If the rear object appears to have moved slightly to the left (2) when panning left and to the right when panning right (3), the nodal slide is too far back. If the rear object appears to have moved to the right when panning left (4) and to the left when panning right (5), the slide is too far forwards. You need to adjust the position of the camera on the slide until the objects remain perfectly aligned (6&7).

Once you've found the optical centre for a specific lens of focal length setting on a zoom, mark its position on the nodal slide. Do this for all the lenses you're going to use to create panoramas, then when you're on location you know exactly where to position the camera so you're rotating it on its optical centre. A length of masking tape can be stuck to the slide and marked with lines denoting each focal length.

Whatever location you shoot, be aware that moving elements can cause problems. If you shoot in low light and have to use long exposures, things like breaking waves may cause alignment problems, as may urban scenes, where there's moving traffic or people. If in doubt, give it a try and see what happens. It may be that you have to do a little retouching in post-production, perhaps using the clone stamp tool to remove unwanted or repeated elements, or to soften visible joins between images. The more experience you gain, the more straightforward these problems are to solve, so don't let the risk of them put you off trying.

A couple of common mistakes that beginners to panoramic photography often make are to leave their DSLR set to autofocus and also leave it set on an automatic exposure mode.

The first error may not cause problems if you're shooting with a wide-ish focal length, set to a small aperture such as f/11 or f/16, because there will usually be sufficient depth-of-field to achieve front-to-back sharpness, even if the lens adjusts focus from frame to frame. That said, it makes sense to switch the camera to manual focus so that once you set focus you know it will stay the same throughout the sequence.

Shooting on auto exposure is more serious, and is almost guaranteed to cause problems, because the camera will adjust exposure for each frame, which means image density varies from one frame to the next and the stitching software will blow a gasket trying to blend the images, failing miserably in the process.

To avoid this, point your camera to a part of the scene you want to shoot that looks fairly average – ie. not the brightest or the darkest area, but rather a mid-tone, and take a test shot. If the exposure looks OK, switch your camera to metered manual mode (M on the exposure mode dial), set the required exposure, and use exactly the same exposure for each frame in the sequence. In high contrast light it may mean that some parts of the panorama are underexposed and others overexposed, but if you want a seamless end result you must keep the exposure consistent.

The final factor is to make sure you overlap each image by at least 30 per cent, so that the stitching software can find a convenient path through each pair of images and blend them together seamlessly. It's clever stuff, this digital technology – it makes me wonder, where it's going to take photography next. ▸

How to create a digital panoramic

So the theory is simple enough: shoot a load of overlapping pictures, then join them together on your computer afterwards. In the past this would have needed specialist software costing quite a few quid, though nowadays Photoshop and Elements can do this themselves, with great results.

Shooting the individual frames that you'll be splicing together is something that's important to get right too. You'll need a tripod (if you are shooting a distant landscape this doesn't have to be specialist panoramic model), and a spirit level will help get things straight. Set an average exposure that is good for the whole scene and lock this in using Manual exposure mode, so that the brightness between frames doesn't change unnaturally.

When you're back at base, it's then a case of taking those individual shots into Photoshop and using the Photomerge command to kick off the merging step. It's an intuitive process that will produce an image that you can fine-tune further using Photoshop's normal editing tools. Let's see how it's done.

1

Mount your camera on a tripod in vertical format and make sure the tripod base is level, so that when you rotate the camera between shots, it remains level. Do a quick practise scan across the scene to decide where you want it to begin and end.

2

Take a test shot from an average part of the scene – not the lightest or the darkest – check the image and histogram, and if all looks OK, set that exposure with your camera in manual mode, so you use exactly the same exposure for each frame.

3

Swing the camera to the far left of the view you want to capture, focus manually and take a shot of your left hand with your fingers pointing to the right. This denotes where the sequence begins so you don't get confused later on.

4

Take the first shot of the sequence, move the camera slightly to the right and make your second exposure. Repeat this until you reach the other end of the scene, making sure you overlap each image by 30-40% to enable easy stitching.

5

Take a shot of your right hand with your fingers pointing to the left to denote the end of the sequence. When you download the files to your computer you'll know that all the images between the two hand shots are in the same sequence.

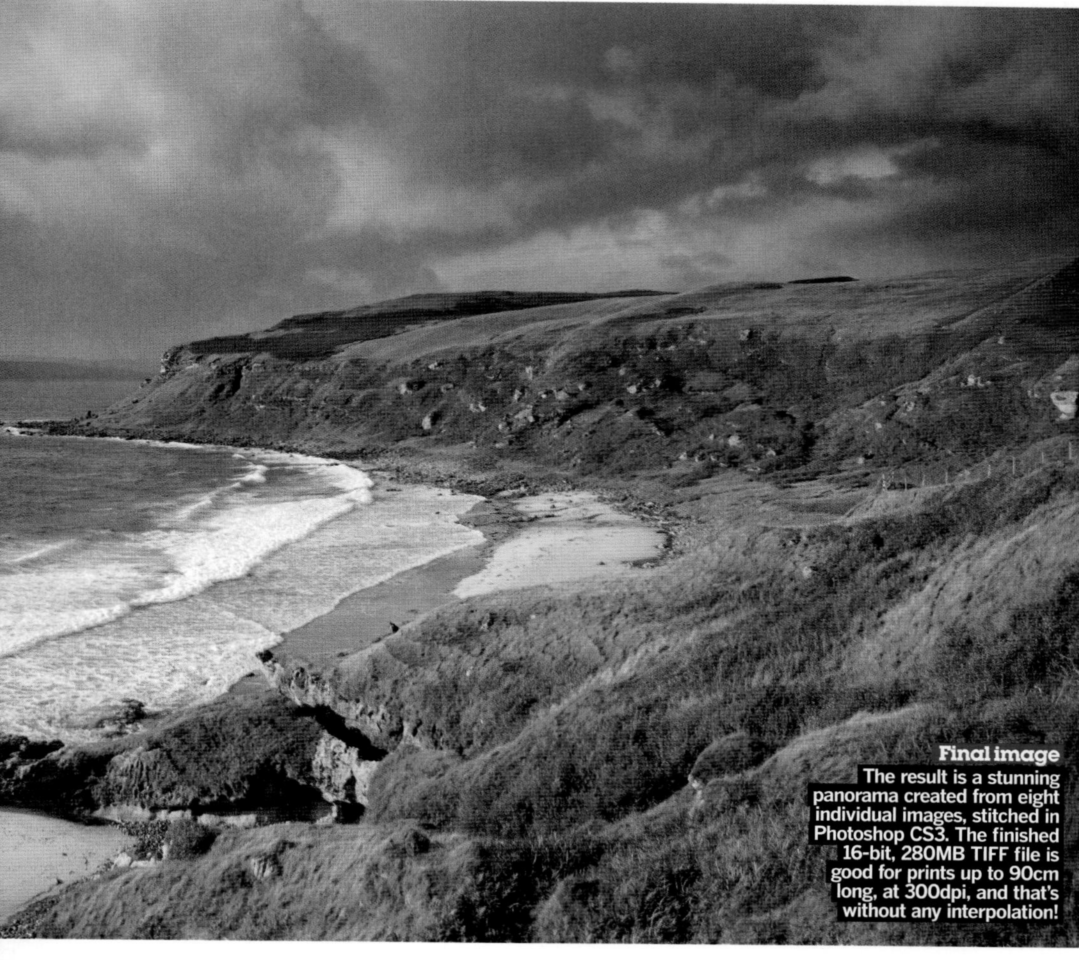

Final image The result is a stunning panorama created from eight individual images, stitched in Photoshop CS3. The finished 16-bit, 280MB TIFF file is good for prints up to 90cm long, at 300dpi, and that's without any interpolation!

Which Photoshop?

PHOTOSHOP CS4
£558 / PC & Mac

This may seem rather an expensive option, purely to do photo-stitching – even at the cheaper upgrade price – but the latest photomerge tool is unbelievably good, even with the most complex of stitches. Obviously you will get much more out of it than just stitching, but if you are starting to take your photography seriously, you will not be disappointed at the potential that this latest version of Photoshop has. Alternatively you may be able to pick up a cheaper version of CS3 that still has an impressive stitcher, too!

ELEMENTS 7
£75 / PC & Mac (v6)

If your budget won't stretch to CS4, then don't worry. The latest versions of Photoshop Elements are also equipped with all the tools you need for an impressive and hassle-free stitch. Both Elements 6 and 7 include the Photomerge command (found under ***File>New>Photomerge Panorama***) and appear to do an equally good job at blending and adjusting images for a panorama – at least to the same standard as CS3. However it doesn't have some of the improved functionality of CS4's photomerge.

6

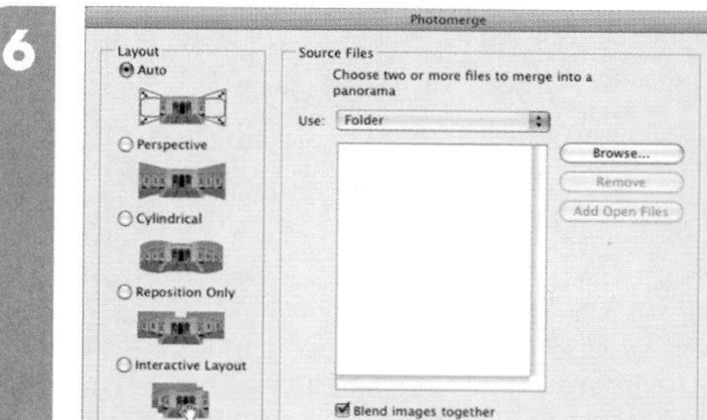

Download the images to a computer. If you shoot in Raw, batch process the Raw files from the sequences so they all receive the same adjustments and corrections, otherwise inconsistencies will creep in. Place those images in a folder.

7

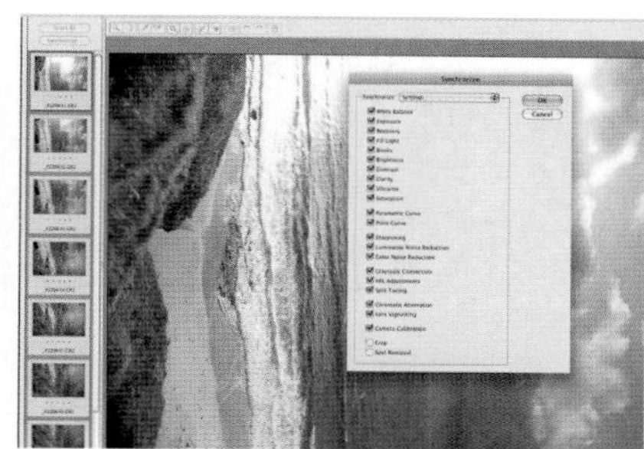

Open Photoshop and go to ***File>Automate>Photomerge***. Select the layout style you desire. Auto usually works fine. You may like to also try Cylindrical and Perspective. Click on the Use tab, select Folders then click on ***Browse***.

8

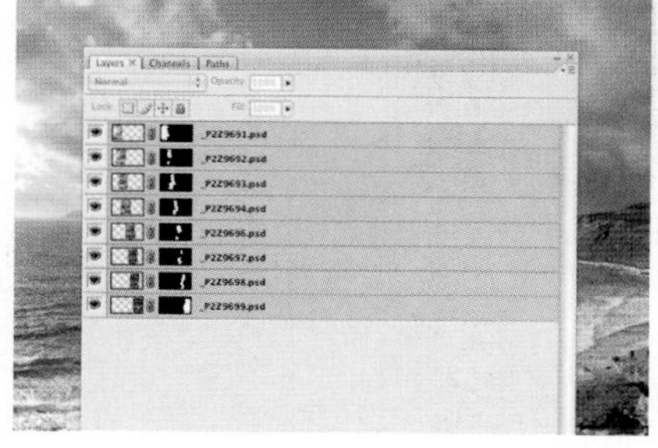

Click on the folder containing the images you want to stitch and they will appear in the Photomerge dialogue box. Click ***OK*** and let Photomerge perform its magic. This can take a few minutes, so put the kettle on and make yourself a cuppa!

9

By the time you're back at your computer the stitch should be complete. You may need to crop the edges to tidy it up. This is common if you don't use a Nodal Point bracket to eliminate parallax error (see panel), but it's nothing to worry about. Only a few more tweaks and you're finished!

10

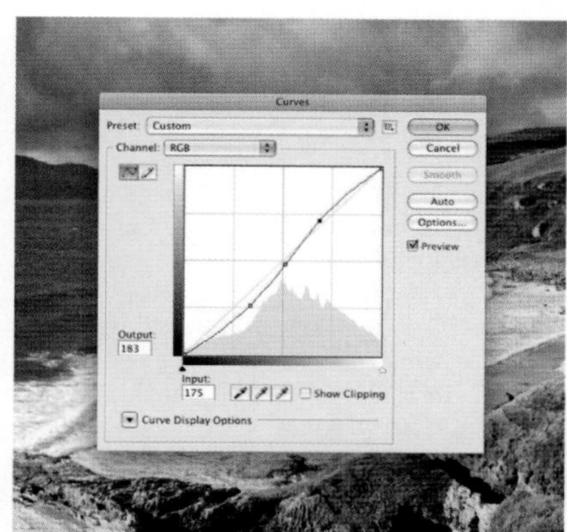

After saving the stitch and flattening the layers (***Layer>Flatten Image***), make any further adjustments until you're happy with the overall look of the image and remove any distracting elements with the Clone Stamp Tool. Job done!

Pro advice: Photospheres

Ian Farrell
Ian is an experienced photographer and a former pro photography magazine editor. Here he shows us how to take your panoramic images further, wrapping images in on themselves to create photospheres.
www.ianfarrell.org

I'VE BEEN A FAN of panoramic photography ever since I got my first digital compact back in 1999: a 3.2-megapixel Nikon Coolpix 885. I would stitch together three or four images in Adobe Photoshop and produce long-thin pictures that seemed to represent what I was seeing with my eyes. As time went on and I read about the subject on the internet, I became fascinated with taking my panoramas wider and wider. I regarded those shooting completely circular 360° images with envy!

It wasn't long before I was doing it myself, though. With a Manfrotto 303 Plus panoramic head that let me rotate my new DSLR with precision, and RealViz Stitcher software to merge the individual shots together, I was getting spectacular results.

I've continued to shoot panoramas ever since, both indoors and out, even having some success selling them as fine-art prints – after all everyone likes an unusual view of something they know well. I experimented with different lenses – settling on a Sigma 10-20mm ultra-wide zoom for much of my work – and even incorporated HDR into some indoor images to help balance extremes of brightness. But after a while, I stared to wonder where else panoramic photography could take me. Having a notoriously short attention span, I wanted a new toy to play with.

As if by magic, I stumbled across the work of Ed Hill, a London based fine-art photographer who also shoots panoramic photography. Instead of presenting his pictures in the traditional long, rectangular format, Hill wraps his thin strip images around in a circle, giving the impression they are scenes on a tiny planet, floating somewhere in space. Ed's one of the number who likes to call it a Photosphere (visit www.glartists.com for many examples of his work). I, of course, became instantly hooked, so I set about finding out how I could create the same effect myself.

Fast forward to 2009. If you search for Photospheres on the internet (or 'Photoplanets', as some are calling them) you'll find a lot of photographers working this way, and producing spectacular results. Creating a circular sphere from a conventional, long-thin panorama is actually fairly straightforward using Adobe Photoshop's Polar Coordinates filter; but the whole process, from start to finish, is fairly involved. Let's have a look at how it's done.

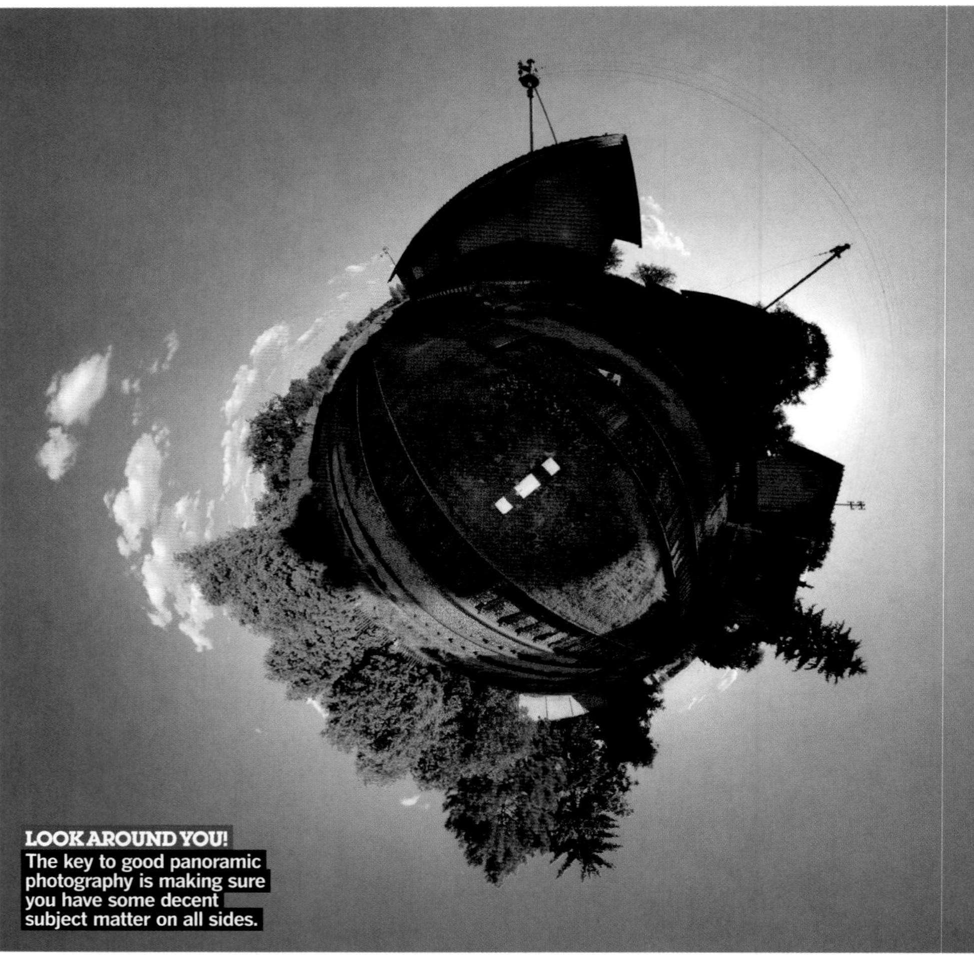

LOOK AROUND YOU!
The key to good panoramic photography is making sure you have some decent subject matter on all sides.

"The final thing to do before you start shooting is set everything on your camera to manual: you really don't want any changes to White Balance or exposure to occur between frames"

STAGE ONE: SHOOTING THE IMAGES

Before you get your camera out of your bag, the first thing to do is to find a good position to shoot from. In contrast to 'normal' composition, you'll need at least some empty foreground in the picture to act as the sphere in the final picture. Shooting in the middle of a field or square is a good option. Also try to make the area directly underneath your tripod a smooth tone that will be easy to work with later in Photoshop; you'll need to remove the tripod legs with the Healing Brush and Clone Stamp tools.

All panoramic photography needs to be shot with a tripod and you'll need to level the camera to avoid getting a wonky horizon in the final shot. What's more, to stitch frames together perfectly you'll need to use a panoramic tripod head. This enables you to rotate the camera around a point that eliminates any lateral side-to-side movement, which can cause parallax errors (see right). Specialist bits of kit like this vary in price, from just under a hundred quid to over £500 for a top of the range model. I've been using the excellent Nodal Ninja 3, which costs about £130. It's well made and lightweight enough to take everywhere.

When it comes to lenses, it's a case of the wider the better for this type of work. The camera is always mounted vertically and you want to get as much top-to-bottom view in as possible. I'm currently using a Nikkor 10.5mm fish-eye on a Fujifilm FinePix S5 Pro, which gives a diagonal field-of-view of 180°. Ultra-wide angle zooms, such as Tamron's SP AF 10-24mm f/3.5-4.5 or Sigma's 10-20mm f/4-5.6 EX are also excellent choices for the job.

When using a lens with such a wide angle-of-view, you don't need to shoot many frames to overlap and form a circle, but it is important to ensure there is enough overlap between each shot for the stitching application to work its magic and join the frames together. I always aim for about a third overlap, just to be sure.

The final thing to do before you start shooting is to set everything on your camera to manual; you really don't want any changes to White Balance or exposure between frames. Set an average exposure for the scene in manual mode. It's also best to opt for a small aperture (say f/22) to maximise depth-of-field.

When you are ready to go, shoot your pictures calmly but quickly, moving in a consistent circle. Be aware of camera shake too – I'd recommend that you use a remote release if your shutter speed is slow enough to mean that you may get camera blur.

To get a perfect photosphere, you'll need to shoot a perfect sphere of coverage, which means shooting two extra shots as well as those that take you round in a circle. You need one looking straight upwards, called a zenith, and one looking straight down, called a nadir. If you don't capture these, it doesn't mean you won't be able to create your photosphere, it just means it will have a kind of 'pinch' in the middle, which can actually look good in the right scene.

STAGE TWO: POST-PRODUCTION

Having captured your images, the really hard work begins back at home in front of your computer. Once you've downloaded your images to your PC or Mac, you'll need to get them into some software capable of stitching together fish-eye or ultra wide-angle images. Specialist software like EasyPano, Panoweaver or Stitcher

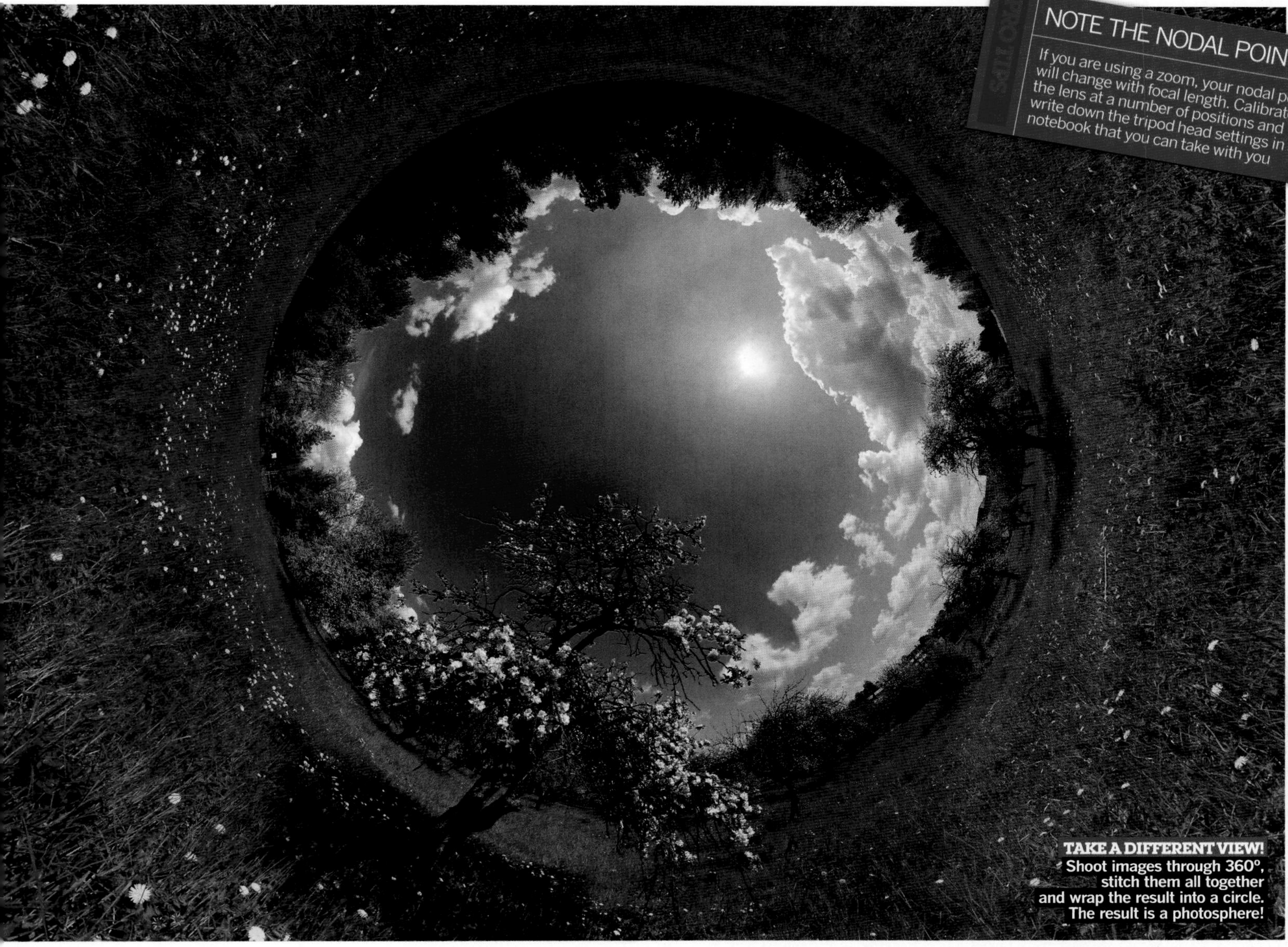

PRO TIPS

NOTE THE NODAL POINTS

If you are using a zoom, your nodal point will change with focal length. Calibrate the lens at a number of positions and write down the tripod head settings in a notebook that you can take with you

TAKE A DIFFERENT VIEW! Shoot images through 360°, stitch them all together and wrap the result into a circle. The result is a photosphere!

from Autodesk (formally RealViz) are good bets, while Photoshop CS4 can also handle such images very well too.

All software works in a slightly different way, but you'll want to stitch the frames together and export the final panorama as a spherical projection – in other words, as if it were projected on the inside of a sphere. This will distort both horizontal and vertical lines wildly but don't worry, this is the kind of effect we are aiming for.

Once the final panorama has been rendered, which can take some time, you'll want to bring the result into Photoshop for the final step of turning it into a sphere – but before this happens, the image must to be made square. Using the Photoshop's Free Transform tool, you'll need to compress the width of the panorama, squashing it up until the width and height are equal. The Info palette can help you here.

The key to transforming the square to a circle lies in the ***Polar Coordinates*** command, which is buried away in the ***Filter>Distort*** menu. The filter bends the picture upwards, so if you want the foreground to be in the middle of the sphere, as if you were looking down from above, you need to rotate it by 180° first. If you don't do this, the sky will be at the centre of the picture and it will appear as if you are looking upwards. Both techniques are worth exploring as often a scene will suit one approach more than the other.

With the sphere constructed, it's time to apply the usual Adobe Photoshop editing tools to tidy things up a bit. I'm talking Curves or Levels adjustment layers, combined with layer masks, to even up exposure, as well as the Healing Tool and Cloning Stamp tools to eliminate the tripod head and your own feet, if these are visible in the middle of your sphere.

As you start to experiment with panoramic photography and photospheres, you'll quickly learn what makes a good subject and what doesn't. Some will suit the traditional linear panorama, while others will look better as a photosphere. I've had most success shooting on bridges and areas surrounded by buildings on all sides, but I'd encourage you to experiment, play and have fun. After all, that's what enjoying photography is all about. ▸

Essential information

UNDERSTANDING NODAL POINT

When you rotate a camera in a circle, part of the movement is rotational (clockwise/anti-clockwise) while part of it is lateral (left/right). It is this lateral component that can cause parallax error, which will wreak havoc when you are stitching frames together.

To get a camera rotating around a point where no side-to-side motion is taking place, you'll need a special panoramic tripod head. This lets you move a DSLR over the centre of a tripod until you find the point where no parallax occurs – the nodal point.

Nodal points are specific to combinations of camera, lens and zoom setting. Finding a nodal point is easy though: simply pick two objects and position your camera so they are in line when viewed over one side of the viewfinder. Now pivot your camera so the objects are on the other side of the frame. If they are still in line, you have found your nodal point; if not then you have parallax error and will need to move the camera forward or backwards until there is no mismatch.

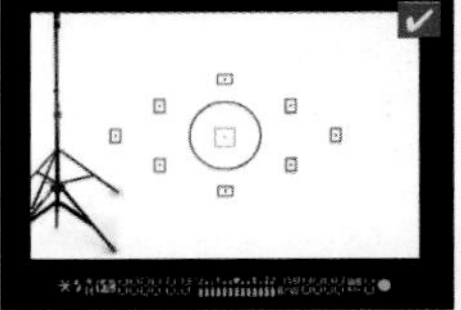
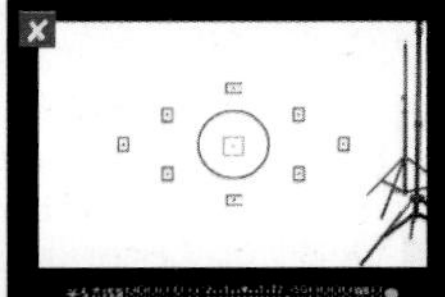
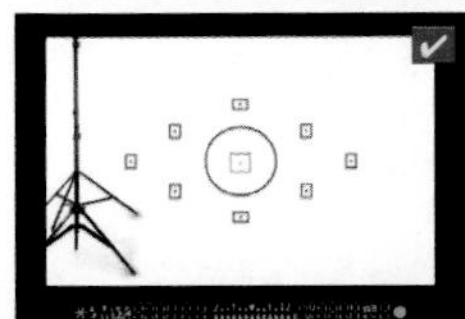
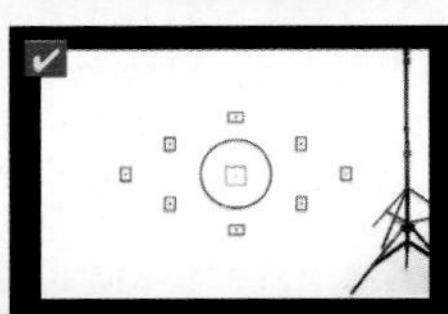

FINDING A NODAL POINT: Pick two objects and arrange them so they appear aligned when on one side of the viewfinder. Now rotate the camera so they are on the other side of the viewfinder. If they remain aligned you have found your nodal point.

Shoot the images for your Photosphere

Shooting a photosphere is not as hard as you might think. First let's look at how the component images are shot. In much the same way as a 'normal' stitched panorama, this is done with the camera turned vertically upwards to make full use of the sensor's longest dimension. It pays to use an ultra wide-angle lens for this, to capture as much as you can in each frame.

Once you've gone round in a complete circle, and have pictures covering 360°, you'll need to shoot two extra images to get a full sphere of coverage: a zenith shot, looking straight upwards, and a nadir, which looks directly down. Then you can move on to the Photoshop stage.

PRO TIPS

WAIT FOR THE WEATHER

Always anticipate what could change during the time you are shooting the component frames. For instance, watch out for the sun going behind a cloud, which could affect your lighting

1

Set up your camera on its calibrated tripod head and make sure your apparatus is level by checking the built-in spirit level. Have a good look around you in a circle, ensuring you have points of interest everywhere, not just in front of you.

2

Lock in a manual White Balance setting and measure an average exposure for the scene in Manual exposure mode. This is easily done by rotating the camera through its circle while keeping an eye on the exposure values on the top plate.

3

You'll want as much front-to-back sharpness in the image as possible, so select a small aperture to maximise depth-of-field. If your lens has a depth-of-field scale, use this to focus hyperfocally. Here I've managed to get everything from 20cm to infinity sharp.

4

When it's time to capture the individual frames, shoot steadily and systematically, moving round in a circle. Pay attention to what is happening in the viewfinder; you don't want to shoot a moving object half out of frame, for instance.

5

Once you've worked your way around in circle, you'll need to cover the top and bottom of the sphere with zenith and nadir shots. For the zenith, orient the camera vertically upwards and duck down so you don't include yourself in the frame.

6

Similarly, point the camera down to shoot the nadir image. This is harder, as you can't avoid including the tripod and your own feet in the shot. For this reason I shoot two images, moving between them so I can merge them later.

Essential information

SHOOTING THE 'ZENITH' AND 'NADIR'

To shoot a whole sphere, you'll need to look up and down as well as left and right. The upward-looking view is called a zenith, while a shot looking down is known as a nadir. Shooting either of these is pretty straightforward, though you'll need a panoramic tripod head that lets you swing the camera up and down as well as side to side. For the zenith, rotate your camera through 90° until it's pointing vertically upwards and take a single shot, taking care not to include yourself in the frame. The nadir is more difficult as there is no way to avoid being in the shot yourself. The easiest way around this is to capture one nadir, move around by 180° before taking a second. Then you can merge the two together in Photoshop or your stitching software, if it has the capability.

Nadir

Zenith

Nadir

Zenith

Producing the Photosphere

With all of your component frames captured and transferred to your computer, it's time to get cracking on the post-production. This can be broken down into two stages: making a rectangular panoramic picture, then wrapping this around on itself to form the finished sphere.

Producing the long, thin panoramic picture from the component images can be done in specialist software or in Photoshop, although it's only CS4's new and improved Photomerge engine that can handle 360° images. Rendering such a picture may take a while because of extra work required to process a complete circle and include the zenith and nadir shots. You'll get there eventually – you might just have to go and make a cup of tea while you wait for your PC to crunch the files.

With the basic panorama complete, the next job is to fold this around on itself to create a sphere. You can do this with Photoshop's Polar Coordinates feature (***Filters> Distort>Polar Coordinates***), which wraps the image upwards to give the impression that you are looking upwards towards the sky. To get the impression of looking down, simply rotate the image by 180° before applying the Polar coordinates filter.

1

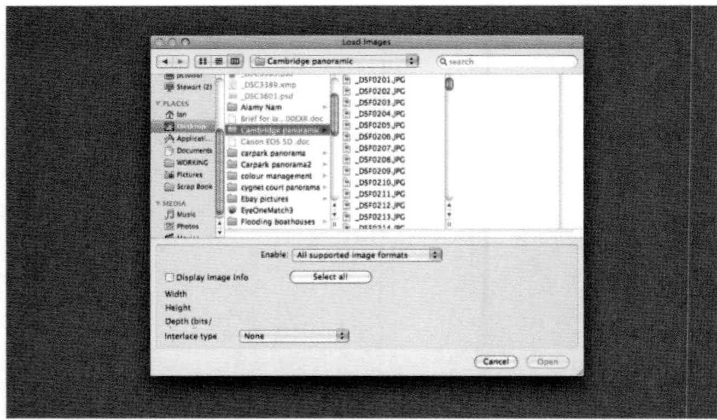

After you have got yourself organised and your images are safely transferred to your PC or Mac, it's time to import them to your stitching software. I'm using Autodesk's Stitcher software (www.autodesk.co.uk), running on a Apple MacBook Pro with 4GB RAM.

2

Stitcher works in different ways, depending on the lens in use and how much distortion is present. I've used a full-frame fish-eye lens, which I specify in the Stitcher's Properties dialogue. Circular fish-eye lenses and rectilinear optics are also supported.

3

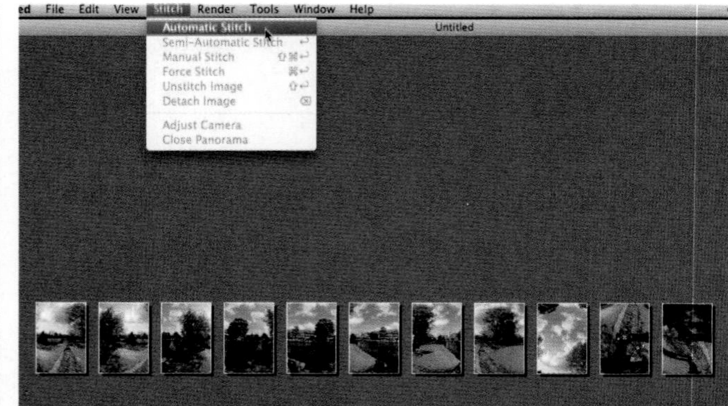

When it comes to fish-eye images, Stitcher only gives you one option: automatic stitching, and this works very well almost all of the time. Thanks to the extent of the distortion, the process is pretty involved and can take a few minutes to complete.

4

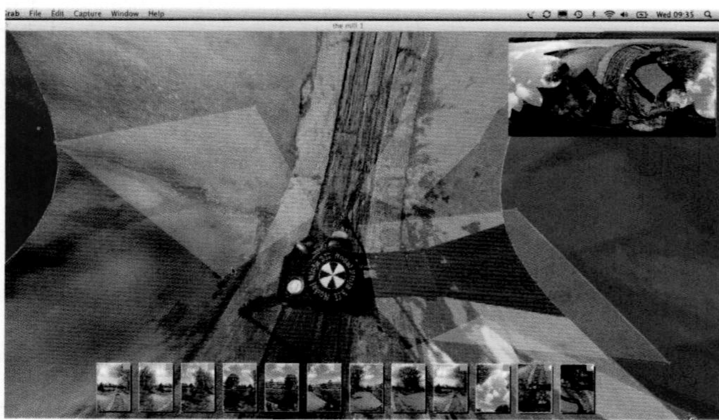

When the initial stitching process is complete, I use Stitcher's stencilling features to exclude my feet from the two nadir shots. Using the polygon tool, I can draw around areas that I want ignored. The application uses detail from other shot instead.

5

Rendering the final panorama can be a time-consuming business, so I use the preview function to check that the final result is what I'm expecting; that all the frames have joined up OK, and that there is no ghosting or double-overlap.

6

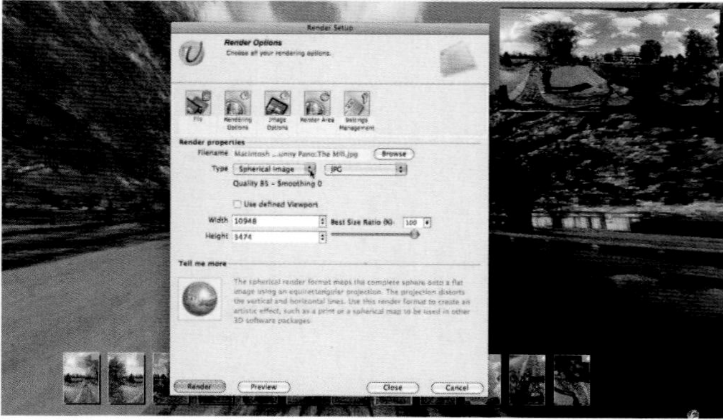

When rendering the final image at 100 per cent, Stitcher can take up to an hour to deliver the goods, even on a fast computer. You'll want to output as a spherical projection in this case, which will distort any straight lines in the pictures wildly.

7

Once you've got the final result, take this into Photoshop and squash up the image into a square, using the Free Transform command. I'm also rotating it through 180° as I want the foreground in the centre of the sphere for a 'looking down' effect.

PRO TIPS

PERSPECTIVE STRETCHING

To make objects at the edge of the sphere more prominent, select the upper part of the panorama and stretch it with a Free Transform before rotating it and applying the polar coordinates filter

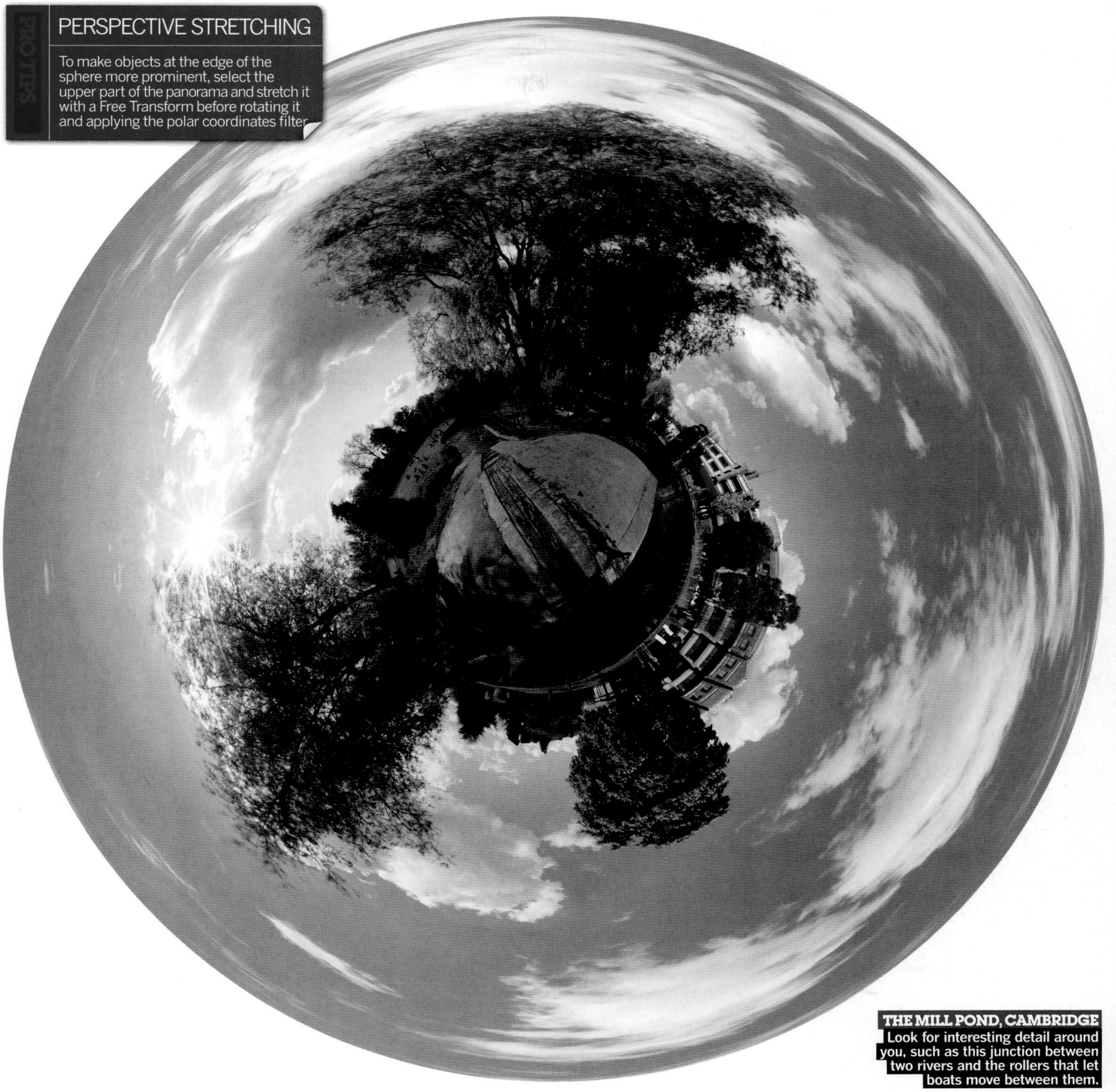

THE MILL POND, CAMBRIDGE
Look for interesting detail around you, such as this junction between two rivers and the rollers that let boats move between them.

8

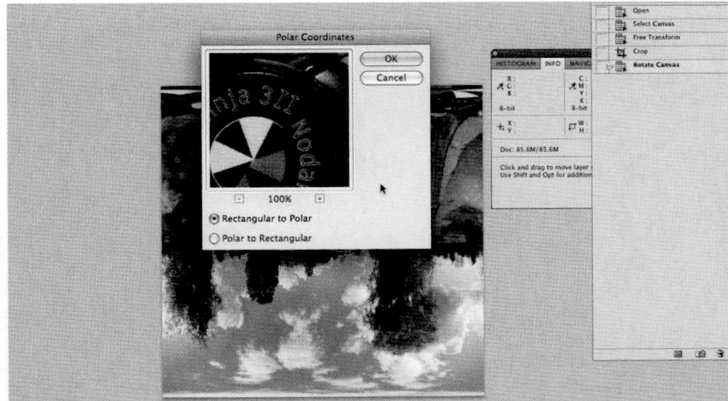

Create the photosphere effect using the Polar Coordinates filter, which you'll find at ***Filters>Distort>Polar Coordinates***. Ensure the Rectangular to Circular option is checked. The preview pane will give you an idea of what to expect when you click OK.

9

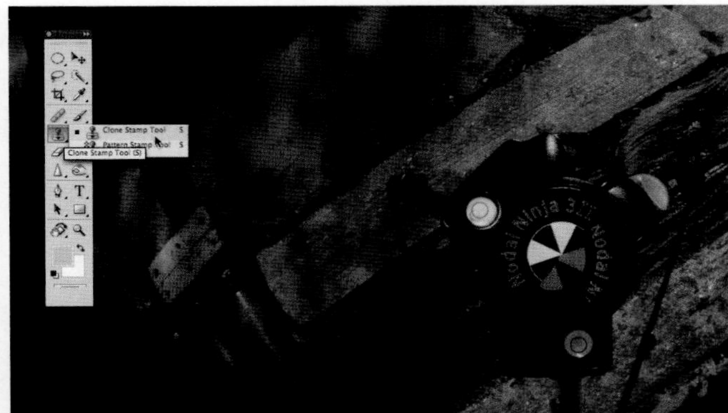

You'll need to use the usual Photoshop tools to fix any glitches – the tripod head and legs need removing with the Clone Stamp, for instance. This is why standing on even-textured ground helps, giving you more pixels to sample from O.while cloning.

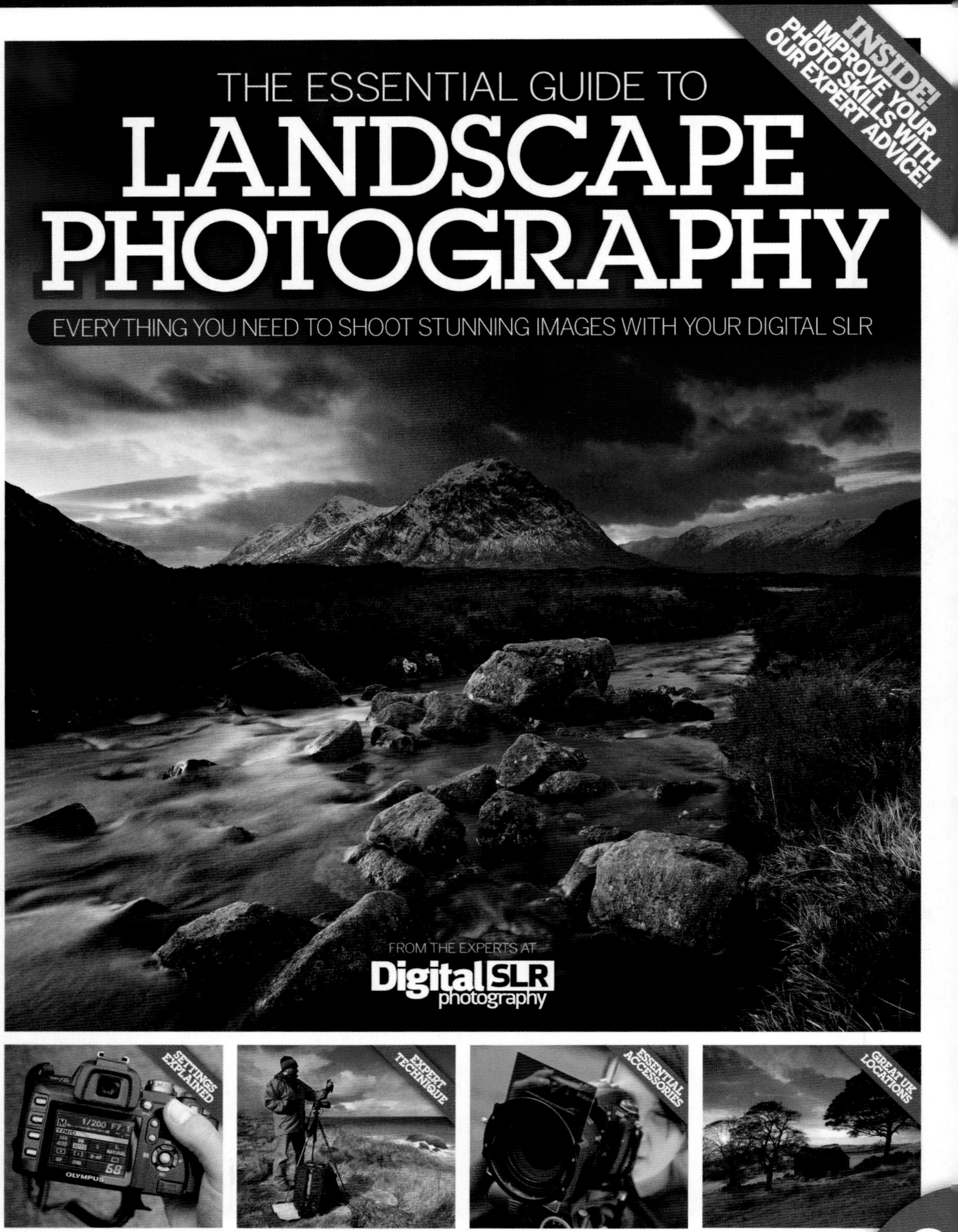